The Bible Speaks Today

Series Editors: J. A. Motyer (OT)
John R. W. Stott (NT)

The Message of Genesis 12—50

From Abraham to Joseph

Kevin Ray

Titles in this series

The Message of Genesis 12—50

From Abraham to Joseph

Joyce G. Baldwin

Inter-Varsity Press
Leicester, England
Downers Grove, Illinois, U.S.A.

Inter-Varsity Press
38 De Montfort Street, Leicester LE1 7GP, England
P.O. Box 1400, Downers Grove, Illinois 60515, U.S.A.

Inter-Varsity Press, England, is the publishing division of the Universities and Colleges Christian Fellowship (formerly the Inter-Varsity Fellowship), a student movement linking Christian Unions in universities and colleges throughout the United Kingdom and the Republic of Ireland, and a member movement of the International Fellowship of Evangelical Students. For information about local and national activities write to UCCF, 38 De Montfort Street, Leicester LE1 7GP.

InterVarsity Press, U.S.A., is the book-publishing division of Inter-Varsity Christian Fellowship, a student movement active on campus at hundreds of universities, colleges and schools of nursing. For information about local and regional activities, write IVCF, 6400 Schroeder Rd., Madison, WI 53707-7895.

Cover photograph: Robert Cushman Hayes

Text set in Great Britain
Printed in the United States of America

UK   ISBN 0-85110-759-1 (paperback)
USA ISBN 0-87784-298-1 (paperback)
USA ISBN 0-87784-925-0 (set of The Bible Speaks Today, paperback)

British Library Cataloguing in Publication Data
Baldwin, Joyce
    The message of Genesis 12—50: From Abraham to Joseph—(The Bible speaks today)
    1. Bible.   O.T.   Genesis XII-L—Commentaries
    I. Title.   II. Series
    222'.1106   BS1235.3
ISBN 0-85110-759-1

Library of Congress Cataloging in Publication Data

Baldwin, Joyce G.
    The message of Genesis 12—50.

    (The Bible speaks today)
    Includes bibliographical references.
    1. Bible.   O.T.   Genesis XII-L—Criticism,
interpretation, etc.   I. Title II. Title:
Message of Genesis twelve-fifty.   III. Series.
BS1235.2.B26   1986   222'.11077   86-10615
ISBN 0-87784-298-1 (U.S.: pbk.)

---

18   17   16   15   14   13   12   11   10   9   8   7   6   5   4

12   11   10   09   08   07   06   05   04   03   02   01   00

Contents

General preface

The Bible Speaks Today describes a series of both Old Testament and New Testament expositions, which are characterized by a threefold ideal: to expound the biblical text with accuracy, to relate it to contemporary life, and to be readable.

These books are, therefore, not 'commentaries', for the commentary seeks rather to elucidate the text than to apply it, and tends to be a work rather of reference than of literature. Nor, on the other hand, do they contain the kinds of 'sermons' which attempt to be contemporary and readable, without taking Scripture seriously enough.

The contributors to this series are all united in their convictions that God still speaks through what he has spoken, and that nothing is more necessary for the life, health and growth of Christians than that they should hear what the Spirit is saying to them through his ancient—yet ever modern—Word.

J. A. MOTYER
J. R. W. STOTT
Series Editors

Author's preface

Ever since I began reading the Bible as a child the book of Genesis has fascinated me. Here were stories that were more than entertainment, for God spoke through them, and I longed to know more. Years of teaching the Old Testament have involved me in further study of these chapters, which retain their charm and continue to provoke thought and questioning, as well as to probe and instruct.

It was the opportunity to give a series of Bible expositions at Trinity College, Bristol, that led me again to these chapters, and eventually to the writing of this book. The Bible expositions were not meant to be an academic exercise, but were given in a context of worship and prayer so that we submitted to the God who speaks through his word today. As I have been preparing this book it has been my hope and prayer that Genesis will indeed speak, not only to those who already know the patriarchs well, but also to those who are still making their acquaintance. I have tried not to presuppose any previous study, and I have endeavoured to indicate some of the background to their lives revealed by archaeology and related studies.

This book has come together slowly, and I am grateful to the Editor, the Rev. Alec Motyer, for his patience, as well as for detailed and painstaking suggestions almost all of which I have adopted. To my husband Jack, who has uncomplainingly done household chores to set me free to write, and then has read the results with helpfully critical eye, I dedicate this volume.

JOYCE BALDWIN

Chief abbreviations

AOOT	*Ancient Orient and Old Testament* by K. A. Kitchen (Tyndale Press, 1966).
AV	Authorized (King James') Version of the Bible (1611).
BA	*Biblical Archaeologist.*
BAR	*Biblical Archaeology Review.*
BASOR	*Bulletin of the American Schools of Oriental Research.*
BDB	*Hebrew-English Lexicon of the Old Testament* by F. Brown, S. R. Driver and C. A. Briggs (1907).
BZAW	*Beihefte zur Zeitschrift für die alttestamentliche Wissenschaft.*
CB	*Cambridge Bible: Genesis* by H. E. Ryle (CUP, 1914).
CBQ	*Catholic Biblical Quarterly.*
EOPN	*Essays on the Patriarchal Narratives* edited by A. R. Millard and D. J. Wiseman (IVP, 1980).
HSS	*Harvard Semitic Studies.*
IBD	*Illustrated Bible Dictionary.* 3 vols. (IVP, 1980).
IDB	*Interpreter's Dictionary of the Bible.* 4 vols. (Nelson, 1962).
JBL	*Journal of Biblical Literature.*
JNES	*Journal of Near Eastern Studies.*
JSOT	*Journal for the Study of the Old Testament.*
LXX	The Septuagint (pre-Christian Greek version of the OT).
NIV	The New International Version of the Bible (1979).
OTA	*Old Testament Abstracts.*
RSV	American Revised Standard Version of the Bible (1952).
RV	English Revised Version of the Bible (1881).
TB	*Tyndale Bulletin.*
TOTC	*Tyndale Old Testament Commentaries: Genesis* by Derek Kidner (Tyndale Press, 1967).
VT	*Vetus Testamentum.*

Introduction

In the beginning ...

Genesis, the book of beginnings, sets the scene for the whole of the Bible, and addresses the whole human race. It anticipates the most basic questions that anyone can ask about the origins of the universe and of all life. Not that the opening chapters tell us by any means all that we should like to know about the process of creation, nor how long it took. Though 'days' of creation mark stages in its development, 'with the Lord one day is as a thousand years, and a thousand years as one day' (2 Pet. 3:8). What the book does insist upon by deliberate use of repetition is the truth that the one and only God was responsible for bringing everything into being. 'He spoke and it was done.' The God who meets us on the very first page of Scripture is the one who speaks, and so lets us know him. In the course of the book of Genesis he speaks to many of the people who are mentioned in the narrative. God communicates with ordinary men and women, and they make their response to him. Fellowship between God and the humans he created is part of God's original intention, and not some strange activity, reserved for those mystically inclined.

This fundamental assertion 'And God said ...', together with the other verbs in Genesis 1, all of which necessarily have God as their subject, has far-reaching implications. Whichever of the many theories about the origin of the universe turns out eventually to be the most likely in the opinion of the specialists, Scripture insists that it did not result from a long series of fortuitous accidents. It was the work of the living, personal God that brought all things into existence. Moreover he had his good purpose in creating mankind.

We may not altogether understand that purpose, but it has to do with the fact that he made us humans 'in his image', capable of loving him and one another. People, therefore, have supreme value. They are more important than systems, philosophies, wealth, or anything else in the universe, because the man and the woman were the crown of God's creation, made in his likeness. People are therefore more important in God's sight than all the rest of creation, and their relationship to him is most precious.

The essential unity of the human race is another of the great themes established at the beginning of the book. *Adam* is both the word for 'humanity' and the name of the first man, the progenitor of the race. However many may be the divisions and distinctions between peoples, all are 'in Adam'. Thus one man stands for all and by the same concept one Man can be Saviour of all. As Paul explained, 'For as in Adam all die, so also in Christ shall all be made alive' (1 Cor. 15:22). One representative man stands for the whole human race. Whereas in society, both ancient and modern, the tendency is for communities to fragment and for individuals to become alienated, the book of Genesis shows that people need each other and belong together. The solidarity of the human race is a biblical concept.

This way of looking at humanity does not in any way detract from the value of the individual. Indeed it is one of the remarkable features of the book of Genesis that ordinary people like the patriarchs, with all their failings as well as their faith, are singled out to be the recipients of God's special care. This is far from being a case of 'favouritism', however; these people were by no means permitted their own way and indulged. As we shall see in the course of our study, the very opposite is the case. Abraham, Isaac and the other patriarchs are selected to become a kind of exhibition to the nations to show them what God can do, and at the same time to be the instrument through which God will work out his intention to provide for all peoples a way of salvation. The family of Abraham was very highly honoured, it is true, but all kinds of unwelcome experiences had to be endured which other people seemed altogether to escape. This was all part of God's training process, both to create the kind of men and women through whom God could reveal his ways, and to demonstrate the principles by which he wanted all men to live.

That the one and only God created all things, and 'made from one every nation of men to live on all the face of the earth' (Acts 17:26), establishes that human existence is not meaningless. For want of this assurance many of our contemporaries are floundering, as the poet Colin Duriez, for example, realizes:

> Where, from where do I come? What am I?
> Where do I go to? Whence? What? Whither?[1]

Nor is it only our contemporaries who have been aware of an agony of bewilderment. Colin Duriez explains that Paul Gauguin painted a picture with the title 'Whence? What? Whither?' in 1897, just before he attempted suicide. Centuries earlier Augustine of Hippo had been aware of a restless searching which he took to be an experience common to humanity. In a well-known prayer he expressed it thus: 'Almighty God, ... [thou] hast made us for thyself, so that our hearts are restless till they find their rest in thee.' Our need to find meaning is wonderfully matched by the revelation of God which begins so purposefully in the book of Genesis.

As that revelation unfolds through the work of Moses and his successors, we soon become clear that what is being presented to us is not merely a series of events, but a connected progression of circumstances through which God reveals his message. Despite the passing of generations there is a recognizable continuity of theme, amid a multiplicity of literary styles and experiences of life. It is almost as if one mind had been responsible for the whole story of Israel's history, and yet that is patently impossible, given such a library as we have in the Old Testament records from Genesis to Chronicles.

The idea of history

So fully have the biblical books shaped the thinking of the western world that we take for granted the word 'history', and presume that people everywhere have always seen that there is some kind of meaning in events. Yet cultures exist still which, while they recount myths of 'days gone by', have no concept of historical time, and expect to see no pattern in events. Even the Romans went no further back than the founding of Rome in their account of history, whereas the opening words of Genesis, 'In the beginning God created ...', set human life in a unified whole, so indicating the need for a universal history. For this the Bible provides the essential

---

[1] *Making Eden Grow* (Scripture Union, 1974), p. 16.

framework, God's purpose to unite all things in Christ being the overarching and all-inclusive theme. In the Bible history has not only a beginning but also an end.

It was through God's dealings with Abraham and his descendants, who became known as Israel, that the truths which make possible a concept of history first became part of human thought. Humanity as such mattered to the one true God who had created it. He had a purpose for it and was well able to fulfil that purpose. He cared even for the individuals who might have considered themselves of no account, for he saw them, not as part of the crowd, but as unique men and women for whom he was deeply concerned. The names of many such are recorded in the Bible's genealogies. They mattered. Each generation mattered, for each one had a distinct role to play in the outworking of the purpose of God, and who knew how soon that purpose would culminate in some special and much-to-be-desired intervention? It was the expectation that God was controlling events with a view to blessing all mankind that eventually gave rise to the concept of history. By the time the earliest records were being written that were to form the basis of the biblical books, the convictions necessary for a concept of historical development were already there.

Looked at from another angle, the dawning realization that life had purpose and meaning arose from a conviction that this world is not self-contained, and therefore cannot be explained in terms of its own existence. More specifically men and women did not find in abstract thought an adequate acccount of their own personalities, endowed as they were with the gift of self-consciousness and the power to assess their own actions. The Greek philosophers were to reason their way to an ultimate logical and impersonal power motivating the universe, whereas in Genesis God reveals himself as a person. 'In the Bible the transcendent truth is dramatic and alive,' writes J. V. Langmead Casserly. 'In the Greek concept of history there is no room for the personal and purposive providence of the Bible. History, in the classical view, is endowed with shape but not direction. It moves, like the planets, in perpetual cyclic revolution, an endless wheel of recurrence.'[2] In the Bible, on the other hand, life's direction is ensured by God who created the world and its peoples; he transcends time and gives to human life and events a significance they could not otherwise have. This is supremely the case in the Old Testament's forward thrust, pointing ahead in plain

[2] J. V. Langmead Casserly, *The Christian in Philosophy* (Faber and Faber, 1949), p. 22.

12

and figurative language which found its culmination in the coming of Christ.

The basis of right and wrong

Another important assumption made in the book of Genesis is concerned with the whole question of right and wrong. Whereas popular thought associates morality with law keeping, Genesis depicts the first human pair enjoying conversation with God, and meant to find happiness in fulfilling the role planned for them by their Creator. The essence of wrongdoing was rebellion against this living, personal God, who had made everything, including man, very good. It is true that law was to play a major part at a later stage, after the exodus from Egypt, but even the law was an expression of the mind of Israel's loving and powerful deliverer (Ex. 20:2–3). Deliberately to disobey it, therefore, was to defy God and incur his reaction in punishment, whereas to obey kept Israel in the place of usefulness, fulfilling the unique vocation that God had planned. The first act of rebellion, with its resulting alienation from God and expulsion from the garden (Gn. 3:22–24), involved the whole human race, but God in his wisdom and love did not break off relations with the people he had made, nor abandon them to their own devices.

Knowledge of God and of his righteous character continued to be a feature of subsequent generations, some of whom so lived as to keep company with him (Gn. 4:4; 5:24). Noah, the second major character in the book, 'found favour in the eyes of the Lord' (Gn. 6:8). The majority, however, corrupted society to such an extent that God's remedy was to send the Flood to destroy that generation, but through Noah he enabled mankind to make a fresh start. All the hope this new beginning engendered was buttressed with God's solemn undertaking that he would never again destroy 'all flesh' nor allow a flood to cover the earth (Gn. 9:9–11), but memories of the catastrophic judgment and the miracle of one family's deliverance made a right relationship with God an urgent matter.

Genealogies summarize the repopulation of the earth; the last of these (Gn. 10:21–31) is the significant one for the continuing narrative, because from the line of Shem, or the Semites, Abraham was to be born. Throughout the first eleven chapters of Genesis the highly selective narrative is leading purposefully towards this important character, Abraham. To him the unchanging God revealed himself, teaching most clearly lessons which are relevant today because they are timeless. And just as a student, reviewing a course for an examination, goes back to the beginning and sees more fully the relevance of much that he was taught in the earliest classes, so it can happen that God's dealings with the patriarchs, and with Abraham especially, enable us to grasp the major themes of Scripture. Despite the lapse of time and the immense differences that separate the world of the patriarchs from our own, their God is our God, and he speaks to us today through his word to them.

We have spoken of the lessons learnt by Abraham being timeless, but that does not mean that their setting is not important. The great strides made in understanding the world of the second millennium BC, and even earlier, through the work of archaeologists immediately raises the question of the dating of the patriarchs and the identification of the places which feature in their lives, as recorded in Genesis. Access to texts, especially when there is similarity of subject-matter or style of writing, is particularly valuable as an aid to putting the biblical writing into a wider context. References to relevant material will be made as the chapters unfold, but some general discussion of the bearing of recent studies on the patriarchs will provide a framework into which the details may be set.

When did the patriarchs live?

There is no quick and easy answer to this question. Indeed many people, including scholars of repute in the theological world, would raise the more basic question whether they should be regarded as historical figures at all. This is largely because, in the nature of the case, personal, family annals do not feature in official histories, even if such histories had survived. The patriarchal narratives give an account of God's dealings with one man, whose descendants found their own lives moulded by the hand of the same God who had called Abraham. A theological unity binds together Israel's history. Has this unity been imposed from the standpoint of a writer late on in the story? This is the assumption of writers such as Martin Noth, John Van Seters and Thomas L. Thompson.[3] Noth, for example, writes of '*heroes eponymi*' [ancestors who gave their names to the

[3] Martin Noth, *The History of Israel* (A. & C. Black, 1958); John Van Seters, *Abraham in History and Tradition* (Yale University Press, 1975); T. L. Thompson, *the Historicity of the Patriarchal Narratives: The Quest for the Historical Abraham* (*BZAW* 133, 1974).

tribes] who, with their common father, are ... simply the personification of the historical situation after the occupation of the land.'[4] He regards Israel as having been composed of separate tribes, each of which had a separate history of its own before being fused together as Israel on the soil of Palestine. Noth cannot, therefore, look upon the patriarchal narratives of Genesis as of any historical worth.

A very different approach was being adopted in America by the so-called 'Albright School'. W. F. Albright had published as early as 1940 *From Stone Age to Christianity*, a popular but scholarly paperback, indicating the bearing of archaeological discoveries on the whole sweep of biblical history. By the time John Bright was writing his history book even more data had come to light, which had a bearing on the patriarchal period,[5] and this was later updated with further revision. In the light of his knowledge of the ancient orient, and especially that gleaned from documents judged to be roughly of the time of the patriarchs, John Bright wrote enthusiastically 'the patriarchal age has been illumined in a manner unbelievable. We now have texts by the literal tens of thousands contemporaneous with the period of Israel's origins. ... And, as the early second millennium has emerged into the light of day, it has become clear that the patriarchal narratives, far from reflecting the circumstances of a later day, fit precisely into the age of which they purport to tell.' He went on to deduce that the patriarchal traditions are very ancient indeed.[6] Bright did not immediately claim to have proved the historicity of the patriarchal narratives, but he called for a more sympathetic evaluation of the traditions, and laid emphasis on the fact that no evidence had come to light contradicting any item in the tradition.

Bright's *History*, with its Prologue headed 'The Ancient Orient before CA. 2000 BC', drew attention to the fact that Abraham came on the world's scene late in time. We too easily assume that in his day the world's population was struggling out of its Stone Age beginnings, whereas 'all across the Bible lands cultures had come to birth, assumed classical form, and run their course for hundreds and even thousands of years before Abraham was born'.[7] The earliest permanent town on the site of ancient Jericho goes back some five

---

[4] *History of Israel*, p. 6. Abraham and Isaac, of course, did *not* give their names to tribes, and Jacob also was a personal name.

[5] John Bright, *A History of Israel* (SCM Press, 1960. Second edition 1972).

[6] *Ibid.*, pp. 69–70.   [7] *Ibid.*, p. 24.

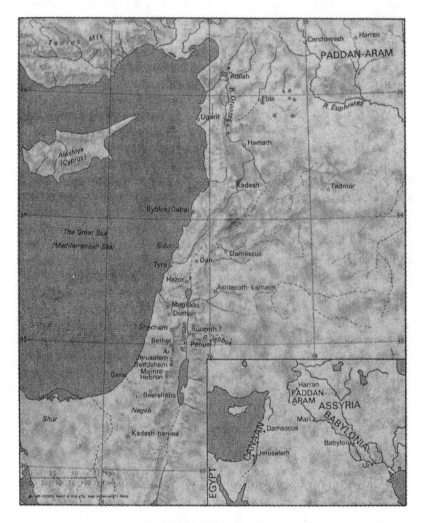

THE TIME OF THE PATRIARCHS

thousand years before Abraham, and from its remains there is evidence of considerable artistic development.

During the fifth millennium pottery began to be made and late in the fourth millennium writing was in use. Alongside these epoch-making inventions all kinds of technical advances were taking place, transforming agriculture by irrigation, and standards of living by trade with other countries. It was the needs of commerce that seem in the first place to have given the impetus to writing skills, but literature flourished also, and from Ebla in north Syria a huge library of texts written on clay tablets in about 2300 BC came to light in 1974–75. Literature had developed in Babylonia and Egypt also, but the importance of the Ebla texts for biblical studies lies in the fact that a local West Semitic language related to Hebrew was used alongside the Sumerian of southern Mesopotamia.[8] Syria–Palestine was already benefiting from its geographical situation between the great cultures of Egypt and Mesopotamia, and drawing upon the resources of both. About 1500 BC an alphabetic script was developing in Canaan, which was eventually to supersede the older pictographs and make reading and writing more accessible to all.

Though Abraham is likely to have moved to Canaan some hundreds of years before 1500 BC, it is clear that this country was no cultural backwater. As can be substantiated from preliminary accounts of the Ebla texts, diplomats travelled the ancient routes from Mesopotamia to Egypt, letters were exchanged and products sold. Since these routes passed through Syria–Palestine, the people who lived there were well aware of international links, language differences and the part played by written documents. The world passed their doorsteps.

The patriarchal narratives reflect this international world. From the Euphrates to the Nile frontiers were open, and free access was taken for granted. Moreover these chapters manifest a tolerance of other peoples which would have been out of character during the period of the exile, and even during the two centuries that preceded the exile. Isaiah's assessment of the Egyptians is scathing: they bring only shame and disgrace (Is. 30:5), and there is no help to be had in any of the so-called great nations. All the pre-exilic prophets proclaimed that God's day of judgment was near for the nations as for Israel. Would anyone who was writing at that time have

[8] A. R. Millard, *The Bible BC* (IVP, 1977), p. 13.

portrayed so peaceful a picture of the lands of the Fertile Crescent, or departed so far from the world he knew, as to speak of Israel's descendants bringing blessing to all the families of the earth? It would have been highly improbable unless he had specific records from which to work. Only when God's people were in exile did life among aliens raise the question of their welfare. Ezekiel in particular shows an ongoing concern that the nations should know the Lord God to be the Lord, repeating the refrain in various forms (*e.g.* Ezk. 30:25; 35:15; 37:28; 38:23). Even so the theological thrust of these statements is far removed from the simplicity of the patriarchal narratives. Bitter experience had taught Israel both the arrogance of foreign armies and the treachery of her own leaders. A terrible lethargy was one of the results (*cf.* Ezk. 33:31–32; 37:11), and it was only with the greatest difficulty that any encouraging word about the future was accepted.

Nevertheless it is the considered view of some recent writers that only in the sixth century BC did Abraham become for the first time the focus of Israel's faith. 'It is to the despairing community of the exile that the unbreakable promises of the patriarchs are addressed, and Abraham becomes the focus of corporate identity and the life-line of their hope and destiny.'[9] Van Seters seeks to demonstrate that the Genesis narratives reflect the historical and cultural perspective of a period later than the second millennium BC, that is, they were composed, as he argues, in the sixth century BC, the time of the exile. According to Van Seters 'there is no unambiguous evidence that points to a great antiquity for this tradition' ... 'one cannot use any part of it in an attempt to reconstruct the primitive period of Israelite history'.[10] The latest stages of the Genesis narrative he would attribute, on grounds of form and content, to the close of the fourth century BC.

This is not the place for a detailed analysis of the arguments and counter-arguments of the specialist world, but at least it is clear that the patriarchs are still the subject of intense interest. Moreover the book of Genesis has come under renewed scrutiny, for it is the date of the book as we have it that is the basis of the observations of Van Seters. Any incentive to return to the study of the book itself is to be welcomed, and in a sense its date of writing is not of great significance if it bears faithful witness to the events it portrays. What we are being asked to believe, however, is that the patriarchal

---

[9] J. Van Seters, *Abraham in History and Tradition*, p. 311.   [10] *Ibid.*, p. 309.

narratives are a late writer's attempt to supply the need of 'roots', an answer to the question of Israelites in exile, 'Who are we?' According to Van Seters there never would have been people answering to the descriptions of Abraham, Isaac and Jacob.

It is not easy to take account of all the implications of so radical a view of Genesis. The book is just the first of a series, and if the first is fictional, what happens to Moses, Joshua and the other great men and women associated with the exodus and conquest of the land? When does the narrative become historical, and how is the transition made so as to show no 'seam'? Experts are needed in the field of archaeology and ancient literature if the bearing of these and other disciplines on the patriarchal narratives is to be accurately assessed. For this painstaking work time is required, but the extreme views of Van Seters and others serve as a stimulus, and some scholarly reactions have already been forthcoming.[11] But the non-specialist, who may not have access to the works of scholars, should not overestimate the importance of following the debate in detail. The book of Genesis itself is of greatest value, and a study of it, as opposed to writings about it, remains a pearl of great price. Whatever its date of writing, and it is doubtful whether we shall ever know that for certain, it deserves to be read and read again. No other book could take its place; its historicity has not been disproved, and its value as a very ancient witness to God's revelation of himself needs to be reasserted.

The extreme scepticism of some scholars about the patriarchs has deflected us from our original quest for the date of Abraham. The fact is that, even if the patriarchal narratives provide little tangible evidence for dating, the Exodus account includes information which can be so utilized. By co-ordinating the periods of the patriarchs and the exodus scholars have arrived at likely solutions to the problem of dates, though certainty is not attainable. The Pharaohs mentioned in the books of Genesis and Exodus are not identified by name. If they had been, the chronology of the period would have been much more easily established. Two other sources of information which provide extensive evidence are archaeological data and texts of the second millennium.

Among the archaeological evidence available is that resulting from the excavation of sites mentioned in the patriarchal narratives. Dr John Bimson lists these individual sites, distinguishing those

[11] *E.g.* A. R. Millard and D. J. Wiseman (Editors), *Essays on the Patriarchal Narratives* (IVP, 1980), to which frequent reference will be made, under the abbreviation *EOPN*.

corresponding to the life of Abraham from those corresponding to the lives of Isaac and Jacob after the death of Abraham.[12] The time-lapse required by the length of their lives is taken into account. He then summarizes what can be known about thirteen of the locations mentioned, and indicates his assessment of the evidence. A distinction between the earlier and later patriarchal period, required by the length of their lives, is shown to be justified. While it needs to be borne in mind that a transition from one style of pottery to another did not take place simultaneously everywhere, and that the two styles overlapped, there is a strong likelihood, according to John Bimson, that the patriarchal period spanned the transition between Middle Bronze I and Middle Bronze II.[13] This means that Abraham's migration from Haran took place around 2092 BC and Jacob with his family moved into Egypt around 1877 BC. Whereas Abraham and Isaac are depicted as wandering as far south as Kadesh and Shur, 'the family of Jacob, after their return from Paddan-Aram, *do not frequent this area at all*, but instead are found in central Palestine, often in the vicinity of Shechem'.[14] He sees this fact corresponding to the depopulation of the Negeb at the end of Middle Bronze I, and the rise in central Palestine of urban centres such as Shechem in Middle Bronze II.

Though this suggested date has to remain tentative, and is subject to alteration in the light of future discoveries, for the purposes of this book we shall place the events of the patriarchal narratives within the twenty-first to nineteenth centuries BC. This is a century or so earlier than Bright indicates for the patriarchs in his chronology.[15]

The chance discovery earlier this century of numerous cuneiform texts from the second millennium made accessible for the first time a social and cultural milieu in which to set the patriarchs. Excavations at Nuzi, near Kirkuk, Iraq, between 1925 and 1931 brought to light several archives which provided a detailed picture of life in an ancient Mesopotamian community over five generations. Significant links between the patriarchal narratives and customs referred to in the Nuzi texts, which belong to the fifteenth-fourteenth centuries

[12] J. J. Bimson, 'Archaeological data and the dating of the patriarchs' in *EOPN*, pp. 59–92, especially pp. 68–80.

[13] These terms, based on changes in the shape of pottery, are not fixed, but are subject to adjustment as more exact evidence is arrived at. The end of MB I is now dated between 2000 and 1900 BC. See John Bimson, *EOPN*, p. 81.

[14] Bimson, 'Archaeological data', p. 80. The italics are his.

[15] *A History of Israel*, p. 477.

BC, are probably to be explained by the persistence of customs over many generations. Abraham did not come from Nuzi, but he came from the same cultural milieu, and social patterns referred to in Genesis are found illustrated in the later text; thus light is shed on their significance. This remains true, despite recent attempts to reduce the connection between the two literatures, and reference will be made to parallels as these occur in the text.

Another important collection of texts came to light in excavations at an ancient site called Mari, excavated by André Parrot from 1933 to 1939 and 1951 to 1964. Mari was situated in SE. Syria, close to the Euphrates river, and was the capital of a major city-state from about 1820 to 1760. Diplomatic texts make up about a quarter of the 22,000 inscribed clay tablets; others, relating to imports of food, hospitality and religious festivals, tell much about daily life. They are written in a Semitic language close to that of the Pentateuch (the first five books of the Bible), and continue to supply important background details of life in the later patriarchal period. Place-names mentioned include Haran (Gn. 11:31–32; 27:43; 29:4), where both Abraham and Jacob lived for some years.

As recently as 1975 the archive of 18,000 texts (mentioned above, p. 17) was discovered by Italian archaeologists at Ebla, about 70 km south of Aleppo, in Syria. It was an important commercial centre between 2400 and 2000 BC, though it had been a city since about 3000 BC. The inscribed cuneiform tablets belong to about 2300 BC, and are written in two languages, Sumerian and a NW. Semitic dialect. Publication of these texts is eagerly awaited, but already reference has been made to accounts of creation, mythologies, hymns; laws and edicts; administrative and economic texts. It is evident that trade was well established in grain, textiles, wood and wine between Ebla, with its quarter of a million inhabitants, and Cyprus, as well as with important capital cities in Palestine and further afield. More than 500 place-names are said to be listed. These texts are too early to have a direct bearing on the patriarchal narratives, but indirectly they fill in background which puts Abraham into a world of developed culture and commerce. He originated in a city, Ur, and though he deliberately avoided city life in Canaan he was well acquainted with the sophistication of life within the close-packed population of a city. What more the Ebla texts will reveal about beliefs and customs, language and literature of Syria in the centuries immediately before Abraham will be awaited with intense interest.

One further collection of texts has a bearing on the patriarchal narratives. At Alalah on the Orontes river in N. Syria the palace archives contained tablets, which in the main consisted of contracts and ration lists; at several points, however, they touch on migrations, social customs and names, such as feature in the Genesis accounts.

All in all, these four major collections of texts from the centuries before and after the patriarchal period provide an astonishingly rich mine of information about the dominant cultures of the Near Eastern world. We shall draw attention to details from this literature when it sheds light on the biblical text, for, though this book is concerned mainly with expounding the text and relating its message for today, the parallels help us to understand the things the patriarchs say and do. The fact that there are parallels strengthens our appreciation of the accuracy of the narrative in reflecting a bygone age, of which we should otherwise know nothing.

Ur of the Chaldeans

Terah took Abram his son and Lot the son of Haran, his grandson, and Sarai his daughter-in-law, his son Abram's wife, and they went forth together from Ur of the Chaldeans to go into the land of Canaan; but when they came to Haran, they settled there (Gn. 11:31).

The first eleven chapters of Genesis are frequently referred to as the 'primeval history', because they describe the outstanding episodes that account for our human condition, and are therefore part of the background of everyman. Yet the narrative suddenly narrows, and by means of a genealogy in chapter 11 introduces Abraham. The patriarchal narrative, the subject of this book, is so closely interwoven with the primeval story that it is impossible to draw a line between them. Terah descended from Noah through the line of Shem, and had three sons, Abram, Nahor and Haran, the last of whom was the father of Lot. Haran died in the land of his birth in Ur of the Chaldeans, but Terah and the rest of the family left Ur for the land of Canaan. This simple statement, so far-reaching in its implications, raises all kinds of questions in our minds. Where was this place of Abram's birth, and what kind of city was it? What was the religion of the place and why did the Lord call Abraham to leave it? He had married Sarai there and they had spent all their married life in this familiar home town.

There can really be little doubt about the identification of Ur.

Some alternatives have been suggested, such as Urfa, a name still found on modern maps of Turkey, near its border with Syria, and several places known as Ura in Asia Minor, but from none of these would Abraham have travelled east to Haran on his way to Canaan. The most generally-accepted identification is with the modern Tell el-Muqayyar on the river Euphrates in S. Iraq, where the famous excavations took place under Sir Leonard Woolley in 1922–34. In documents found there nothing further was needed to identify it beyond the name Ur, but since this meant 'city' it is not surprising that eventually other places bore the name, and the phrase 'of the Chaldeans' was added for clarification. The middle of the third millennium BC (2700–2250) was the classic period of the Sumerians who dominated S. Mesopotamia until about 1750 BC, and Ur was one of their four main cities. Knowledge of the city during this period is provided by the treasures from the royal tombs and from contemporary inscriptions. The city fell in c. 2250 to the famous Sargon of Agade, but rose to become the capital during the Neo-Sumerian period (2100–1960). According to our estimate of Abraham's dates, he would have been leaving Ur at the beginning of this revival of prosperity for the city.

The exquisite art treasures from the tombs at Ur belong to an earlier age than that of Abraham, but it is unlikely that the skills that produced them had been entirely lost. Details of the city he knew in 2100 BC are known from 'more than a hundred thousand clay tablets written in both Sumerian and the Semitic Babylonian dialects. Most have been found in Ur itself and in the neighbouring towns'.[16] The population at this time numbered at least a quarter of a million whose well-being depended on commerce and manufacture. Raw materials from as far away as India were transhipped in the Persian Gulf and carried up-river to the harbours at Ur. In the busy market the different trades occupied their separate quarters; one firm of weavers produced twelve different grades of cloth; the jewellers worked in gold and silver, mother-of-pearl and lapis-lazuli; copper-workers, carpenters, shipbuilders, potters and leather-workers were among the many other tradesmen to be found there.

The new city was dominated by a huge temple-tower, or ziggurat, 'three stages of which rose to one hundred and fifty feet above street level. On the top, surrounded by terraces lined with trees, stood a blue and silver temple dedicated to Nannar, also called

[16] D. J. Wiseman, *The Word of God for Abraham and Today*, Dr G. Campbell Morgan Memorial Lecture Number 11, 1959, p. 6, to which I am indebted for many details about Ur.

Suen or Sin, the moon-god and the principal deity served by many classes of priests.' The temple area was itself a vast market, and housed also a library and school, from which literature, pupils' exercises and teachers' reports survive. 'Religion in Babylonia at this time was polytheism of the grossest type ... more than three hundred distinct gods were worshipped.' 'According to Jewish tradition Abraham's father traded in these idols and this polytheism was a feature of Abraham's early home life from which he revolted.'[17] This is borne out by the reference to Terah, the father of Abraham, in Joshua's farewell address (Jos. 24:2): 'Your fathers ... served other gods.'

From this background God called Abraham. Despite the predominant materialism and money-making, life in Ur was culturally rich and comfortable, and there must have been many good reasons for wanting to stay there. On the other hand religious rituals in Ur were degrading, with their involvement in magic, superstition and prostitution. If a break were to be made, and the light of God's truth followed, physical removal from the whole environment was essential.

Haran

But when they came to Haran, they settled there (11:31).
The trade route from Ur to Haran was one of many used by merchants and salesmen as they promoted their products in new markets in Syria and Turkey (as we now call these countries). There is no uncertainty about the city of Haran, a name which has been perpetuated through the centuries, and the identification of which has been confirmed by discoveries on the site. Its name means 'crossroads', and it was the meeting-place of routes from Nineveh to the east and from Aleppo to the west, as well as from Babylon and Ur in the south. References to Haran in texts of *c.* 2000 BC indicate that it was noted for its temple, where the moon-god Sin was worshipped. The fact that it had something in common with religion at Ur may have tempted Terah to terminate his journey there, and settle down. Nahor's family resided permanently in that area, as we know from the Genesis story (24:15; 28:5), but Abraham was to be called to go further, into the land the Lord had promised to give to him.

[17] *Ibid.*, pp. 7–8

24

The life-span of the patriarchs

Not everyone who begins reading the Bible at Genesis is troubled by historical and geographical questions, both of which require some specialist knowledge, but everyone notes with astonishment the ages attained by the patriarchs and their forebears. As Derek Kidner comments, 'the patriarchal life-span was ... approximately double our own (this seems to have been a special providence (cf. Dt. 34:7): there is no indication that it was general).'[18] The pre-Flood era is so long ago that no-one is in any position to question the great ages of men like the ancestors of Noah, but, as has already been pointed out, Abraham belongs within the period of written documents and archaeological investigation. What can one make of his great age of 175?

It is a fact, of course, that there are people who, without any special recourse to scientific discoveries, attain long life in our own day. 'According to a Social Security Administration Report, there were 10,700 centenarians across the nation in 1976' (i.e. in the U.S.A.).[19] Granting that there may in certain cases be a lack of accurate documentation, 'yet there are enough well-documented cases of old people to prove that longevity can be achieved under many different climatic and social conditions'. Among several instances described is one from the seventeenth century: 'In 1638, an Englishman, Thomas Parr, was summoned to London by Charles I because it had been reported to the king that church records and other circumstantial evidence showed "Old Parr" ... to be 152 years old.' After his death an autopsy showed that his organs were 'as healthy as the day he was born'. René Dubos draws on specialist studies of old age and reaches certain general conclusions. In addition to 'a certain genetic constitution', ability to reach a very old age is correlated with 'a rather frugal diet but of well-balanced composition, vigorous and continued physical activity, and involvement in community affairs to the end of one's life'. There is one other factor he mentions, 'the will to live that mobilizes the body's natural mechanisms of resistance to disease'. This last may be the significant factor in the long life of men like Abraham, who had a future goal for their descendants, and in whom the other conditions

[18] *Genesis. TOTC.* p. 117.

[19] This and other quotations in this section are from the Introduction by René Dubos to *Anatomy of an Illness as Perceived by the Patient – Reflections on Healing and Regeneration* by Norman Cousins (Bantam Books, 1979), pp. 12ff. As the title indicates, this book was not written with the Genesis record in mind.

mentioned were probably fulfilled to a marked degree. There was a connection between long life and 'the fear of the LORD' (Ps. 34:11– 14), even if exceptions to the outworking of that principle could be found, but more important as an incentive for living was the desire to see the Lord's goodness upon children's children (Gn. 50:23).

Recent scholars have given themselves to the study of the patriarchal life-span, specifically because this has a bearing on the dating of the patriarchs. Some are sceptical: 'That Abraham lived 175 years has to be taken seriously, but it is nonsense from an historical perspective',[20] whereas others draw attention to longevity among peasant communities, and suggest that 'it is not impossible that environmental conditions in the third to early second millennium BC were such as to allow great ages to be reached frequently in the ancient near east. ... The Egyptians considered a lifespan of 110 years to be the ideal, and it seems reasonable to suggest that this notion arose at a time when men sometimes reached such an age without the ravages of extreme senility.'[21] The length of the patriarchal period required by the Bible's chronology of Abraham, Isaac and Jacob fits in with the dating suggested by the archaeological background, and therefore should not lightly be dismissed as impossible.

Quite apart from the arguments we have been considering, the Genesis narrative implies that there was something very exceptional about the experience of Abraham and Sarah, expressly because the Lord was establishing with them his everlasting covenant. It was imperative that they should learn the lesson of trust in their God, by which all their descendants were to live, and by which salvation was to be secured for all, to this day. Paul argues this point very fully in Romans 4: salvation 'depends on faith, in order that the promise may rest on grace and be guaranteed to all his descendants ... for he is the father of us all' (Rom. 4:16). It is hard to see how so important a principle could be established without the testings, which in Abraham's case involved a lengthened lifespan, and unusual generative powers in old age. The continued vigour of the patriarchs 'shows that this was no mere postponement of death but a spreading-out of the whole life process',[22] not for its own sake but to establish the corner-stone of salvation, faith, and its close association with life more abundant.

---

[20] T. L. Thompson, *Historicity of the Patriarchal Narratives*, p. 13. See *EOPN*, p. 84.

[21] Bimson, *EOPN*, p. 91. Source material is acknowledged, but Bimson admits that further research is needed to throw more light on the situation. [22] *Genesis, TOTC*, p. 117.

Part I
ABRAHAM
(Genesis 12 – 20)

Genesis 12:1–9

The decisive journey

Now the Lord said to Abram, 'Go from your country and your kindred and your father's house to the land that I will show you. ²And I will make of you a great nation, and I will bless you, and make your name great, so that you will be a blessing. ³I will bless those who bless you, and him who curses you I will curse; and by you all the families of the earth shall bless themselves.'

⁴So Abram went, as the Lord had told him; and Lot went with him. Abram was seventy-five years old when he departed from Haran. ⁵And Abram took Sarai his wife, and Lot his brother's son, and all their possessions which they had gathered, and the persons that they had gotten in Haran; and they set forth to go to the land of Canaan. When they had come to the land of Canaan, ⁶Abram passed through the land to the place at Shechem, to the oak of Moreh. At that time the Canaanites were in the land. ⁷Then the Lord appeared to Abram, and said, 'To your descendants I will give this land.' So he built there an altar to the Lord, who had appeared to him. ⁸Thence he removed to the mountain on the east of Bethel, and pitched his tent, with Bethel on the west and Ai on the east; and there he built an altar to the Lord and called on the name of the Lord. ⁹And Abram journeyed on, still going toward the Negeb.

These words mark a fresh start in the narrative of the book of

Genesis. Three times in the first eleven chapters God's judgment had fallen: mankind was banished from the garden of God (3:23–24), destroyed by the Flood (chs. 6 – 9), and divided by diverse languages (11:1–9). There were also five primal curses. The serpent was cursed and proclaimed to be the enemy of the woman (3:14–15); the ground was cursed (3:17); Cain was condemned to doubtful harvests and anxious wandering (4:11–12) and Canaan to servitude (9:25–27); linguistic distinctions ensured chaotic misunderstandings between the nations (11:1–9). True, there had also been blessing (1:28; 9:1); but in relation to God the predominance of divine displeasure, resulting in judgment, made for fear and uncertainty. Now a new departure is about to be made which will remove the doubt about God's intention to bridge the gulf between himself and mankind.

The first step had already been taken under the leadership of Terah, who had taken the family from Ur of the Chaldeans on the decisive stage to Haran. Only four people are named in 11:31, but clearly Nahor and his wife and children were included because they continued to live in Haran (*cf.* 24:10, 'the city of Nahor'). The extended household may well have numbered many more. It would be interesting to know the circumstances of the removal from Ur, and all that it entailed. The narrative implies that a settled life in the vicinity of a populous area was more congenial than venturing farther into the unknown.

It has often been thought that Abraham should be described as a nomad. A distinction has been made between long-distance nomads of Central Asia and the semi-nomads, who lived on the edge of settled communities making seasonal movements in order to find pasture for their flocks and herds. But Abraham does not fit neatly into either category. He and his father had been city dwellers, for whom the long move northwards marked a strenuous uprooting. For Terah and Abraham it was a once-for-all journey into a new environment. Their agreed destination was the land of Canaan, but 'when they came to Haran, they settled there' (11:31). This overwhelming desire to stay in one place is uncharacteristic of nomads, whose possessions are portable and who live on the move. They have no land to call their own, whereas Abram was making for a country that God promised to him. If his company seemed to be often on the road it was necessity that drove Abram on, not love of freedom to travel. Since the only land he ever owned was the field that contained the cave of Machpelah, where Sarah was buried

(23:20), it is not surprising that there is no mention of Abraham growing crops, but Isaac and his sons were to do so (26:12; 30:14; 37:7). In view of God's promise they took advantage of every opportunity to stake their claim to farming land, thinking, perhaps, that by assimilation the promised territory would become their possession. For the sake of accuracy, then, we should not think of the patriarchs as typical nomads. The long journeys they made were once-for-all removals, epoch-making events that marked the turning-points in their lives. The records in Genesis pass over these journeys without comment until the land of Canaan comes into view.

The reluctance of Terah and Nahor to proceed beyond Haran highlights the obedience of Abram. Not only was he prepared to take to the road again when the remainder of the family had settled down, but also he was going into the unknown without a map and, as it turned out, was not to enjoy a settled abode again. This was the price of obedience, as it is for many who respond to God's call today. There is, however, this difference, that those who cross national barriers now at the call of God do so in order that others may know the benefits of the gospel; Abram was leaving all in order that there should *be* a people of God and a Saviour. He was to make a decisive break with the past in order to be open to God's truth.

By leaving Ur and Haran, where moon worship was the dominant cult (the name Terah is related to the Hebrew for 'moon'), Abram would be set free from the drag of a familiar culture which would be positively harmful and detrimental to any new start. The break with his family would minimize the influence of ancestral traditions in so far as these were idolatrous. Foreign gods were amongst the belongings that Jacob's family took with them from Haran to Bethel (35:2), and the same was true of those who gathered at Shechem under Joshua. Religious practices are persistent, and some of the Israelites who entered Canaan with Joshua were still clinging to the gods their fathers served 'beyond the River', that is, in Mesopotamia, beyond the Euphrates (Jos. 24:14, 23). Though the leaders were clear about the supremacy of the one true God, popular superstitions were never far below the surface, and emerged in times of crisis.

The wrench of leaving the family and going out into the unknown, with all its uncertainty and associated hardships, is familiar to every pioneer. In the case of Abram God was weaning him away from everything that would remind him of his cultural roots, and testing his faith so that it would develop muscle. This could best happen when the softening influences of familiar surroundings had been removed, and every step required dependence on the God who had called him.

The break with the past, then, has a place in the future purposes of God. Thus far Abram has heard the call of God, but his knowledge of him is limited. The place where God will reveal himself in a fuller way is not Haran but a hitherto unknown country, away to the south-west, on the route to Egypt. Without the separation there will be no further revelation. In a similar way Jesus called his disciples to 'leave their nets' and follow him (Mk. 1:17–18). There is a sense in which every believer has to abandon the past, make an about turn and start afresh in the service of Jesus. This may not entail a literal journey, and circumstances may remain just as they were before, but nevertheless to forsake all in order to serve the Lord is as decisive a step as was Abram's move from Haran, and as full of potential for good. It is therefore important not to turn a deaf ear to the insistent promptings through which God speaks, but instead to recognize their source and to act upon them. Terah shows what happened to one man who held back. Having left the moon cult behind him in Ur he came to it again in Haran, and failed to make the decisive break with idolatry. 'Where he halted he also died.'[1]

God disclosed to Abram not only his commands but two far-reaching promises. Indeed the commands of God and the promises of God belong together.

The *land* is the first-mentioned promise of God in connection with the *blessing*, a word that sums up God's great design for the lost to be restored. By anchoring blessing in a land God made the promise tangible. A land had boundaries, geography, inhabitants; it had to be possessed, occupied and fortified against attack; it needed cultivation and conservation if it was to support a population. Indeed every aspect of life was involved with the land. God committed himself to fulfil a programme which could be tabulated; the blessing was not to be in any way nebulous, but measured in relation to crops and stock. Success or failure would be obvious to all. Because the land was expressly God's gift every harvest was his loving supply. If disaster struck, God would be administering a rebuke. Material and spiritual values met in the ordinary events of the workaday world, and God was very close at hand.

[1] U. Cassuto, *A Commentary on the Book of Genesis*, II (Jerusalem, 1949; English Translation israel Abrahams, 1964), p. 283.

The second half of the promise, '*I will make of you a great nation*', was equally subject to observation, and seemed as unlikely to be fulfilled as the promise of land. 'Sarai was barren; she had no child' (11:30). This very disqualification became in God's hand a tool for his purpose. Though Abram was 'as good as dead' (Rom. 4:19), because it looked as if his family was about to die out, the God 'who gives life to the dead and calls into existence the things that do not exist' (Rom. 4:17) taught Abram and all succeeding generations to trust him to fulfil his word, despite all the adverse indications. It is situations of human helplessness that provide occasions for God's power to be demonstrated and recognized.

And I will bless you, and make your name great, so that you will be a blessing (12:2).
According to these words, when God is allowed to be the director of Abram's life the evidence of his working will become obvious to all. In the short term maybe only Abram was aware of it, through an inner reassurance, and he was soon to have that reassurance tested by famine and therefore by hunger; in the course of his lifetime, however, he was to know beyond the shadow of a doubt that the Lord who had spoken to him was true to his word. He had said, '*I will bless you.*' Five times in two verses the word 'bless' (in various forms) insists that the Lord is going to shower his goodness upon Abram, and though troubles were sure to come for him as for everyone else, if God was for him, all would ultimately be well. Two aspects of this blessing, land and descendants, had already been named, but the short human lifespan would not permit Abram himself to live to see such outworkings of God's purpose.

How then could Abram recognize the blessing of God in his life? As the narrative unfolds the answers will appear, but they will be of two kinds: *a*. personal and private and *b*. outward and visible. Abram will make time for communion with God and will find that God frequently speaks to him; what other people would see would be his increasing prosperity and his 'success'. The blessing of God Almighty is not nebulous, but clear and definite.

That Abram's name became great can hardly by denied. Its meaning 'exalted father' probably implies that he came from an exalted family, but it could also draw attention to God as his great Father. There is the further possibility, if the name is derived from Akkadian, that it means 'he loved the Father'.[2] This would explain

[2] U. Cassuto, *Genesis*, II, p. 267.

31

the references to Abram in later literature as 'the friend of God' (2 Ch. 20:7; Is. 41:8), a lovely name that was appropriate for one to whom the Lord confided his secrets (Gn. 18:17).

Blessing was not restricted narrowly to the one to whom it was promised. It overflowed to others. In the first place those who happened to come into contact with Abram were to have a share in the blessing; simply by meeting and knowing him, because he lived close to his God, others would become aware of the living reality of the Lord. '*You will be a blessing.*' But there was a special benediction for those who recognized his worth and 'blessed' him with their help and support. They too would experience the enriching touch of the Lord on their lives. Conversely, any who alienated themselves from Abram, for whatever reason, would find the opposite of prosperity coming their way, so enabling them to conclude that they were on the wrong road, and encouraging them to side with Abram. Both the blessing and the curse were appointed signposts. According to Ryle the singular 'him who curses you' implies that his foes were few, but, attractive as that thought is, the inference is probably not justified. The singular is more likely to be a stylistic variation meaning 'every single one who curses you will be cursed'.

But the extent of the blessing was greater yet. It was to embrace *all the families of the earth*, an aspect of the promise that could not have been formulated after the event, whether the Genesis text dates from the sixth century BC, or from a time nearer to Abram's day, for it anticipates the gospel of Jesus Christ. Translations bring out two possible ways of understanding the Hebrew of the last clause of verse 3. On the one hand there is the rather more restrictive translation, which understands the verb as a 'middle' or reflexive mood: 'by you all the families of the earth will bless themselves' (RSV). The idea would be that people would formulate blessings incorporating the name of Abram. On the other hand the verb has usually been taken to be passive, hence, 'in thee shall all the families of the earth *be blessed*' (AV, RV; and *cf.* NIV). Both renderings can be supported, and in the last analysis there is not much difference in the sense, for both testify to a universal blessing through Abram. His fame will everywhere be associated with all the good things that the blessing of the Lord implies, and, as Ryle points out, Abram is thus given a place in the divine scheme of redemption.[3]

From our vantage-point in the Christian era we are well placed to assess the promise to Abram. The letters of Paul overflow with the

[3] H. E. Ryle, *Genesis*, CB, p. 156.

wonder of the mystery of God's purpose, 'which he set forth in Christ as a plan for the fullness of time, to unite all things in him, things in heaven and things on earth' (Eph. 1:9–10). The obedience of one man was to make possible the beginning of God's cosmic plan of salvation, which in Christ was to open out into undreamed of riches for all who hoped in Christ. The gifts of land and posterity were real blessings, but they were also tokens of blessings as yet unmentioned, which were in store, kept ready by the God and Father of our Lord Jesus Christ as love gifts that he alone could bestow. His bounty surpasses all our calculations, rebuking our little faith and halting obedience. But God did not reckon two thousand years too long in order to bring his plan to fulfilment, and Abram had to move forward by taking what must have seemed to him to be a step in the dark.

So Abram went, as the Lord had told him. ... Then the Lord appeared to Abram (12:4, 7).
The trek which had taken the family to Haran now had to be continued under Abram's leadership, while Terah remained at the half-way post. Lot and Sarai are mentioned by name because they are to be prominent in future events, but it is clear that both Abram and Lot were heads of sizeable communities 'gotten in Haran', and, to judge by the 318 trained men whom Abram could muster in time of need (14:14), we should think in terms of hundreds rather than tens on the move with Abram and Lot. Despite this, or perhaps because of their numerical strength, they were allowed to travel unmolested as they crossed the Euphrates and made their way south. The desert road via Tadmor was shorter but more demanding than the main route through Aleppo and Qatna. Both took in Damascus and Hazor. No-one dared to plot his own route, but travelled by the traditional ways taken by merchants and armies through the centuries. 'Movements in stages by groups of persons, possibly merchants, are attested by records of Old Babylonian itineraries.'[4] At regular intervals staging-posts marked the resting-places along all the ancient routes. Taking the well-defined road in the direction of Egypt, Abram and his company came in due course, after covering some 400 miles, to the Jordan valley, and from there the road took them into the mountainous terrain, later to belong to the

---

[4] D. J. Wiseman, 'Abraham in History and Tradition', *Bibliotheca Sacra* (1977), p. 125. He makes reference to W. W. Hallo, 'The Road to Emar', *Journal of Cuneiform Studies* 18 (1964), pp. 57–88.

Joseph tribes. The twisting valleys led to the pass between Mount Ebal and Mount Gerizim, which commands the route to the Mediterranean and the north-west, and southwards the way led over the hills to Hebron and Beersheba. It was at this important junction that Abram visited *the oak of Moreh* at Shechem, or Sichem (AV). The name Shechem means 'shoulder', and a shoulder of Mount Gerizim dominates the western horizon of the city. The remains of the ancient city are known today as Tell Balata, a mound in the eastern suburbs of modern Nablus. A copious spring situated nearby has ensured the importance of the spot through the ages.

Excavation has shown that the story of Shechem goes back to *c.* 3500 BC, so it was well over a thousand years old by the time Abram saw the place. We should think of it in his day as an unwalled village of considerable size, dominated by the 'oak' or terebinth (turpentine tree) for which it was famous. The *place* at Shechem is possibly a technical term for 'sanctuary', and the special tree, referred to in Genesis 35:4 and Joshua 24:26, may have been connected with teaching at the shrine, for *Moreh* is a name connected with the Hebrew word for 'instruction'. If so there was special point in saying *the Canaanites were in the land*. The area was dominated by alien gods, like many cities of the world today. They were worshipped as if they were the owners of the territory, but the reality was otherwise. The Lord was not in competition with any other god, for he owned the whole created order and had in his gift every country of the world. Therefore he could say categorically, '*To your descendants I will give this land.*' He reigned even where he was not acknowledged. As a sign that this was certain Abram paid formal tribute to the Lord by erecting a special memorial and by worshipping the Lord. He thus claimed on behalf of his posterity the fulfilment of the promise he would not live to see. But he was in the heart of the land which his family would later inhabit, and he could look about him and with the eye of faith appreciate its possibilities.

On the way farther south Abram avoided both Bethel and Ai, preferring to frequent the unoccupied hills, now that he was within reach of wells and food supplies. Despite long periods of excavation on sites thought to be Bethel and Ai, the evidence has raised problems which have not satisfactorily been solved, and the possibility that Bethel should be identified with modern Bireh is currently being explored. Whereas Abram is not mentioned as returning to Shechem, the vicinity of Bethel was his goal after his escapade in Egypt (13:3), and seems to have been specially significant to him as a place of worship, as it was to be for Jacob also (28:19; 35:1).

For the first time Abram is mentioned as *pitching his tent* on the east of Bethel, and this has usually been taken to indicate that he and his company were regularly tent-dwellers. Yet no mention has been made of tents through the story of the long journey thus far, probably because places of hospitality were available at villages along the way. Now, however, Abram is leaving the frequented route for the hills, and it is here that he both pitched his tent and built an altar to the Lord, acts which 'may be symbolic of assuming territorial possession or at least of the adoption of the territory for the tribe, for those same acts are noted with some emphasis as "the place where his tent had been at the beginning and where he had made an altar at the first ... and had called on the name of the Lord" (Gn. 13:3–4).'[5] This new way of life, then, marks Abram's faith. He stakes his claim to the land God has promised by setting up camp. He is forced into the less habitable hill country because the valleys are already occupied, but he does not expect to become prosperous. It is enough to have the promise of God that his 'seed' will possess the land. With this assurance Abram turns his back on the security of a house in a town or village to become a tent-dweller.

It has been argued recently that, contrary to popular supposition, mention of tents is more indicative of a first millennium origin for the patriarchal narratives than a date in the second millennium.[6] Abram has been assumed to have been a nomad, rather like the modern bedouin, but the tent encampments of the bedouin are a distinctive feature by the mid-first millennium BC. It is the assumption which has been misleading. Abram was looking for a land which his descendants would inherit and, as Van Seters rightly argues, the theme of land-inheritance is utterly foreign to the nomadic way of life. Nor does the text of Genesis suggest that Abram was taking part in a widespread migration; rather the reverse. He was doing the extraordinary thing at the command of God, and moving into what was, humanly speaking, the unknown. The call of God to each individual is intensely personal, for no two of his children are taken by quite the same path, but the outcome of obedience is far reaching. In the case of Abram it was to be pivotal for the whole of history.

[5] D. J. Wiseman, 'They Lived in Tents', in *Biblical and Near Eastern Studies: Essays in Honor of William Sanford Lasor*. Ed. C. A. Tuttle (Eerdmans, 1978), p. 198.
[6] J. Van Seters, *Abraham in History and Tradition*, p. 16.

Genesis 12:10 – 13:1

Abram in danger

*Now there was a famine in the land. So Abram went down to Egypt to
sojourn there, for the famine was severe in the land.* [11]*When he was about to
enter Egypt, he said to Sarai his wife, 'I know that you are a woman
beautiful to behold;* [12]*and when the Egyptians see you, they will say, "This
is his wife"; then they will kill me, but they will let you live.* [13]*Say you are
my sister, that it may go well with me because of you, and that my life may
be spared on your account.'* [14]*When Abram entered Egypt the Egyptians saw
that the woman was very beautiful.* [15]*And when the princes of Pharaoh saw
her, they praised her to Pharaoh. And the woman was taken into Pharaoh's
house.* [16]*And for her sake he dealt well with Abram; and he had sheep,
oxen, he-asses, menservants, maidservants, she-asses, and camels.*

[17]*But the Lord afflicted Pharaoh and his house with great plagues
because of Sarai, Abram's wife.* [18]*So Pharaoh called Abram, and said,
'What is this you have done to me? Why did you not tell me that she was
your wife?* [19]*Why did you say, "She is my sister," so that I took her for my
wife? Now then, here is your wife, take her, and be gone.'* [20]*And Pharaoh
gave men orders concerning him; and they set him on the way, with his wife
and all that he had.*

[13:1] *So Abram went up from Egypt, he and his wife, and all that he had,
and Lot with him, into the Negeb.*

Abram did not stay long in the vicinity of Bethel, but, in the
reassurance of the Lord's disclosure to him at Shechem that he was
now in the land the Lord intended to give him, he set out to explore
its southern extremities. It was there that he encountered a severe
famine. Anyone who has ventured into the barren country south of
Beersheba will wonder that the Negeb, or 'south', was ever anything
but desert. The rainfall of the area has evidently varied considerably
at different periods, and there is a theory that between *c.*2200 and
*c.*1900 BC an extension in the polar ice caused a southerly shift in the
line of the flow of cyclones from the west, which would have
brought a much better rainfall to the eastern Mediterranean
countries than they enjoy at present.[7] Even so the Negeb, like the
sub-Saharan belt across Africa, must always have been a marginal
region, and we can take it that there was a divine purpose that led
Abram into famine conditions.

Early on in his spiritual experience Abram was discovering that to
be in the place of God's appointment is not to be exempt from

suffering. As the psalmist found, the person who declares his trust in the Lord sometimes seems to be singled out for trouble, while the godless prosper (Ps. 73:2–14). There are indications in Scripture that spiritual 'high points', when God draws near or speaks in a special way, are often followed by unusual testings. Outstanding in this respect is the experience of Elijah after the public vindication of his lone stand for God on Mount Carmel. It was followed by a threat on his life and by deep depression (1 Ki. 19:1–4). Even more telling is the way Jesus was sent by the Spirit after his baptism out into the desert to be tempted by Satan (Mk. 1:12–13). The personal reassurance for Jesus, 'You are my Son, whom I love; with you I am well pleased', seems to be a preparation for the severe forty-day testing in the bleak and lonely desert, when Jesus clung to God's word, and so defeated Satan (Mt. 4:11). Abraham, on the other hand, appears to have been caught off his guard by the famine conditions.

So Abram went down to Egypt to sojourn there. The plain factual statement leaves open the question of motivation, and we do not know whether this journey was part of God's purpose for Abram or not. His grandson, Jacob, was to be told expressly to go to Egypt (Gn. 46:3–4), and the angel told Joseph to take the child Jesus and his mother into Egypt to escape the murderous intentions of Herod (Mt. 2:13). Abram, pioneering the way of faith, could not have known that Egypt was to become for his descendants a place of bondage, and probably took the advice of travellers, who told him that food was plentiful in Egypt, without expressly seeking God's guidance. In view of the fact that he knew he was in the land of promise, and had only recently had a special revelation of the fact (verse 7), to leave it so promptly the minute difficulty loomed ahead 'has every appearance of an unbelieving flight from circumstantial difficulty, a desertion of faith in favour of logic'.[8] He thereby lost the opportunity to discover that the Lord could provide for his people not only a land but also necessary food.

In all probability the glories of Egypt had been general knowledge to Abram when he lived in Ur. Now he was within reach of this fabulous country, created in a desert by the Nile floods, did he have an urge to see it for himself? Its ancient culture had reached its peak of splendour in the Old Kingdom period (2680–2180 BC), during which the pyramids were built, and religious and wisdom

[7] Denis Baly, *The Geography of the Bible* (Lutterworth, 1957), p. 73.

[8] J. A. Motyer, in a personal note to the author.

literature flourished. Already there were impressive sights to attract the traveller. Indeed the first great step pyramid, the first major structure of cut stone in history, was by Abram's time some 600 years old. Moreover, the Pharaohs of the period, unlike the kings in Canaan who ruled over city states, were rulers of all Egypt and wielded great power.

If Abram arrived in Egypt about 2090 BC, as is possible if he travelled from Haran to Canaan about 2092, the centre of power would have been a city state called Herakleopolis, about 60 miles south of Memphis. Some 40 years later he would have had to travel further south still, to Thebes; in either case, since he had direct dealings with the Pharaoh, he must have penetrated far beyond Goshen and up the Nile valley to the royal capital of his time.

On the borders of Egypt Abram began to be plagued by fear. Asiatic infiltrators like himself had caused trouble in the Delta region of Egypt some decades earlier, creating political upheaval. It would not be surprising, therefore, if Asiatics continued to be viewed with some suspicion and were subject to harassment. As a foreigner in search of food Abram was aware that he had no rights in Egypt, and he feared for his life. In particular he was aware that the Pharaohs were always interested in adding beautiful women to their harem, and that they paid handsomely for the privilege. He judged that his wife, Sarai, would attract notice. What was to prevent Egyptians putting him to death in order to present Sarai to their monarch? With a brutal disregard for Sarai, and a total lapse from faith in his Lord, Abram resorted to deceit in order to save his own skin. Sarai was in fact his half-sister as well as his wife (20:12), so, while it was not altogether a lie to pass her off as his sister, it was a deliberate deception, intended to enable him to escape danger and incidentally to enrich himself. But it was a despicable ruse, and one which might have endangered the birth of his promised son. He reveals his self-centred reasoning, *that it may go well with me ... and that my life may be spared*, no matter what happened to his wife.

The Bible is totally candid about the failings of those whom the Lord chose to be his servants. Abraham, the great man of faith, knew what it was to desert the way of faith, and experienced fear and fell into temptation. The Pharaoh, to Abram's shame, administered a stern rebuke, so revealing that his code of ethics was higher than Abram had supposed. He would not wittingly have stolen another man's wife. Now Abram must take his wife and be gone. Still in possession of the bride-price the Pharaoh had paid in flocks and herds, Abram left the country. He never ventured to Egypt again. The danger of shortage in Canaan was to be preferred to the moral and spiritual dangers he had hardly been aware of when he went to Egypt. Indeed it was a sin of omission in the first instance which had ultimately involved him in cowardice and betrayal of his wife: he had failed to draw near to the Lord, and had failed therefore to trust him, when trouble struck. The source of his danger was confidence in his own judgment. Like Abram, we have to learn that it is all too easy to find ourselves off the track, simply because we have trusted our own reasoning instead of consulting our guide. All kinds of dangers follow.

Marvellously there was a way back, for the Lord had not given up on Abram, despite his lapse, any more than he abandons his defeated servants today. Abram was allowed to leave Egypt without suffering any recriminations; unaccountably, the Pharaoh allowed him to keep all his *sheep, oxen, he-asses, menservants, maidservants, she-asses, and camels* (12:16), and take them back to Canaan. The only explanation was that the Lord had spoken to the Pharaoh, forbidding him to touch his 'anointed ones' (Ps. 105:15). The return journey brought Abram into the south of Canaan, but he was not content to stay there, for he had a mind to head for Bethel and Ai, 'where he had made an altar at the first' (13:4). Instinctively Abram sensed his need of forgiveness, cleansing and renewal, and he sought them at the place where he had already owned and worshipped the Lord. It is important to notice that he came back, that the way was open for him to come back, and that the Lord received him back, as the continuing story proves.

Genesis 13:2 – 18

Be separate

Now Abram was very rich in cattle, in silver, and in gold. ³And he journeyed on from the Negeb as far as Bethel, to the place where his tent had been at the beginning, between Bethel and Ai, ⁴to the place where he made an altar at the first; and there Abram called on the name of the Lord. ⁵And Lot, who went with Abram, also had flocks and herds and tents, ⁶so that the land could not support both of them dwelling together; for their possessions were so great that they could not dwell together, ⁷and there was strife between the herdsmen of Abram's cattle and the herdsmen of Lot's cattle. At that time the Canaanites and the Perizzites dwelt in the land.

8Then Abram said to Lot, 'Let there be no strife between you and me, and between your herdsmen and my herdsmen; for we are kinsmen. 9Is not the whole land before you? Separate yourself from me. If you take the left hand, then I will go to the right; or if you take the right hand, then I will go to the left.' 10And Lot lifted up his eyes, and saw that the Jordan valley was well watered everywhere like the garden of the Lord, like the land of Egypt, in the direction of Zoar; this was before the Lord destroyed Sodom and Gomorrah. 11So Lot chose for himself all the Jordan valley, and Lot journeyed east; thus they separated from each other. 12Abram dwelt in the land of Canaan, while Lot dwelt among the cities of the valley and moved his tent as far as Sodom. 13Now the men of Sodom were wicked, great sinners against the Lord.

14The Lord said to Abram, after Lot had separated from him, 'Lift up your eyes, and look from the place where you are, northward and southward and eastward and westward; 15for all the land which you see I will give to you and to your descendants for ever. 16I will make your descendants as the dust of the earth; so that if one can count the dust of the earth, your descendants also can be counted. 17Arise, walk through the length and the breadth of the land, for I will give it to you.' 18So Abram moved his tent, and came and dwelt by the oaks of Mamre, which are at Hebron; and there he built an altar to the Lord.

And Lot ... went with Abram (verse 5). The Genesis narrator seems to be insisting on the fact that, though Abram was called to leave his father's household, Lot went with him (12:1, 4). When Abram went up from Egypt ... Lot went with him (13:1). This nephew of his, as becomes apparent in this chapter, did not appreciate what motivated his uncle in leaving the rest of the family in response to God's call. Though he travelled with Abram he did not share his vision, and at some point it was inevitable that a separation between them would occur. While Abram was slowly learning the way of faith, Lot learnt about Egypt from his uncle's misguided journey (verse 10), and in general picked up from him the wrong kind of example.

Only now is mention made of Abram's wealth. It is likely that he was already rich in silver and gold after selling his property in Haran; now, as a result of his escapade in Egypt, he had a greatly increased household and stock of animals. It was on account of their increased prosperity that Abram and Lot found themselves at loggerheads. Pasture was at a premium on the bare limestone hills, and friction arose between the herdsmen of the two families, a thing unheard of earlier, when their possessions were few. The Canaanites and Perizzites (possibly the town-dwellers and the country folk respectively) represented a threat which increased now that Abram and Lot were becoming more powerful. The possibility of armed attack had to be reckoned with, but if they separated they would not arouse the same degree of suspicion in the population around them. On two counts, therefore, it was expedient that Abram and Lot should go their separate ways. The question arises whether Abram should in the first place have permitted Lot to accompany him. What Abram now saw clearly was that separation was inevitable. As head of the family he had the right to direct where Lot should live, but on this occasion he behaved with exemplary selflessness, and gave Lot the choice.

Lot took full advantage of this option and predictably chose the most fertile land in sight, *well watered everywhere like the garden of the Lord, like the land of Egypt.* He was attracted by the promise of prosperous farming, and the improved standard of living he and his family would enjoy in the sub-tropical fertility of the Jordan valley. Where rivers or springs created oases, the growth of vegetation, including trees and luscious fruits, contrasted with the barrenness of the hills all round. Lot had visions of the good life as he had witnessed it in Egypt, with all the latest in artistic and technological development, and time and leisure to enjoy it. He would be a fool to miss the opportunity of self-advancement and assured prosperity! The separation of Lot was final. He went eastwards, down the steep drop of some 3,000 feet into the rift valley to seek his fortune in the plain of Jordan. There he lived *among the cities of the plain,* namely Sodom, Gomorrah, Admah, Zeboiim and Bela (or Zoar), as they are listed in 14:2, but *he pitched his tent near Sodom,* undeterred by its foul reputation, and when next he is mentioned he is living *in* Sodom (14:12). What he did not reckon with was the downward pull of evil around him, and the enervating effect of prosperous ease on a self-centred life. He had made his choice, and it would soon become apparent whether Lot found the advantages he was hoping for in his new surroundings.

Meanwhile Abram, looking intentionally in every direction from a vantage-point in the hills, was musing upon his nephew's opportunism and his own isolated way of life. It was after he had parted with one of the most desirable areas of the land promised to him that he was reassured by a word from the Lord. *'All* (not part of) *the land which you see I will give to you and to your descendants for ever.'*

He could not in the long run deprive himself of what God had promised him, and neither can we. The late Fred Mitchell, Home Director of the China Inland Mission from 1943 to 1953, quoted the experience of a donor to the Müller Orphan Homes who gave over and above a tenth of his income, as time went on and his family commitments were less demanding. He found that the more he gave the more he received, so that he could not ultimately impoverish himself.[9] His testimony is a striking illustration of the statement of Jesus, 'Give, and it will be given to you; good measure, pressed down, shaken together, running over, will be put into your lap. For the measure you give will be the measure you get back' (Lk. 6:38). It is open to everyone to take Jesus at his word.

Abram, unlike Lot, had not chosen for himself (verse 11), but, far from losing out, he had the word of the Lord, *'I will give* to you and your descendants all the land.' Those descendants, moreover, would become so numerous that no census would be able to count them. The reiterated promises and the recurring themes of people and land enabled him to believe that it would be as the Lord had said. Now he is to make a pilgrimage of faith, and walk the length and breadth of the land to claim it as his own, according to the Lord's command. In other words, he is to appropriate and enjoy the gift God has given him, appreciating all that it entails. Our New Testament heritage is even more astonishing, for God has 'blessed us in Christ with every spiritual blessing in the heavenly places ...' (Eph. 1:3), and only by conscious application of that truth in our particular circumstances do we begin to enter into our inheritance.

Abram's immediate response was to move from Bethel to a site much further south, *near the great trees of Mamre at Hebron* (NIV), which were already sacred, like the 'place' at Shechem. Here Abram built an altar, appropriate in his day as a symbol of worship, and dedicated to the Lord who had made the solemn promise to give him the land. In this way he claimed the area as the Lord's gift to his posterity, and for considerable periods he lived there himself in conscious possession of the land-right.

On a factual note, the Old Testament informs us that the city of Hebron had not yet been built (Nu. 13:22). The information that it was built seven years before Zoan in Egypt suggests, according to the specialists, a date about 1720 BC. Evidently the text was finalized after this date, when Hebron was a well-known city that

---

[9] F. Mitchell, *The Stewardship of Money* (Inter-Varsity Fellowship, 1951), p. 33.

helped to locate the older Mamre. The modern visitor is taken to the traditional site of Mamre, 3 kilometres north of present-day Hebron, where Herodian ruins remain to mark the enclosure round a well at Ramet el-Khalil, meaning 'the high-place of the friend'. Pottery found there indicates that this site was already frequented in the third millennium BC, before the time of Abram. It has not proved easy to locate ancient Hebron, which should be to the east of Mamre (Gn. 23:17, 19; 49:30; 50:13), if the ancient mosque in Hebron is built over the cave of Machpelah, as tradition claims. Perhaps the original Hebron now lies within the confines of the present city, in which case possibilities of excavation are severely limited.

Genesis 14:1–24

A just war?

In the days of Amraphel king of Shinar, Arioch king of Ellasar, Chedorlaomer king of Elam, and Tidal king of Goiim, ²these kings made war with Bera king of Sodom, Birsha king of Gomorrah, Shinab king of Admah, Shemeber king of Zeboiim, and the king of Bela (that is, Zoar). ³And all these joined forces in the Valley of Siddim (that is, the Salt Sea). ⁴Twelve years they had served Chedorlaomer, but in the thirteenth year they rebelled. ⁵In the fourteenth year Chedorlaomer and the kings who were with him came and subdued the Rephaim in Ashteroth-karnaim, the Zuzim in Ham, the Emin in Shaveh-kiriathaim, ⁶and the Horites in their Mount Seir as far as El-paran on the border of the wilderness; ⁷then they turned back and came to En-mishpat (that is, Kadesh), and subdued all the country of the Amalekites, and also the Amorites who dwelt in Hazazon-tamar. ⁸Then the king of Sodom, the king of Gomorrah, the king of Admah, the king of Zeboiim, and the king of Bela (that is, Zoar) went out, and they joined battle in the Valley of Siddim ⁹with Chedorlaomer king of Elam, Tidal king of Goiim, Amraphel king of Shinar, and Arioch king of Ellasar, four kings against five. ¹⁰Now the Valley of Siddim was full of bitumen pits; and as the kings of Sodom and Gomorrah fled, some fell into them, and the rest fled to the mountain. ¹¹So the enemy took all the goods of Sodom and Gomorrah, and all their provisions, and went their way; ¹²they also took Lot, the son of Abram's brother, who dwelt in Sodom, and his goods, and departed.
¹³Then one who had escaped came, and told Abram the Hebrew, who was living by the oaks of Mamre the Amorite, brother of Eshcol and of Aner;

these were allies of Abram. [14]*When Abram heard that his kinsman had been taken captive, he led forth his trained men, born in his house, three hundred and eighteen of them, and went in pursuit as far as Dan.* [15]*And he divided his forces against them by night, he and his servants, and routed them and pursued them to Hobah, north of Damascus.* [16]*Then he brought back all the goods, and also brought back his kinsman Lot with his goods, and the women and the people.*

[17]*After his return from the defeat of Chedorlaomer and the kings who were with him, the king of Sodom went out to meet him at the Valley of Shaveh (that is, the King's Valley).* [18]*And Melchizedek king of Salem brought out bread and wine; he was priest of God Most High.* [19]*And he blessed him and said,*

> *'Blessed be Abram by God Most High,*
> *maker of heaven and earth;*
> [20]*and blessed be God Most High,*
> *who has delivered your enemies into your hand!'*

And Abram gave him a tenth of everything. [21]*And the king of Sodom said to Abram, 'Give me the persons, but take the goods for yourself.'* [22]*But Abram said to the king of Sodom, 'I have sworn to the Lord God Most High, maker of heaven and earth,* [23]*that I would not take a thread or a sandal-thong or anything that is yours, lest you should say, "I have made Abram rich."* [24]*I will take nothing but what the young men have eaten, and the share of the men who went with me; let Aner, Eshcol, and Mamre take their share.'*

International events impinged on the life of ordinary peace-loving citizens even in the days of Abram, and the incident related in this chapter is the only one that touches on world politics. As it happens the Bible has perpetuated knowledge of the event when few other sources of information have survived, which is not surprising considering that, according to one scholar, the account was written 'scarcely later ... than the middle of the second millennium'.[10] His argument is that the names of the foreign invaders and their respective countries have an authentic ring and one of them at least (Arioch) takes us back to the Old Babylonian age. This name belonged to a vassal of Zimri-lim at Mari, its linguistic background is Hurrian (the mountainous area north-east of Haran), and it is not attested after the middle of the second millennium. When account

---

[10] E. A. Speiser, *Genesis*, p. 106. He weighs carefully the evidence of the names, indications of Akkadian influence and the geographic details, and concludes, 'Abraham was not a nebulous literary figure but a real person who was attested in contemporary sources' (p. 108).

is taken of the Mesopotamian power alliances and the coalition of Canaanite city states, the likely date of the incident, according to one specialist historian, is narrowed to between 2000 and 1750 BC.[11]

Present-day visitors to Israel have a good view of the geographical area invaded by the coalition of the four alien kings when they look across the Dead Sea from Masada. A tongue of land, known as the Lisan peninsula (Lisan means 'tongue'), almost divides the Dead Sea in two, and in Roman times it was possible to ford the strait. Masada guarded the crossing. The plain at the foot of the mountain ridge beyond the unproductive marl of the Lisan is a prolonged oasis, producing fruits, grain and cotton, and supporting sheep, goats and cattle. The region may well have been even more fertile before the catastrophe that overtook Sodom and Gomorrah. The inaccessibility of the plain, and its intense heat, were normally a deterrent to invaders. South of the Lisan peninsula the water of the Dead Sea 'is never more than three feet deep, and it has been suggested that it is of fairly recent formation, having been created by an earthquake. ... It is held that if this did happen, it would explain the destruction of the five cities of the plain (Gn. 19:15–28)',[12] though no supporting evidence for this theory has been forth-coming.

The chapter covers a timespan of fourteen years (verse 5). It was the familiar story of oppression by a coalition of stronger powers. Chedorlaomer of Elam, the country to the east of Sumer in which Ur was situated, and bordering on the Persian Gulf, headed a coalition of Mesopotamian states. Ironically, those rulers whose domain Abram had left were making a bid for the very land which the Lord had promised to Abram. Even political events conspired to obstruct God's purposes. The cities represented by the five kings are likely to have been in the vicinity of the Dead Sea (*the Salt Sea*, verse 3). Though these kings duly paid tribute for twelve years, in the thirteenth they refused, hence the invasion in the fourteenth year. This is depicted as part of a much more extensive campaign of conquest. The army followed the eastern road south from Damascus, through Ashteroth-karnaim (5), situated in the hills to the east of the Sea of Galilee, and through the territory of Zuzim, Emim and

---

[11] K. A. Kitchen, *The Bible in its World*, p. 72. Speiser opted for 'approximately the eighteenth century B.C.' (p. 109), though F. F. Bruce has estimated the date as 2080. *Cf. Places they knew. Abraham and David* (Scripture Union, 1984), p. 14.

[12] Denis Baly, *The Geography of the Bible*, p. 205.

Horites, east of Jordan, to El-paran (6), on the Gulf of Aqaba.[13] From there they moved north-west to Kadesh, and then north-east to the southern end of the Dead Sea. The fact that names are brought up to date with alternatives in brackets suggests that we have to do with an ancient record, whose references were no longer meaningful when the book was finalized.

The overthrow of the five city states of the Dead Sea region was swiftly accomplished and would soon have been forgotten but for the fact that Lot, who by this time had moved into Sodom, was taken captive together with his family and possessions. Others managed to escape capture, only to stumble into bitumen wells in their panic. The value of bitumen ('slime', AV, RV) for building purposes had long been appreciated (11:3).

Abram in Hebron may well have been aware of the movement of powerful troops in the vicinity, but he would not have known of Lot's plight apart from the message brought him by a fugitive. Nor would Abram's gallantry and skill in fighting have been known apart from this incident. The title *Abram the Hebrew* suggests an independent account, for it was a designation used by others and not by Israelites, except as an accommodation to other people's usage, as in 40:15 (though see also Ex. 21:2; Dt. 15:12). It seems to have had a derogatory tone about it, and to have meant something like 'the migrant', implying that he did not really belong. Nevertheless he had been settled there for long enough to have won the confidence of his neighbours *Mamre, Eshcol* and *Aner*. Their covenant of mutual support meant that they went with Abram into battle (*cf.* verse 24), for a kinsman's need was a call to arms. By the time Abram had mobilized his retainers,[14] *born in his house* and therefore fully loyal (as opposed to purchased slaves who might resent their lot and rebel), the enemy had covered some 180 kilometres. By strategic deployment of his small army, and with the element of surprise in his favour, Abram succeeded in throwing the enemy into confusion. Having pursued them for a further 100 kilometres as a precaution against their return, he collected both the captives and their belongings to return them to their homes. Especially mentioned are

---

[13] Egyptian texts from the 20th and 19th centuries BC, which are inscribed on sherds, mention the names of enemies of Egypt's rule in Palestine, accompanied by curses. Amongst cities named are Jerusalem, Ashtaroth, and possibly Kadesh.

[14] The word *ḥᵃnîkāw*, translated 'retainers', occurs nowhere else in the Bible, but it is found in Egyptian Execration Texts (*cf.* footnote 13, above), denoting a Palestine chieftain's retainers, exactly as here.

Lot and *the women*, whose sufferings in such conditions did not bear thinking about.

The victory was already being celebrated before the return of the army, and two very different characters, Melchizedek and the king of Sodom, went to meet the triumphant Abram at the otherwise unknown Valley of Shaveh (though the King's Valley is mentioned in 2 Sa. 18:18). That a landless stranger should liberate the inhabitants was in itself an event of note, that deserved recognition. But more than that is entailed here.

Melchizedek

It is necessary to dwell a little on Melchizedek because of the references to him later in Scripture. His name means 'king of righteousness' and he is king of Salem, meaning 'peace'; it was a significant link between the two concepts, for there can be peace only where there is righteousness, but it was an astonishing name for any human being to bear. A later king of Jerusalem had *zedek* as part of his name, Adoni-zedek, 'lord of righteousness' (Jos. 10:1), so Salem has usually been thought to be Jerusalem; though other places bore the name (Shaalim, 1 Sa. 9:4, and Salim, Jn. 3:23, could be alternative spellings). Psalm 76:2 uses Salem as Jerusalem, seat of the Mighty God, while in Psalm 110 Melchizedek was originator of the priesthood the Lord had purposed to found. In the New Testament the writer to the Hebrews saw in Melchizedek the foreshadowing of the king-priest, the Lord Jesus Christ, who far surpassed all others, and Jerusalem witnessed his priestly self-offering.

In the light of all this, we return with added interest to examine what the Genesis writer has to say about so exalted a person. The surprise is that he says very little. Melchizedek appears from nowhere; his parentage is not given, even though Genesis excels in genealogies. Yet even this omission is deliberate, for, according to the writer to the Hebrews, it signifies an eternal priesthood (Heb. 7:3). What our writer does say is that Melchizedek brought bread and wine to sustain the victor, and that he was *priest of God Most High* (Heb. *'Ēl 'Elyôn*), that is, the supreme God, whom he identified as creator of heaven and earth (verse 19). It was in the name of the supreme God that he blessed Abram, and gave glory back to God Most High for delivering Abram from his enemies. Abram, conqueror of the kings of the east and deliverer of the kings of the Dead Sea region, was now 'king of kings', had he wished to assert his position, yet he received the blessing of Melchizedek, and recognized his superiority by giving him a tenth of all the spoils. Abram recognized him as a worshipper of his own Lord, Yahweh, under the title of God Most High (verse 22), a witness to 'his eternal power and deity', revealed to mankind since the beginning of time (Rom. 1:19–20), a revelation which served only to render sin inexcusable, as Paul points out.

Through Abram God was to provide a way of redemption; 'Abram represents the new spiritual force that has entered the world's history',[15] and yet, mysteriously, Melchizedek represented an order of priesthood that far surpassed the levitical priesthood that descended from Abram. It was an eternal priesthood, foreshadowing that of the Son of God himself (Ps. 110:1, 4; Heb. 7:15–17); and 'we have such a high priest, one who is seated at the right hand of the throne of the Majesty in heaven' (Heb. 8:1). Thus Melchizedek is part of the Bible's rich and intricate tapestry, a recurring theme that leads to the principal priest-king, the Lord Jesus Christ.

The other king who met Abram that day was a very different character, representing all the evil for which Sodom was already famous. Since Abram had defeated his conquerors, the king of Sodom was at Abram's mercy, yet he took the initiative in attempting to make a deal by asking to receive back his subjects, whom Abram had rescued. In this way he made a show of generosity by offering to let Abram keep the spoils, which in any case were Abram's by right of conquest. It was a clever ploy, but Abram had already in his mind renounced any thought of keeping the plundered goods, and had *sworn to the Lord God Most High, maker of heaven and earth*, that he would not take so much as a shoe-lace from the king of Sodom, lest he should say, '*I have made Abram rich.*' This was both a declaration of allegiance to his Lord, and a testimony to the Lord's ability to provide the needs of his servant. Goods from Sodom would be the ultimate in all that was desirable in the luxury of the time. Abram had no use for them as he worked out a counter-culture on the bare hills. He saw that his allies and suppliers were reimbursed, but he voluntarily forfeited his reward. His logic was explicable only to the eye of faith, but the Lord was not slow to see and reassure him.

[15] H. E. Ryle, *Genesis*, p. 182.

Genesis 15:1–21

A sovereign Protector

After these things the word of the Lord came to Abram in a vision, 'Fear not, Abram, I am your shield; your reward shall be very great.' ²But Abram said, 'O Lord God, what wilt thou give me, for I continue childless, and the heir of my house is Eliezer of Damascus?' ³And Abram said, 'Behold, thou hast given me no offspring; and a slave born in my house will be my heir.' ⁴And behold, the word of the Lord came to him, 'This man shall not be your heir; your own son shall be your heir.' ⁵And he brought him outside and said, 'Look toward heaven, and number the stars, if you are able to number them.' Then he said to him, 'So shall your descendants be.' ⁶And he believed the Lord; and he reckoned it to him as righteousness.

⁷And he said to him. 'I am the Lord who brought you from Ur of the Chaldeans, to give you this land to possess.' ⁸But he said, 'O Lord God, how am I to know that I shall possess it?' ⁹He said to him, 'Bring me a heifer three years old, a she-goat three years old, a ram three years old, a turtledove, and a young pigeon.' ¹⁰And he brought him all these, cut them in two, and laid each half over against the other; but he did not cut the birds in two. ¹¹And when birds of prey came down upon the carcasses, Abram drove them away.

¹²As the sun was going down, a deep sleep fell on Abram; and lo, a dread and great darkness fell upon him. ¹³Then the Lord said to Abram, 'Know of a surety that your descendants will be sojourners in a land that is not theirs, and will be slaves there, and they will be oppressed for four hundred years; ¹⁴but I will bring judgment on the nation which they serve, and afterward they shall come out with great possessions. ¹⁵As for yourself, you shall go to your fathers in peace; you shall be buried in a good old age. ¹⁶And they shall come back here in the fourth generation; for the iniquity of the Amorites is not yet complete.'

¹⁷When the sun had gone down and it was dark, behold, a smoking fire pot and a flaming torch passed between these pieces. ¹⁸On that day the Lord made a covenant with Abram, saying, 'To your descendants I give this land, from the river of Egypt to the great river, the river Euphrates, ¹⁹the land of the Kenites, the Kenizzites, the Kadmonites, ²⁰the Hittites, the Perizzites, the Rephaim, ²¹the Amorites, the Canaanites, the Girgashites and the Jebusites.'

The battle, with its prolonged period of exertion and tension, was followed by morbid fears and a sense of failure. It had been all very well to win a surprise victory, but in doing so Abram had exposed himself to a hostile attack from kings who had proudly avenged the mere failure to pay taxes. He could expect fierce retaliation for his daring attack, and he was understandably afraid.

It would not be surprising if he also had misgivings about the wisdom of allowing the king of Sodom to take all Abram's share of the spoils, when he could have come to a compromise with him.

While Abram was going through this turmoil of confused thoughts, the Lord chose to give Abram a vision of himself, and *the word of the Lord came to Abram*. This particular phraseology, so characteristic of the prophetic books, is repeated in verse 4, but comes nowhere else in the Pentateuch. In effect it marks Abram out as a prophet (20:7; *cf*. Ps. 105:15). The whole episode, which begins in the night (for Abram is directed to the stars), and lasts through the day following till sundown and another night (12, 17), is to be seen as the word of the Lord. No event of Abram's life surpasses this in importance.

The Lord takes the initiative, comes to his servant and speaks directly to his need: '*Fear not ... I am your shield*.' Any outstanding act of faith sets a precedent and causes the man of God to feel exposed and under threat. Though Abram cannot see God's shield covering him, he is to count on its presence and dismiss his fears. He will not be the loser, because he has trusted in the living God and put God's honour before his own. The thought of a great reward brings to the surface all Abram's pent-up questions concerning the promise, which, inasmuch as it presupposes a son, seems as unrealistic as ever. While he remained childless the promise had no possibility of fulfilment, unless his adopted son was intended by the Lord to inherit the promise.

On his way from Haran Abram's route would have taken him through the fertile plain of Damascus, an oasis where people have lived from time immemorial. This may have been the occasion when the parents of Eliezer became part of Abram's household. Among the extant collections of written records of the second millennium BC it is remarkable that there should be a mention of the practice of adoption in the Nuzi texts. Admittedly these belong to NE Mesopotamia and are later than Abram's time, but the custom may well have been widespread and ancient. Childless couples adopted a son, who would be their servant and would eventually inherit their possessions. Hurrian law (discovered at Nuzi) distinguished between the direct heir and the substitute heir. There was no doubt in Abram's mind that the latter was second best, and that if subsequently a natural son was born he would become the heir, as Hurrian law laid down.

It was helpful that Abram had voiced his misgivings. The Psalms record a whole range of human reactions to life's experiences, and encourage frank admission of the enigmas that arise when God seems far away, or appears to have allowed wrong doing to succeed. Freedom to express our misgivings leads on to the Lord's response, not in rebuke, but in redoubled promises, as happened here. Abram said, '*I continue childless ...; and a slave born in my house will be my heir*'; but the word of the Lord came to him, '*Your own son shall be your heir.*'

Abram was learning the basic lesson that every believer in turn has to learn, namely that God's delays are not denials. Though the years were passing and many of his contemporaries were already dead, Abram had continued to rely on the word the Lord had given him concerning a son. But the time of waiting was agonizingly long, and the Lord, who had taken note of his servant's need of renewed assurance, said, '*Look toward heaven, and number the stars, if you are able to number them*', which, of course, he was not able to do with the naked eye. Even with sophisticated telescopes the task is never finished. How appropriate, therefore, was the sign; the Lord would give to Abram not only physical descendants, but also the children of faith in every generation and of every nation (Rom. 4:16–17).

And he believed the Lord. The Hebrew verb 'believe', from the same root as the word *Amen*, conveys the security of a faithful and established relationship. Abram might easily have pointed to his excellent reasons for doubting whether the Lord could mean his word to be taken literally. In view of Sarai's childlessness all through the years, he might have asked what hope there was of her bearing a son in her old age. And he himself was so old as to be as good as dead. Unbelief comes readily, whereas faith fears a disappointment and tends to hesitate. But Abram was convinced in the depth of his being that the Lord was true, and his word valid. He therefore expected to have a son, as the Lord had promised, despite all the adverse circumstances, being 'fully convinced that God was able to do what he had promised' (Rom. 4:21).

The incident highlights for us one of the main truths of the gospel, for faith is central to its message. Abram had received a specific promise from God, but he did not seem to receive what was promised and he could do nothing to achieve it. He was helpless, so much so that the promise appeared to mock him. Yet his response was to look to the greatness of the One who had spoken and to accept that *he* took responsibility for the fulfilment of his promise. Faith rests on the fact that God is faithful, and when we take God at his word we prove for ourselves his faithfulness. After further years of waiting Abram received the promise, but through faith he found immediate acceptance with God, who *reckoned it to him as righteousness.*

Paul saw clearly how fundamental was the way of faith, from the time of Abram and right through the Old Testament period into the New. He goes so far as to say that verse 6 was written for Christian believers, 'to whom God will credit righteousness – for us who believe in him who raised our Lord from the dead' (Rom. 4:23–24, NIV). Christian believers know that, because they are 'in Christ', his righteousness is extended to them, as it was to Abram, faith being the link that causes them to be accepted and blessed in Christ, and granted the promises. Those who do not yet know him may learn from the example of Abram and believe God's word, resting on God's reliability which will never let anyone down. Those who know the way of faith will nevertheless find God leading into ever new circumstances in which to trust him.

How am I to know?

Abram needed not only a sovereign Protector but also a sovereign Lord of history, if the promise to his family was to be sure of fulfilment. The divine promise concerned both inheritance of the land and a son to succeed him. Already Abram had been reassured about the coming heir and his descendants; now the Lord makes a further affirmation, '*I am the Lord who brought you from Ur of the Chaldeans, to give you this land to possess*' (7). By pronouncing his name and mighty acts the Lord ensures that Abram knows his identity, his proved reliability and his continuing work in his servant. God's faithfulness was the foundation rock on which Abram could rely; he had only to recall the many times he had proved it in his experience since leaving Ur. It is good and necessary for us frequently to recall the works of the Lord, and in the light of all he has done move on to new acts of faith. As the popular old hymn reminds us, if we 'count our many blessings, name them one by one, then it will surprise us what the Lord has done'. We shall also find boldness to look ahead to his purposes which are largely hidden from us. New ventures create new tensions for us because they call us into the unknown.

Abram, unable to see how the Lord was going to give him the land, asked for some evidence that history would work out according to God's word. Far from rebuking him, the Lord responds by entering into a solemn treaty to ratify his word. Such treaties or 'covenants' were a common feature of life throughout the ancient Near East. The Lord used for his purpose a well-known political and social convention, the most binding form of agreement among men, to reinforce the certainty of his promise. This treaty is the original form of the salvation covenant which gives the Old Testament ('will' or 'covenant') its name. Whereas the covenant made after the Flood had established that God would not again destroy life on the earth (Gn. 8:21–22), this covenant marks the beginning of God's plan of salvation. God makes himself known by his personal name to Abram, '*I am the Lord*' (verse 7), *Yahweh*, the One who *is* (for the name is connected with the verb 'to be', and is explained as I AM in Ex. 3:14). He is the source of all life, the unchanging one, controller of man's destiny, and therefore well able to design his salvation. The Lord's ability to disclose to Abram the oppression of his people before they inherit the land is a small thing by comparison. He is identified with God Most High, maker of heaven and earth (14:22). Melchizedek knew the Creator; Abram meets with the Saviour of mankind.

First Abram is required to bring five sacrifices. Why these particular animals and birds were commanded we do not know, and little is known about the rites connected with covenant making in the ancient Near East, except that the animal was killed, divided and used partly in a burnt offering to the deity and partly for a communal feast. The Bible itself is the best source of further detail. Abram cut each of the sacrifices into two, and with the parts made two heaps. The Hebrew technical term to 'cut a covenant' reflects this part of the ritual, with its inevitable shedding of blood. The picture is filled in by the prophet Jeremiah in the course of berating the king for breaking a covenant he had initiated to secure the freeing of slaves in Jerusalem (Je. 34:18–19). The solemn commitment was made by passing between the parts of the sacrifice, and those who broke their word the Lord would 'make like the calf which they cut in two and passed between its parts'. In other words, death awaited the person who broke a covenant.

The 'cutting' of the covenant was the point at which the covenant was inaugurated, and two other verbs, used of making a covenant in chapter 17, bring this meaning to the fore. 'I will make my covenant between me and you' (verse 2) has, instead of 'cut', the Hebrew verb 'give', or 'put'. Thus God lays down the terms of the covenant as well as taking the initiative, and later he says, 'I will *establish* my covenant' (verse 7), where the verb adds to the idea of entering into a covenant the element of security and changelessness. Human covenants were often broken, and still are, but this covenant was established by the unchanging God, and was consequently ordered and secure.

Abram had asked, '*How am I to know ... ?*' The Lord replies, '*Know of a surety*', without any shadow of doubt. Abram does not receive a direct answer to his question; instead he is given an outline of the events that must take place before his descendants inherit the land. First they are to become exiles, then slaves, in a land that is not their own. The oppression will last four hundred years, after which judgment will fall on the nation they serve, and they will emerge with great possessions. Abram would die in peace and be buried in the land, which was already inhabited. The time had not yet come for him to occupy the land. He had not the military strength needed to overcome the inhabitants, nor could he adequately occupy it; in any case the time had not yet come for judgment to fall on the land, *for the iniquity of the Amorites is not yet complete.*

The Judge of all the earth knows the moral state of each of the nations. He will not hesitate to subject his people to bondage, nor will he precipitate the death of the Canaanites. In God's mastery of history the exodus from Egypt and the destruction of the Canaanites would be timed to coincide, and the Israelite invasion, which required of Joshua unusual courage (Jos. 1:6–7, 9), was the outworking of God's justice. Israel could know that slavery in Egypt was no accident, and that it would come to an end in God's time; those who defied God, and his moral ordering of the universe, would know defeat and death. There was no favouritism in this respect, as Israel was to discover when the northern kingdom was conquered by the Assyrians, and the southern by the Babylonians. Thus the Lord is shown to be governing with total impartiality the affairs of the nations, effecting with infinite patience his moral purposes.

Abram received the Lord's disclosure of future events, of his own death, and of the sufferings his people would have to endure for a time, before they eventually possessed the land. He was still guarding the sacrificial offerings when darkness fell again, and he watched as 'an oven of smoke and a flame of fire' passed between the pieces (17). The furnace of fire symbolized the presence of the living God with whom Abram was being brought into fellowship. It was an awesome symbol, which Moses was to encounter at Sinai on a grander scale, and one which the people were to associate with God's holiness (Ex. 19:18–23). He was not a God who could be trifled with, and yet he would go with them in a pillar of cloud and of fire (Ex. 40:38), guiding and protecting them.

For Abram all this was implicit as, all alone, he felt the heat of the flame that passed so near to him. He would be aware that, if this had been a treaty made by a human king, both parties to it would have passed between the pieces of the sacrifice. As it was Abram was merely the passive observer, while the Lord, symbolized by the fire, walked between the sacrificial offerings, so taking upon himself the curse implicit in the ritual: 'Thus be it done to me' if the terms of the covenant are broken. Though the reason for these particular offerings is not known to us, the principle that a sacrifice lay at the base of a covenant is already shown to be fundamental. The Lord 'cut' a covenant with Abram that day, using the most solemn form of oath, to ensure the certainty of the fulfilment of his word: *To your descendants I give this land* (18). In principle it was his already, from its southern border along the river that formed the boundary with Egypt northwards to the great curve of the Euphrates to the north-east of Hamath, though it was occupied by other peoples.

The centrality of faith

This remarkable prophecy sets the human life-span in perspective. Even the man whom the Lord singles out to bless in a special way, and to make the father of his people, will see little of the fulfilment of the promise, first made directly to him. Nor can he contribute anything towards its fulfilment. He and his wife do not even have children, yet all around him are other people's children in abundance. The discrepancy between his present plight and the word of God could hardly have been greater, nor his helplessness more marked. But faith requires testing if it is to grow. Even more fundamentally, faith can be exercised only when its focus is unseen; once its object materializes faith 'vanishes into sight', and God, who has called forth faith, is proved faithful. The point of the exercise is to trust God because he has promised, and to act on his word before there is external evidence that he will do as he has said. This is

Abram's crowning achievement, that he understood what the Lord was teaching him through his perversely impossible circumstances, continued to believe nevertheless, and so became 'the father of all who believe' (Rom. 4:11).

In view of the fact that faith is the outstanding topic throughout the Abram narrative, there is evidence here that faith is the primary response required by God of everyone, before the coming of Christ as well as after. Paul saw this clearly. He pointed out that Abram was not given the law; a further 430 years were to elapse before the law would be given (Gal. 3:17–18), and yet Abram received the promise. The idea of salvation by law-keeping appeals because it gives us an illusion of self-help, but it is not effective. It cannot make us right with God, nor acceptable to him. That is why it has to be by faith in his promises that salvation is granted. Obedience to God's law may be an evidence of faith, but it is the faith that God requires, supremely faith in Christ Jesus. 'And if you are Christ's, then you are Abraham's offspring, heirs according to promise' (Gal. 3:29). Indeed, Paul argues that Abram's 'seed' (singular in the Hebrew, as in English) is Christ (Gal. 3:16).

It was in anticipation of Christ's life, death and resurrection that Abram received such blessing, and, under the tuition of Jesus himself, we learn that Abram had life eternal. The expression *go to your fathers* (Gn. 15:15) is probably a current circumlocution for death, but it is suggestive of continuing consciousness and fellowship beyond the grave. Used in the mouth of God it already implies ongoing life. Jesus, however, is more emphatic. Speaking to the theologians of his day, he expected them to read 'the God of Abraham, and the God of Isaac, and the God of Jacob' in the light of the fact that God is not the God of the dead but of the living. In the eyes of Jesus these experts knew 'neither the scriptures nor the power of God' (Mk. 12:24–27). They should not have doubted that the living God would raise from the dead those who trusted in him.

Genesis 16:1–16

Marital stress

Now Sarai, Abram's wife, bore him no children. She had an Egyptian maid whose name was Hagar; ²and Sarai said to Abram, 'Behold now, the Lord has prevented me from bearing children; go in to my maid; it may be that I shall obtain children by her.' And Abram hearkened to the voice of

Sarai. ³So, after Abram had dwelt ten years in the land of Canaan, Sarai, Abram's wife, took Hagar the Egyptian, her maid, and gave her to Abram her husband as a wife. ⁴And he went in to Hagar, and she conceived; and when she saw that she had conceived, she looked with contempt on her mistress. ⁵And Sarai said to Abram, 'May the wrong done to me be on you! I gave my maid to your embrace, and when she saw that she had conceived, she looked on me with contempt. May the Lord judge between you and me!' ⁶But Abram said to Sarai, 'Behold, your maid is in your power; do to her as you please.' Then Sarai dealt harshly with her, and she fled from her.

⁷The angel of the Lord found her by a spring of water in the wilderness, the spring on the way to Shur. ⁸And he said, 'Hagar, maid of Sarai, where have you come from and where are you going?' She said, 'I am fleeing from my mistress Sarai.' ⁹The angel of the Lord said to her, 'Return to your mistress, and submit to her.' ¹⁰The angel of the Lord also said to her, 'I will so greatly multiply your descendants that they cannot be numbered for multitude.' ¹¹And the angel of the Lord said to her, 'Behold, you are with child, and shall bear a son; you shall call his name Ishmael; because the Lord has given heed to your affliction. ¹²He shall be a wild ass of a man, his hand against every man and every man's hand against him; and he shall dwell over against all his kinsmen.' ¹³So she called the name of the Lord who spoke to her, 'Thou art a God of seeing'; for she said, 'Have I really seen God and remained alive after seeing him?' ¹⁴Therefore the well was called Beer-lahai-roi; it lies between Kadesh and Bered.

¹⁵And Hagar bore Abram a son; and Abram called the name of his son, whom Hagar bore, Ishmael. ¹⁶Abram was eighty-six years old when Hagar bore Ishmael to Abram.

The more clearly God's promises were spelt out to Abram, the more clearly Sarai saw herself as the failure. Though she continued to preside over the household, which may by this time have included some of the concubines and their sons (Gn. 25:1–6), and though she was the legal wife, she felt keenly the humiliation of her barrenness. Each passing year diminished her hopes of becoming a mother and of giving to Abram the son of the promise. She saw no answer to her prayers and may easily have come to the conclusion that she had for some reason forfeited the Lord's favour. If so, she was wrong. The very reverse was true, but reason, in conflict with faith, for the time being won the day.

Only now is mention made of Sarai's Egyptian servant-girl, Hagar. There were ways in which a childless couple could acceptably meet their need of a child. One was by adoption, and Abram had evidently adopted Eliezer (15:2). Another, mentioned in the Laws of Hammurapi, was for the wife to present one of her slave-girls to her husband to bear a son for the marriage.[16] It was understood that in this case the wife, and not the mother, had jurisdiction over the child, whose right of inheritance was uncertain until he was legally adopted. When Sarai suggested that Hagar might become the substitute mother of her child she was, therefore, following a socially acceptable precedent, though there was some doubt in her mind as to whether such a child would be the son of the promise: '*it may be that I shall obtain children by her*' (verse 2).

Abram's compliance is reminiscent of that of Adam (Gn. 3:6). Even in so important a matter it's a case of 'As you say, dear', and once again the result is disruption of relationships. The response of faith would have been that, if the Lord had prevented conception thus far, he would be the one to bring it about in accordance with his word. But ten years was a long time to wait and patience was at an end.

What Sarai had not bargained for was the emotional upheaval which the new situation would involve. The once-amenable Hagar found she had one up on her mistress, because she was to bear Abram a child. Though the Law of Hammurapi forbade a slave-girl to exalt herself to equality with her mistress (and it is likely that an unwritten law had said the same through the ages), the fact of pregnancy brought Hagar a new status and a new hope, which legislation was powerless to crush. Sarai clearly felt that she had a cause for grievance against Abram, and expected him to put Hagar firmly in her place. 'You are responsible for the wrong I am suffering' (5, NIV), she said, unreasonably, to Abram. As his lawful and beloved wife she looked for his understanding and support in her just resentment against Hagar, forgetting that she had first suggested that he should take Hagar. But Abram put the onus on Sarai and shrugged off his wife's problem. Sarai's frustration worked itself out in such an abusive attitude that Hagar ran away. What had seemed to be reasonable, permissible by law, and expedient, was disrupting the family and causing a rift between husband and wife. In retrospect it was obvious that her attempt to remedy their childlessness had not been part of God's plan, a realization that added to her bitterness and led her to blame Abram rather than to admit that she had been wrong. It is always easier to put the blame on someone else than to face up to our own faults, which, as in

[16] *EOPN*, p. 127.

Sarai's case, may have led to the friction in the first place.

The spotlight now falls on Hagar, who instinctively made for home. The road to *Shur* (7), the eastern district of Egypt (Gn. 25:18), cut across the desert to the southern tip of the Nile delta, but it would be a tiring and lonely journey. The text suggests that there was only one spring where drinking-water could be found along that road, and there *the angel of the Lord found her*. Does it come as a surprise that the Lord should appear to an Egyptian, and a woman at that? The revelation she was to receive was as specific as that to Abram had been, for 'God shows no partiality' (Acts 10:34). Her first reassurance was to meet someone who took notice of her and asked about her journey. The questions may have been stereotyped ones, for her answer mentioned no place-names. Indeed Hagar disclosed the reason for her plight, *'I am fleeing from my mistress Sarai'* (8), and she received the instruction to return and submit to her. It was a hard thing to go back to face her problems and to 'eat humble pie'; it involved 'turning', the basic move in repentance, and the first stage in finding God's way. The Lord delights to show mercy and give relief to the oppressed, but he also confronts them with their responsibilities.

Hagar was irrevocably involved with the Lord's promise to Abram and now heard words which may have reminded her of words she had heard from his lips. Though she was just a slave-girl, God's promise to Abram stood, and she would be the mother of multitudes without number (10). What the Lord does *not* say is significant also: he omits the familiar sequel that all the nations will be blessed. That culmination of the promise belonged to the son of the free wife.

A little poetic oracle follows, disclosing something more about the unborn child. His name, *Ishmael*, meaning 'God hears', would for ever remind Hagar that God had heard her prayer and had been aware of her misery (11). Her son's character is described in terms that evoke the wide-open spaces: the *wild ass* loves freedom, and is noted in Scripture not for stupidity but for fierce independence, stubborn pride and untameable strength (*cf.* Jb. 39:5–8; Ho. 8:9). These qualities will set him apart from his kith and kin; he will live *over against* them, near and yet opposing them. Even today the Arab descendants of Ishmael are in dispute with their neighbours who have descended from Isaac, and manifest a rugged independence which makes co-operation with anyone uncertain and precarious. By these pronouncements the angel prepared Hagar for a future separation from Abram and Isaac.

Hagar was greatly privileged, for the one whom she had met on the road, who was originally referred to as *the angel of the Lord*, is now called *the LORD*, the name which Abram used of the Most High God (14:22). Hagar recognized that she had seen God and, equally wonderfully, he had seen her need and had appeared to her. The astonishing thing was that she had survived unscathed. She could not have known that one day God was to come to earth as a man, and that long before he was born to Mary in Bethlehem he appeared in human form to certain men and women who needed his word. He was to appear also to Abram and give him an urgent message concerning Sodom (Gn. 18). Hagar had indeed seen God, and she commemorated the event by noting the name of the well, *Beer-lahai-roi*, 'the well of one who sees and lives' (RSV mg.) or 'well of the Living One who sees me' (NIV mg.). The writer does not actually say that Hagar named the well; in the desert the ability to spot a well could make all the difference between life and death, hence the appropriate name; but for Hagar it would take on a fuller meaning. She had in the first place seen the well, but more than that God had seen her, for he had answered her prayer, and she had seen God. The treble pun, with all its appeal to the eastern mind, would live on for generations.

So Hagar returned, enriched by the experience she had had of the wonderful protection and care of the Lord and knowing that he was not far away, but at hand and accessible. She had so much to tell Abram, not least that she would have a son and that he was to be called Ishmael, while Abram had a further insight into the ways of the Lord. In due time Hagar's son was born, and *Abram called the name of his son ... Ishmael*, so endorsing the revelation to Hagar as from the Lord, and also accepting a father's responsibility for the child.

Originally it had been Sarai's intention to adopt the slave-girl's baby as her own (2), but she did not do so. The Lord in his encounter with Hagar had prepared the way for the break that was to come between Ishmael and Isaac, and in any case it is doubtful whether Sarai would have wanted to adopt the boy after clashing so violently with his mother.

Genesis 17:1–27

New names and a covenant sign

When Abram was ninety-nine years old the Lord appeared to Abram, and said to him, 'I am God Almighty; walk before me, and be blameless. [2]And I will make my covenant between me and you, and will multiply you exceedingly.' [3]Then Abram fell on his face; and God said to him, [4]'Behold, my covenant is with you, and you shall be the father of a multitude of nations. [5]No longer shall your name be Abram, but your name shall be Abraham; for I have made you the father of a multitude of nations. [6]I will make you exceedingly fruitful; and I will make nations of you, and kings shall come forth from you. [7]And I will establish my covenant between me and you and your descendants after you throughout their generations for an everlasting covenant, to be God to you and to your descendants after you. [8]And I will give to you, and to your descendants after you, the land of your sojournings, all the land of Canaan, for an everlasting possession; and I will be their God.'

[9]And God said to Abraham, 'As for you, you shall keep my covenant, you and your descendants after you throughout their generations. [10]This is my covenant, which you shall keep, between me and you and your descendants after you: Every male among you shall be circumcised. [11]You shall be circumcised in the flesh of your foreskins, and it shall be a sign of the covenant between me and you.

[12]He that is eight days old among you shall be circumcised; every male throughout your generations, whether born in your house, or bought with your money from any foreigner who is not of your offspring, [13]both he that is born in your house and he that is bought with your money, shall be circumcised. So shall my covenant be in your flesh an everlasting covenant. [14]Any uncircumcised male who is not circumcised in the flesh of his foreskin shall be cut off from his people; he has broken my covenant.'

[15]And God said to Abraham, 'As for Sarai your wife, you shall not call her name Sarai, but Sarah shall be her name. [16]I will bless her, and moreover I will give you a son by her; I will bless her, and she shall be a mother of nations; kings of peoples shall come from her.' [17]Then Abraham fell on his face and laughed, and said to himself, 'Shall a child be born to a man who is a hundred years old? Shall Sarah, who is ninety years old, bear a child?' [18]And Abraham said to God, 'O that Ishmael might live in thy sight!' [19]God said, 'No, but Sarah your wife shall bear you a son, and you shall call his name Isaac. I will establish my covenant with him as an everlasting covenant for his descendants after him. [20]As for Ishmael, I have heard you; behold, I will bless him and make him fruitful and multiply him

exceedingly; he shall be the father of twelve princes, and I will make him a great nation. ²¹But I will establish my covenant with Isaac, whom Sarah shall bear to you at this season next year.'

²²When he had finished talking with him, God went up from Abraham. ²³Then Abraham took Ishmael his son and all the slaves born in his house or bought with his money, every male among the men of Abraham's house, and he circumcised the flesh of their foreskins that very day, as God had said to him. ²⁴Abraham was ninety-nine years old when he was circumcised in the flesh of his foreskin. ²⁵And Ishmael his son was thirteen years old when he was circumcised in the flesh of his foreskin. ²⁶That very day Abraham and his son Ishmael were circumcised; ²⁷and all the men of his house, those born in the house and those bought with money from a foreigner, were circumcised with him.

Though the covenant had already been sealed by sacrifice (chapter 15), one more preparatory stage remained to be fulfilled before the birth of the promised son. Whereas in chapter 15 the covenant made with Abram was private and personal to him alone, now the time had come for the matter to be made public. Society had to be aware of this new development, just as, centuries later, the private anointing of Saul (1 Sa. 10:1) would eventually be recognized by public acclaim (1 Sa. 10:20–24) and proved in experience (1 Sa. 11).[17] The covenant sacrifice established that the covenant was an unconditional act of God in which Abram had no part to play, and to which he could make no contribution. Now his response is stipulated, albeit in one all-embracing command. In Exodus the Passover sacrifice established the Lord's provision of the way of escape from death: 'When I see the blood, I will pass over you' (Ex. 12:13). Subsequently at Sinai the fuller response of obedience to the law's stipulations was spelt out. In both cases the initiative was God's; he pronounced what he would do, and established the certainty of his purpose in a sacrifice. Only afterwards was the

[17] A different explanation of the relationship between chapters 15 and 17 is given by those who think that Genesis is a compilation of documents from different sources. According to this 'documentary hypothesis' these two chapters represent the same subject looked at from the point of view of different writers, designated J and P (J for Jahweh and P for 'priestly'). This chapter is the main source in Genesis from which the features of P are deduced. Compared with chapter 15 it is said to be 'ritualistic and impersonal' (E. A. Speiser, *Genesis*, p. 126), and its style is likened to the legalistic material in Leviticus. There is some similarity of subject-matter, because the rite of circumcision became part of the ritual for which regulations were required. There is, however, no reason why it should not have come from the patriarchal period, for Abraham needed to know which members of his household should be included in the ceremony. Moreover, there is nothing impersonal about this chapter.

command given, in obedience to which the full blessings of the covenant could be enjoyed.

Mention of Abram's age (86 when Hagar bore Ishmael (16:16), and 99 when the Lord appeared to him again) indicates the passing of the years and the resulting pressure on his faith. By this time Abram was 'as good as dead' (Heb. 11:12), yet God had not written him off, nor had he forgotten him. The long wait was necessary to prove beyond a shadow of doubt that the God of the covenant was *El Shaddai*, God Almighty, who was well able to perform what he had promised, even against all odds. The meaning of the word *Shaddai* is obscure, but the translation 'Almighty' is apposite because the name is used in contexts which lay stress on God's power, as opposed to human helplessness. 'It was the claim of El Shaddai to be powerful where man was weakest, and He exerts this claim supremely by promising to an obscure and numerically tiny family that they should one day possess and populate a land which, in their day, was inhabited and owned by people immeasurably their superiors in number and power.'[18] In this first use of the name God's almighty power is to be demonstrated in two specific ways. He is, on the one hand, in control of the nations and their territory, and on the other he is able to give to Abram and Sarai a son in their old age. But first a way of life is prescribed for him and his family.

Walk before me, and be blameless (1)
Though no divine law was formulated as yet, God required those who were in covenant with him to live in such a way as to please him. The verb 'walk', used already of the Lord God in the garden (3:8), of Enoch, who 'walked with God' (5:24), and of Noah (6:9), is a reminder that all of life is an ongoing pilgrimage. There can be no 'once for all' formula for instant holiness, because life's circumstances and demands keep changing, like the different phases of a journey. In all of them the Lord wants his people to please him by walking *before him*, that is, in his presence, with nothing to hide from him. Abram is to live so as to win God's approval, and be *blameless* (Heb. *tāmîm*). The word is used of Noah in 6:9; its root meaning is 'whole', 'integrated', as a person is whole who puts all his energies into one pursuit. Abram is to be wholly dedicated to God's cause. He is not free to live like the Canaanites around him, nor to be half-hearted in his service of God, but is to be 'perfect and complete' (Jas. 1:4). James uses the word *telaios*, 'whole', 'perfect',

[18] J. A. Motyer, *The Revelation of the Divine Name* (Tyndale Press, 1959), pp. 29–30.

to capture the force of the Hebrew word; the call is for whole-heartedness. For Abram holiness was to be an intrinsic part of his life, as one whom God had called, chosen and justified. The gospel of salvation by faith does not jeopardize right living. Rather it activates the conscience, freed from fear by forgiveness, and provides a new directive for a good life. With all the single-mindedness of the athlete, the believer makes it his aim to please his Lord. The good he does is not an end in itself, something of which to be proud, but a by-product of the greater, overriding aim, to be a whole-hearted disciple.

A new name (4–8)
This time Abram does not argue, but instead falls down in worship, and hears the Lord address him again: *'Behold, my covenant is with you.'* Abram has been individually singled out, and the Lord's word to him is intensely personal, resting on the covenant *'between me and you'*. The covenant changes his status, a fact which requires a new name that will point to the promise, just as the Christian name, given in baptism, indicates a person's standing in Christ. Whereas Abram meant 'father exalted', the new name, *Abraham*, meant 'father of many' (*hᵃmôn*), so echoing the Lord's words, *'you shall be the father of a multitude of nations'*. Had he been able to look into the distant future, Abram would have seen the countless millions of the Christian church world-wide, saved like Abram by faith, who were to look to him as their father in the faith (Rom. 4:16).

While it was a personal word that the Lord spoke to Abram, its impact was by no means confined to him. It had an immediate impact upon his domestic life, for the reference to 'nations' takes account of Ishmael's claim on the promise to Abram's descendants. He too will become a nation with his own territory and destiny. The Lord's promise is not restricted in its scope, but is capable of embracing Ishmael also, and other children of Abram (25:1–4). Abram was to be quite literally 'the father of many nations', and the change of name would for ever be a reminder of the ever-extending scope of the covenant.

There is, however, further emphasis on the size and organization of the nations that will issue from Abram's line. He was to be the father of kings, a fact which exalted Abram himself to royal status. Each of the nations directly descended from him was to have its kings: Midian (25:2), Ishmael (25:16, 'princes'), Edom (36:31) and, of course, Israel. But to be in communion with the King of kings bestowed a status that was infinitely higher, and that would continue through the generations.

The covenant God was making with Abram was, moreover, spiritual. It was therefore not limited to this life, but had eternity in its scope, and extended throughout the generations of Abram's descendants after him *for an everlasting covenant* (7). God Almighty, who demonstrated his mighty power through human helplessness, undertook *'to be God to you and to your descendants after you'*. Here was hope indeed, based on the word of God who could not fail, on a covenant that would be binding and lasting.

Finally, this covenant was territorial: *'I will give to you, and to your descendants after you, the land of ... Canaan, for an everlasting possession'* (8). With all its distant implications, the covenant was nevertheless earthed in a geographical area, the very land that Abram inhabited. If he was ever tempted to wonder whether he had followed a whim of his own imagining, the ground beneath his feet would tell him otherwise. Had it not been the Lord who had brought him to this land? And was he not dependent on the Lord to give him the son without whom the promises could not stand? These were tangible evidences that gave reassurance, and enabled him to be confident in his God when faith might have faltered. God's commitment to Abram was certainly far in excess of anything he in his wildest dreams would ever have imagined.

From this point on the new name is used. Other people in the market-place would note the change of name and as likely as not have a joke at Abraham's expense, in view of the fact that his wife was barren. As the Lord explained it to Abraham, however, the stress was upon all that the Lord was going to do. *'I have made you ...'*, *'I will make ...'*, *'I will make ...'*, *'I will establish ...'*. God Almighty is making Abraham a new man, with new powers spiritually engrafted. The new name is symbolic of his regeneration, with all the new possibilities this implies.

A covenant sign (9–27)
As for you, you shall keep my covenant, you and your descendants after you throughout their generations. God's unconditional commitment to Abraham had again been stated and defined, but now Abraham had to commit himself and his heirs equally unconditionally to their God, and to his covenant. Many people today object to the idea of involving their children in any kind of commitment, intending instead to allow them to make their own way, unencumbered by

parental values. There is wisdom in this to the extent that coercion is often counter-productive. Each generation has to find its own identity and adopt its personal lifestyle. Among Christians there have been misgivings about the baptism of infants, partly because this had become in some cases a mere social convention, but partly also because newly converted adult Christians wanted to be baptized publicly to symbolize their new status in Christ, but were debarred from doing so by their infant baptism. They preferred therefore to withhold baptism from their own children until they made their own confession of faith in Christ. In this way the rite of baptism would be meaningful, fulfilling its function as a symbol of cleansing from sin and of new life in Christ and in the church.

Understandable as this reasoning is, Abraham found that God's covenant was not confined to his own generation, but extended to generations yet unborn. This was the way God's gift operated; who was Abraham to deny that gift to his children? It did not even occur to him to question the principle of family solidarity on which God's purpose of salvation rested. God's grace reached out more widely than human reasoning would have supposed, and the sign of God's favour was the indelible mark of circumcision, to be set upon 'every male among you'. Once again the inclusiveness of God's grace reaches to the babies of eight days old; whether they are slaves or free, the children of foreigners or of Abraham, all are included. Mercifully women were not subjected to any cutting, as they have been in some parts of the world; this did not mean that they were excluded from the covenant, for they were an integral part of the family, and were accepted with their fathers, husbands and brothers. For every male, circumcision was obligatory. It was no merely optional sign of the covenant, but a symbol that stood so completely for the total covenant that it could be referred to as 'my covenant' (10). To refuse the sign was to break the covenant and to forfeit its promises (14).

While it is true that some other peoples of western Asia and of Egypt practised circumcision, it was not known in the Mesopotamian world, and Abraham had not up to this point been circumcised, though the idea would not have been strange to him. In other countries it was a puberty rite, marking the transition to full adult status, and at Shechem it was 'all who went out of the gate of his city', that is, all adult males, who were circumcised (Gn. 34:24). It was the extension of this rite to infants that characterized as different the role of circumcision in Israel. If infants are to be circumcised, the essence of circumcision must be what the Lord is saying to them, for they can say nothing to him. Indeed circumcision is the sign of God's covenant, not of any human response to the covenant; it signifies what God is saying, in terms of promises, to each one who is circumcised, and the sign conveyed and sealed those promises to the candidate. In other words it is an acted oracle. The similarities between circumcision and the New Testment covenant signs of baptism and the Lord's Supper are obvious. They also signify what the Lord has done for us and has invited all who believe to appropriate for themselves. In the case of adult baptism the ceremony may provide a suitable occasion for a response on the part of the candidate, but, as in the case of circumcision, the sign speaks of the promises made by God to the candidate.

Just as infants and children were included within the covenant sign, so were people of other races and social classes. Any who were associated with Abram as members of his household, *whether born in his house or bought with his money*, were to be circumcised. In this way foreigners who were not born of Abraham were from the start grafted into the people of God, in keeping with the Lord's declared intention of blessing all the families of the earth.

As for Sarai your wife ... The promise of a son and descendants to Abraham was equally a promise to Sarai. She had discovered the hard way that no substitute wife would do. It was as important that she should be the mother of the promised son as that Abraham should be his father. Now the Lord reveals this to be so; not to Sarai direct but to Abraham. As a symbol of her share in the covenant she too receives a slight change in her name. *Sarai* becomes *Sarah*, probably an updated form of the same name, meaning 'princess'. Through the son she will bear she too will be *a mother of nations* and of kings. Her name is therefore prophetic, a sign that the reiterated *'I will bless her'* has been fulfilled.

For the second time (*cf.* verse 3) Abraham fell on his face. That he should do so in worship is predictable, but now he laughed! God's words to him touched the point of tension, where deep emotion quickly welled up into an excited leap of faith, only to be checked by an element of fear lest he should have misunderstood the divine disclosure. Aware of the improbability of begetting a son at his and Sarah's advanced age, he must first eliminate the possibility that the Lord had Ishmael in mind by praying for Ishmael's acceptance and special protection. His exploratory reaction prompted the unmistakable reassurance he was seeking. Sarah herself would bear him a son;

there was no mistake. His name *Isaac* (Heb. *yishāq*) is suggested by Abraham's laughter, for it means 'he laughs' or 'may he laugh (or smile) upon him'. The latter meaning is suggested by the name Ishmael, 'may God hear' (*cf.* 20, and the pun on the name), just as Jacob was connected with a current name meaning 'may God protect'. Names with several meanings were popular, and the laughter caused by his promised birth (Sarah also laughed, 21:6) was not to be compared with the joy that accompanied the fulfilment of the promise, and so confirmed long-tested faith.

Abraham's prayer for Ishmael did not go unnoticed either. The answer is an emphatic affirmative, assuring Abraham that Ishmael will know divine blessing, fruitfulness and numerical strength, so that he also will become a nation with twelve tribal princes. But the covenant proper, with its bestowal of land and its promise of blessing to others, is reserved for Isaac, whose birth is to take place within the year. As the prophecy was worked out in history, the point of divergence between Ishmael and Isaac was focused in the promised 'seed' (Gal. 3:16), for the Christ was to be born among the descendants of Isaac.

Nevertheless in the last verses of this chapter (22–27) the inclusiveness of the first circumcision ceremony receives emphasis. In particular Egypt was represented through Hagar, Ishmael's mother. From this time on the ceremony would be performed in the various branches of the family on every male child at the age of eight days, thus testifying that God's grace, not human merit, under-girded the covenant, and that that grace enfolded the children of those who believed. Grace also bound together those who were committed to the covenant, and created the community of believers who became the church of Old Testament times, centred originally round Abraham, 'the father of all who believe' (Rom. 4:11). Paul saw that God had been working on the selfsame principle from the beginning, namely that of faith, though for a period the rabbis, teaching that meticulous law-keeping was the way of salvation, lost sight of it. But the righteousness granted to Abraham preceded the law and preceded circumcision; it depended on neither, but depended instead on his belief in God's promises. In the same way the Christian is reckoned righteous because he believes that God raised from the dead the Lord Jesus Christ (Rom. 4:22–25). The ways of God do not change.

Genesis 18:1–15

Unexpected visitors

And the Lord appeared to him by the oaks of Mamre, as he sat at the door of his tent in the heat of the day. [2]He lifted up his eyes and looked, and behold, three men stood in front of him. When he saw them, he ran from the tent door to meet them, and bowed himself to the earth, [3]and said, 'My lord, if I have found favour in your sight, do not pass by your servant. [4]Let a little water be brought, and wash your feet, and rest yourselves under the tree, [5]while I fetch a morsel of bread, that you may refresh yourselves, and after that you may pass on — since you have come to your servant.' So they said, 'Do as you have said.' [6]And Abraham hastened into the tent to Sarah, and said, 'Make ready quickly three measures of fine meal, knead it, and make cakes.' [7]And Abraham ran to the herd, and took a calf, tender and good, and gave it to the servant, who hastened to prepare it. [8]Then he took curds, and milk, and the calf which he had prepared, and set it before them; and he stood by them under the tree while they ate.

[9]They said to him, 'Where is Sarah your wife?' And he said, 'She is in the tent.' [10]The Lord said, 'I will surely return to you in the spring, and Sarah your wife shall have a son.' And Sarah was listening at the tent door behind him. [11]Now Abraham and Sarah were old, advanced in age; it had ceased to be with Sarah after the manner of women. [12]So Sarah laughed to herself, saying, 'After I have grown old, shall I have pleasure?' [13]The Lord said to Abraham, 'Why did Sarah laugh, and say, "Shall I indeed bear a child, now that I am old?" [14]Is anything too hard for the Lord? At the appointed time I will return to you, in the spring, and Sarah shall have a son.' [15]But Sarah denied, saying, 'I did not laugh'; for she was afraid. He said, 'No, but you did laugh.'

The three men who came into view that hot day and stood opposite Abraham as he was having his siesta looked like ordinary travellers, but there was more than ordinary politeness, even by eastern standards, in Abraham's eagerness to entertain them. First he ran, despite the heat, to detain them, and then bowed down before them to pay his respects, particularly to the one whom he recognized as their leader. Did some second sense tell him what the writer tells us, that it was the Lord who appeared to him that day by the oaks of Mamre? Abraham indicated how honoured he would be if *my lord* (Heb. *"donai*) would deign to accept his hospitality. He would provide water for hot tired feet, rest in the cool of the shady tree, and some light refreshment. All this he promised on the spur of the moment, for he had been taken by surprise. When his offer was accepted he hurried off to rouse the household to cook a meal fit for honoured guests, and he himself killed the best calf. This was hospitality on a lavish scale, and Abraham himself waited at table and served his guests.

'*Where is Sarah your wife?*' (9) was a startling question, if only because the visitor knew her name. She was, as usual, in the kitchen, but not a word of the conversation escaped her as she eavesdropped behind the flap of the tent. Why did Abraham not fetch her and introduce her to the divine guest, who had a special message for her? In the end she emerged, but at a disadvantage because she had been baking in the heat of the day, and because she had been overhearing news which was of primary importance to her as well as to Abraham. After all the years of childlessness it was hard to believe that in old age a son would be born to them, hence Sarah's chuckle of incredulity as she reacted in the light of innumerable disappointments. Understandable as we may consider this reaction to be, it failed to take seriously the word of the Lord which had been specifically addressed to her (Gn. 17:15–16). '*After I am worn out and my master is old, will I now have this pleasure?*' (12, NIV) captures her thoughts, as she guarded against being disappointed yet again. But the Lord was better than her fears, and altogether greater than she had thus far grasped.

The guest had not only known her name but had even read her thoughts, thus indicating that he was no ordinary visitor. Now he draws attention to Sarah's unbelief by asking the significant question, '*Is anything too hard for the Lord?*' (14). What could be too hard for the one who had created all things? Simply to pose the question shows how ludicrous it is to think of the Lord in terms of human limitations. Of course Sarah had not meant to imply that God could not override the usual expectations of the human life-cycle, and, forgetting for a moment the proprieties, she joined in the conversation with a useless denial that she had laughed. Though it is usual to link Sarah's laughter with the name Isaac, there is no mention of the name in this narrative, but only an assurance that Sarah will indeed have a son.

Prayers that receive no immediate answer, though they are based on God's word, can be a source of considerable unease. Like Sarah, the praying person may conclude that God has either not heard the petition or is limited in his capabilities, whereas the explanation in this incident lay in quite another direction. Now that Sarah is past the usual age for childbearing, the son of her womb will be in an unusual sense the child of promise. In similar terms the angel Gabriel was to speak of Elizabeth's conception, 'for with God nothing will be impossible' (Lk. 1:37). Thus John the Baptist, like Isaac, was to be a man with a special role to play in relation to the Messiah, born at God's exactly planned moment in history. The delay, far from indicating any limitation of God's power, showed rather God's total control over events. The prayer of Abraham and Sarah that they might have a son was entirely within the will of the Lord, because it was based on his direct and unmistakable promise. To wait for its fulfilment proved to be a trial almost beyond endurance, but to wait with contentment is an activity of faith which gives glory to God, and is not be be confused with passivity. Suddenly, when God's time comes, his purposes blossom like a long-awaited spring.

The Lord's time had come. He would return *at the appointed time*, and Sarah's son would be born, despite her unbelief.

Genesis 18:16–33

Tenacious intercession

Then the men set out from there, and they looked toward Sodom; and Abraham went with them to set them on their way. [17]*The Lord said, 'Shall I hide from Abraham what I am about to do,* [18]*seeing that Abraham shall become a great and mighty nation, and all the nations of the earth shall bless themselves by him?* [19]*No, for I have chosen him, that he may charge his children and his household after him to keep the way of the Lord by doing righteousness and justice; so that the Lord may bring to Abraham what he has promised him.'* [20]*Then the Lord said, 'Because the outcry against Sodom and Gomorrah is great and their sin is very grave,* [21]*I will go down to see whether they have done altogether according to the outcry which has come to me; and if not, I will know.'*

[22]*So the men turned from there, and went toward Sodom; but Abraham still stood before the Lord.* [23]*Then Abraham drew near, and said, 'Wilt thou indeed destroy the righteous with the wicked?* [24]*Suppose there are fifty righteous within the city; wilt thou then destroy the place and not spare it for the fifty righteous who are in it?* [25]*Far be it from thee to do such a thing, to slay the righteous with the wicked, so that the righteous fare as the wicked! Far be that from thee! Shall not the Judge of all the earth do right?'* [26]*And the Lord said, 'If I find at Sodom fifty righteous in the city, I will spare the*

whole place for their sake.' ²⁷*Abraham answered, 'Behold, I have taken upon myself to speak to the Lord, I who am but dust and ashes.* ²⁸*Suppose five of the fifty righteous are lacking? Wilt thou destroy the whole city for lack of five? And he said, 'I will not destroy it if I find forty-five there.'* ²⁹*Again he spoke to him, and said, 'Suppose forty are found there.' He answered, 'For the sake of forty I will not do it.'* ³⁰*Then he said, 'Oh let not the Lord be angry, and I will speak. Suppose thirty are found there.' He answered, 'I will not do it, if I find thirty there.'* ³¹*He said, 'Behold, I have taken upon myself to speak to the Lord. Suppose twenty are found there.' He answered, 'For the sake of twenty I will not destroy it.'* ³²*Then he said, 'Oh let not the Lord be angry, and I will speak again but this once. Suppose ten are found there.' He answered, 'For the sake of ten I will not destroy it.'* ³³*And the Lord went his way, when he had finished speaking to Abraham; and Abraham returned to his place.*

This graphic example of the man of God at prayer illustrates the mystery of interceding for others with the living God, whose sovereign purposes have already been disclosed. Can it be permissible even to want to change any detail of those purposes? In view of the fact that God has already determined what he will do, can human pleading in any way change his mind? It is instructive to study this first full-scale prayer of the Bible to see how it was answered.

Their message concerning Sarah safely delivered, the visitors prepared to depart, and Abraham's never-failing courtesy took him far enough along the road with them to realize that they were making for Sodom, where his nephew and family lived. As he stood with the heavenly messengers, looking from the Judean hills across the Dead Sea, he was granted the extra special privilege of such intimacy with the Lord that the Lord shared his intentions with Abraham, as friend shares with friend. It was as though for a few moments they were again in the garden of Eden. In the light of all that Abraham was to become, and the blessing he was to be to all the peoples of the earth, this extra privilege was included as part of the relationship. The fact that Abraham was to be let into the secret of God's future purposes confirmed his status as a prophet (20:7). Not only that, for Abraham would train his family in *the way of the Lord* by doing what was right and just. Though the covenant was truly unconditional, to be brought into fellowship with God involved nothing less than becoming like him in all goodness. The same insistence on what is just and right recurs in Isaiah 56:1, reminding a later generation that nothing less than maintaining justice and practising righteousness will do if God's blessing is to be enjoyed.

The outcry against Sodom and Gomorrah (20) is not spelt out. Perhaps it was already proverbial. Even so, no judgment would be pronounced against it until the Lord had satisfied himself that the reports that had reached him were accurate. *'I will go down to see whether they have done altogether according to the outcry which has come to me; and if not, I will know'* (21). He seems reluctant to believe them; he will not judge on hearsay; he looks for evidence which human opinion has left out of account, and he intends to examine all the facts. Abraham is learning how the Judge of all the earth sifts the total evidence and knows the situation for himself before he pronounces his verdict. How presumptuous we are when we question God's judgments, and yet Abraham would not be rebuked for so doing.

Abraham has his own impression of the state of affairs in Sodom. He watches as the two men, who are referred to as 'angels' or messengers in 19:1, walk on towards the doomed city, and finds himself standing in the presence of the Lord. It was an invitation to respond in intercession, as well as to enjoy his company. Scripture shows us that it is the Lord who prompts his children to pray (*cf.* Gal. 4:6), and one of the purposes of disclosures about events still future is to supply an incentive for intercession, for a loving God, not blind fate, is in control.

Despite his intimacy with the Lord, Abraham never becomes familiar. He opens the conversation with a question which shows that he has thought about the Lord's determination to see for himself the state of affairs in Sodom (verses 20–21). He will not attribute to the Lord less of a sense of justice than he himself possesses. Surely the Lord would not destroy the righteous with the wicked. Abraham is making a desperate bid to save Lot and his family, who, by association with Abraham, had known blessing and had experienced deliverance from captivity. In addition, perhaps there were others in Sodom who could be described as righteous; in his mind's eye Abraham recalled Sodom's king and his terrified subjects whom he had come to know in his rescue campaign. Were they all to be indiscriminately obliterated? If so, he would have difficulty in reconciling such a judgment with a righteous God, and it is the agony of this intractable problem that drives him to prayer. If God himself is unjust, then the very foundation of all life's values is pulled from under our feet. Abraham shrinks from contemplating such a collapse of confidence. *'Far be it from thee to do such a thing, to slay the righteous with the wicked ...! Shall not the Judge of all the earth do right?'* (25).

Though a man stood before Abraham, by divinely given insight Abraham called him Lord, and seemed to have no problem in discerning that this man was the ultimate Judge of all men, the one true God. Later in Scripture the plea was often to be made, especially by the psalmists, that the Lord should deliver the innocent and slay the guilty, and the prayer reflects observed injustices in the outworking of providence in our world. There are many disasters we can neither understand ourselves nor explain to others; we shall be wise to avoid the mistake of Job's friends, who set themselves up as interpreters of God's ways, and take refuge rather in the insight of Abraham, who appealed to the Lord to vindicate his righteousness.

Abraham's terrifying boldness met with a reassuring response. If the Lord found *fifty* righteous people in the city he would spare it for their sakes. But the problem had not been resolved, because the injustice would remain even if there were less than fifty righteous people there. Who was Abraham to question the integrity of the God of all the earth? He realized that he was *but dust and ashes* (27) in relation to God, and that he risked provoking him to a stormy reaction (30), but such was his agony of spirit that he was driven to speak again and again. Whereas humans resent any inference that they are less than just, the Lord showed no such resentment, but assured his servant that he would not destroy Sodom if *ten* righteous were found there. Beyond that Abraham did not dare to go, and it appears that the Lord closed the conversation.

What had begun as intercession turned into an urgent probing of the character of God. But this was the same God who had come to visit Abraham, so *inviting* him to converse with him as his friend, and who had shared with Abraham what he was about to do. The Lord not only tolerated his questions, but, by revealing his intentions, positively evoked them. He welcomes the response we make, and wants to hear about our fears, misgivings and even our objections to what he seems to us to be doing. The Lord did not move off, but remained with Abraham while he framed his questions so that *Abraham still stood before the Lord* (22). Though we do not see him as Abraham did, we who are 'in Christ' have immediate access to the Father by virtue of our status, and those not yet in Christ are right in believing that 'In him we live and move and have our being' (Acts 17:28, words of the Greek Epimenides, quoted by Paul). God is not far from each one of us.

This episode in Abraham's walk with God has yet more to tell us about prayer. We see how *frank* he was in expressing his misgivings. Job was to be bolder still in his accusations against the ways of God, and even he was in the end commended for speaking what was right about God (Jb. 42:7). We cannot hide from him our true feelings, and Scripture encourages us to voice them, albeit humbly, to God himself. We see also that Abraham built his prayer upon what he knew of God's character, and argued on the basis of God's integrity. God cannot deny himself, and therefore to take him at his word and expect him to honour it is to corroborate his good name. Once our prayers are squarely based on God's word we can, like Abraham, be bold and persevering, and continue until we receive the Lord's reassurance. The Bible makes no promises that intellectual problems will be met by reasoned arguments; God does not defend himself to you and to me. Instead he reveals himself as the God who knows and cares, whose providential ordering of our lives shows beyond doubt that he is in control, and that 'he rewards those who seek him' (Heb. 11:6).

Genesis 19:1–29

Sodom's day of destiny

The two angels came to Sodom in the evening; and Lot was sitting in the gate of Sodom. When Lot saw them, he rose to meet them, and bowed himself with his face to the earth, ²and said, 'My lords, turn aside, I pray you, to your servant's house and spend the night, and wash your feet; then you may rise up early and go on your way.' They said, 'No; we will spend the night in the street.' ³But he urged them strongly; so they turned aside to him and entered his house; and he made them a feast, and baked unleavened bread, and they ate. ⁴But before they lay down, the men of the city, the men of Sodom, both young and old, all the people to the last man, surrounded the house; ⁵and they called to Lot, 'Where are the men who came to you tonight? Bring them out to us, that we may know them.' ⁶Lot went out of the door to the men, shut the door after him, ⁷and said, 'I beg you, my brothers, do not act so wickedly. ⁸Behold, I have two daughters who have not known man; let me bring them out to you, and do to them as you please; only do nothing to these men, for they have come under the shelter of my roof.' ⁹But they said,

75

'Stand back!' And they said, 'This fellow came to sojourn, and he would play the judge! Now we will deal worse with you than with them.' Then they pressed hard against the man Lot, and drew near to break the door. [10]But the men put forth their hands and brought Lot into the house to them, and shut the door. [11]And they struck with blindness the men who were at the door of the house, both small and great, so that they wearied themselves groping for the door.

[12]Then the men said to Lot, 'Have you any one else here? Sons-in-law, sons, daughters, or any one you have in the city, bring them out of the place; [13]for we are about to destroy this place, because the outcry against its people has become great before the Lord, and the Lord has sent us to destroy it.' [14]So Lot went out and said to his sons-in-law, who were to marry his daughters, 'Up, get out of this place; for the Lord is about to destroy the city.' But he seemed to his sons-in-law to be jesting.

[15]When morning dawned, the angels urged Lot, saying, 'Arise, take your wife and your two daughters who are here, lest you be consumed in the punishment of the city.' [16]But he lingered; so the men seized him and his wife and his two daughters by the hand, the Lord being merciful to him, and they brought him forth and set him outside the city. [17]And when they had brought them forth, they said, 'Flee for your life; do not look back or stop anywhere in the valley; flee to the hills, lest you be consumed.' [18]And Lot said to them, 'Oh, no, my lords; [19]behold, your servant has found favour in your sight, and you have shown me great kindness in saving my life; but I cannot flee to the hills, lest the disaster overtake me, and I die. [20]Behold, yonder city is near enough to flee to, and it is a little one. Let me escape there — is it not a little one? — and my life will be saved!' [21]He said to him, 'Behold, I grant you this favour also, that I will not overthrow the city of which you have spoken. [22]Make haste, escape there; for I can do nothing until you arrive there.' Therefore the name of the city was called Zoar. [23]The sun had risen on the earth when Lot came to Zoar.

[24]Then the Lord rained on Sodom and Gomorrah brimstone and fire from the Lord out of heaven; [25]and he overthrew those cities, and all the valley, and all the inhabitants of the cities, and what grew on the ground. [26]But Lot's wife behind him looked back, and she became a pillar of salt. [27]And Abraham went early in the morning to the place where he had stood before the Lord; [28]and he looked down toward Sodom and Gomorrah and toward all the land of the valley, and beheld, and lo, the smoke of the land went up like the smoke of a furnace.

[29]So it was that, when God destroyed the cities of the valley, God remembered Abraham, and sent Lot out of the midst of the overthrow, when he overthrew the cities in which Lot dwelt.

76

It had been business as usual in Sodom, and the usual evening activities were afoot when the messengers arrived, to be greeted by Lot, who *was sitting in the gate of Sodom*, where it was customary for the dignitaries of the city to gather.[19] From that fatal day when Lot made his choice to better himself in the luscious valley he had become more and more involved in moral compromise. In disregard of his uncle he had chosen what he thought to be the best of the land; his motive had been self-seeking, and he had taken no warning from the evil reputation of the cities of the plain. He had originally set up his tent close to Sodom (13:12) but was soon resident within the city (14:12), hence the capture of Lot and his family by the invading kings. Even after that warning he remained in Sodom, where he had become one of the city fathers. Even so, as a foreigner with different standards that were bitterly resented, he was not altogether trusted (19:9), and his influence was negligible.

There was nothing in the circumstances of that evening to give a hint that catastrophe was looming over the city, and Lot had no idea that he had been prominent in his uncle's intercessions. As soon as he saw the visitors entering the gate of the city he was quick to offer them hospitality. He had immediately assessed them to be honest men, unsuspecting travellers, whose dignity and integrity caused him to prostrate himself before them in genuine appreciation of their worth. He hoped to shield them from the worse aspects of night-life in the city by taking them to his home. He would not detain them in the morning.

Lot's determination to protect the visitors nearly cost him his life. When the whole of the male population made a hostile attack on his home, in craven self-defence he offered them his daughters in the forlorn hope that the crowd would disperse. Had he but realized it, those he was protecting were able to deliver him, but it was by a miraculous intervention. Suddenly those who had threatened to break down the door could no longer see, and so were helpless.[20]

Lot had been delivered already by his association with Abraham, and now he is invited to warn anyone in the city who is related to him, even indirectly, of its imminent overthrow. In the wideness of

---

[19] Excavation has revealed, notably at Dan and Acco, a courtyard between an inner and outer gate of the city. A stone bench, still *in situ* round the walls, may have been used by the elders of the community.

[20] The word for 'blindness' is not the usual Hebrew word, but a loan word from Akkadian, translated by Speiser 'blinding light'. As in the experience of Saul of Tarsus (Acts 9:8), a flash of blinding light was responsible for the alarming, if temporary, loss of sight.

God's mercy he would spare as many as possible. *But he seemed to his sons-in-law to be jesting* (14). This may imply that Lot already had married daughters, whose sons opposed their departure (Speiser, for example, takes the text this way), or that these are prospective sons-in-law (so RSV). To them the threat of destruction was ludicrous. But those who had come to the city as divine assessors needed no further evidence: its guilt was established, and as the Lord's messengers they had the mandate to destroy Sodom.

At first light the reason for urgency is disclosed. Not a moment can be spared if anyone is to escape the doom of the city; but Lot and his family lack the will to escape. Familiar things seem indispensable and doubly precious. Lot becomes vague and irresolute, and the family escapes only because the men forcibly compel them to leave, *the Lord being merciful to him*. For Lot's sake the family is spared, and safely conducted outside the gates, but from that point on they are expected to complete their escape from the doomed valley by running with all speed to the hills. When every second counted Lot puts forward his own plan. In his fear reason deserts him. He has failed to understand that danger is confined to the plain, and he dreads the hills. He is given permission to take refuge in Zoar (called Bela in 14:2). The name Zoar is similar to the Hebrew noun *mis'ār*, 'a small thing'; the pun reinforces his plea that he is really not asking much. The traditional site of Zoar is close to the modern Sāfi, which is in the valley south of the Dead Sea. Lot's 'little' request amounted to no less than the reversal of the instructions he was first given, but his choice of Zoar meant that that city was spared (21), and even Sodom and Gomorrah were safe until Lot reached Zoar.

Brimstone and fire from the Lord out of heaven (24) is a vivid description of the final catastrophe that brought to an end the cities of the plain. The significance of the event is more important than a geological explanation, and the prophets made frequent reference to the fate of 'the cities which the Lord overthrew without pity' (Je. 20:16), Sodom and Gomorrah (Je. 23:14), Admah and Zeboiim (Ho. 11:8), seeing it as typifying the destruction of Samaria and Jerusalem in their turn. 'Exudations of bitumen, petroleum and probably natural gas (since the last named is generally an accompaniment of these substances) ... catching fire from lightning or human action, would adequately account for recorded phenomena ...'[21] It was not only that whole populations died in the overthrow

---

[21] F.G. Clapp, 'Geology and Bitumens of the Dead Sea Area, Palestine and Transjordan', *BASOR* XX: 7 (1936), pp. 881–909; quoted in *Biblical Archaeologist Reader* 1 (1961), p. 69.

of their cities, but that the total area was rendered infertile by the cataclysm. Such fruit as subsequently grew upon that ground was inedible (Dt. 32:32); prolonged burning (28) destroyed the natural properties of the soil and the falling rocks turned it into desert. The judgment of God on human rebellion fell also on nature's life so that the area became abandoned, apparently for ever. Yet Jesus spoke of a judgment worse than that of Sodom and Gomorrah (Lk. 17:28–32). Those who had seen his miracles and failed to receive him had less excuse than Sodom (Mt. 11:23–24), and Ezekiel had even foreseen the restoration of the region of the Dead Sea (Ezk. 47:8), and the rebuilding of 'Sodom and her daughters' (Ezk. 16:53, 55). In the gospel there is hope for even the most degraded.

An up-to-date example which can be fully authenticated shows how the gospel brought new hope to some tribal groups in the island of Sarawak. So rotten were these people with alcoholism and disease that their government had given up on them, and was content to allow them to die out. Missionaries of the Borneo Evangelical Mission witnessed an amazing transformation of these hopeless tribes into a society of healthy, purposeful men and women of God.[22] Examples of the transforming work of God's Spirit are to be found nearer home by those with eyes to see. But no-one is transformed by the kind of compromise attempted by Lot. Instead of fraternizing he should have preached repentance.

But Lot's wife ... looked back (26). Even a miraculous escape from the city was insufficient to overcome the nostalgia she felt for all she had left behind. Her hesitation was fatal, for she was caught up in the molten tide that swept across the plain like volcanic lava. Thus she became fossilized among the many grotesque peaks of rock that are a feature of the southern end of the Dead Sea valley. Our consumer society, with its enormous range of possible possessions, needs the warning of Jesus, 'Remember Lot's wife' (Lk. 17:32).

What of Abraham's intercession? As he watched from a distance all he could tell was that God's judgment had certainly overwhelmed the Dead Sea plain, which had become an inferno. The city for which he had prayed could now be no more, but in due course he would find out that God had wonderfully *sent Lot out of the midst of the overthrow* (29). Though Sodom could not be spared God's judgment, *God remembered Abraham*. His prayer had been no mistaken effort, and Lot had been 'consecrated' through his faith (*cf.* 1 Cor. 7:14).

---

[22] The account of their conversion, and of the changes that followed, has been written up by Shirley Lees, *Drunk Before Dawn* (Overseas Missionary Fellowship, 1979).

Genesis 19:30–38

The end of Lot's story

Now Lot went up out of Zoar, and dwelt in the hills with his two daughters, for he was afraid to dwell in Zoar; so he dwelt in a cave with his two daughters. ³¹And the first-born said to the younger, 'Our father is old, and there is not a man on earth to come in to us after the manner of all the earth. ³²Come, let us make our father drink wine, and we will lie with him, that we may preserve offspring through our father.' ³³So they made their father drink wine that night; and the first-born went in, and lay with her father; he did not know when she lay down or when she arose. ³⁴And on the next day, the first-born said to the younger, 'Behold, I lay last night with my father; let us make him drink wine tonight also; then you go in and lie with him, that we may preserve offspring through our father.' ³⁵So they made their father drink wine that night also; and the younger arose, and lay with him; and he did not know when she lay down or when she arose. ³⁶Thus both the daughters of Lot were with child by their father. ³⁷The first-born bore a son, and called his name Moab; he is the father of the Moabites to this day. ³⁸The younger also bore a son, and called his name Ben-ammi; he is the father of the Ammonites to this day.

Though the Lord had assured Lot that he could safely settle in Zoar, Lot was uneasy, the victim of many fears (30). He therefore fled to the hills after all, and set up home in a cave. His two daughters, young and deprived of their prospective husbands, had not been brought up in Sodom for nothing. Despite their godly father they adopted the standards of their friends in Sodom. By exploiting the weakness of their easygoing father they could have their way and evade his disapproval. Their two sons, children of Lot, were to become nations, near neighbours of Abraham's descendants, related to them but standing for a totally different and incompatible way of life.

The Moabites worshipped a fertility god and indulged in orgies which beguiled the Israelites on their way into the promised land (Nu. 25). Ammon became noted for cruelty not only in war (Am. 1:13) but even in religious observance (Lv. 18:21), for Molech was the Ammonite god who demanded child sacrifice.

To be born into one of these nations did not, however, imply an automatic exclusion from God's people. The story of Ruth stands as a memorial to the efficacy of faith in the living God, for, though she belonged to Moab, she became the ancestress of both David and

Jesus himself (Mt. 1:5). The door of salvation is open to all who are willing to enter in penitence and faith, no matter what their background.

Genesis 20:1–18

Abraham's fears reassert themselves

From there Abraham journeyed toward the territory of the Negeb, and dwelt between Kadesh and Shur; and he sojourned in Gerar. [2]And Abraham said of Sarah his wife, 'She is my sister.' And Abimelech king of Gerar sent and took Sarah. [3]But God came to Abimelech in a dream by night, and said to him, 'Behold, you are a dead man, because of the woman whom you have taken; for she is a man's wife.' [4]Now Abimelech had not approached her; so he said, 'Lord, wilt thou slay an innocent people? [5]Did he not himself say to me, "She is my sister"? And she herself said, "He is my brother." In the integrity of my heart and the innocence of my hands I have done this.' [6]Then God said to him in the dream, 'Yes, I know that you have done this in the integrity of your heart, and it was I who kept you from sinning against me; therefore I did not let you touch her. [7]Now then restore the man's wife; for he is a prophet, and he will pray for you, and you shall live. But if you do not restore her, know that you shall surely die, and all that are yours.'

[8]So Abimelech rose early in the morning, and called all his servants, and told them all these things; and the men were very much afraid. [9]Then Abimelech called Abraham, and said to him, 'What have you done to us? And how have I sinned against you, that you have brought on me and my kingdom a great sin? You have done to me things that ought not to be done.' [10]And Abimelech said to Abraham, 'What were you thinking of, that you did this thing?' [11]Abraham said, 'I did it because I thought, There is no fear of God at all in this place, and they will kill me because of my wife. [12]Besides she is indeed my sister, the daughter of my father but not the daughter of my mother; and she became my wife. [13]And when God caused me to wander from my father's house, I said to her, "This is the kindness you must do me; at every place to which we come, say of me, He is my brother."' [14]Then Abimelech took sheep and oxen, and male and female slaves, and gave them to Abraham, and restored Sarah his wife to him. [15]And Abimelech said, 'Behold, my land is before you; dwell where it pleases you.' [16]To Sarah he said, 'Behold, I have given your brother a thousand pieces of silver; it is your vindication in the eyes of all who are with you; and before every one you are righted.' [17]Then Abraham prayed to God; and God healed Abimelech, and also healed his wife and female slaves so that they bore

children. *¹⁸For the Lord had closed all the wombs of the house of Abimelech because of Sarah, Abraham's wife.*

Abraham was committed to a pilgrim life and therefore to travelling, but he was obsessed in foreign cities by the idea that local rulers would want to marry Sarah, and therefore would kill him. From the outset he had tried to overcome his phobia by planning with Sarah to claim, as they had done in Egypt (12:11–13), their brother-sister relationship rather than their married status. It was a dangerous deception, jeopardizing again the paternity of their promised son, and the world's hope of salvation. But irrational fears do not just go away, and when, after venturing on the road towards Egypt, reminiscences triggered his fears anew (*cf.* 12:10–20), he adopted his earlier remedy. The man who was pioneering the way of faith, and who was learning the basic lessons that generations to follow were to observe from his life, faltered over a relatively small danger because he was gripped by fear. The incident is utterly true to life, and shows how vulnerable Abraham was.

Gerar was an important caravan centre on the border between Canaan and Egypt, but it was also a royal city, where Abimelech was king. Abraham intended to stay there only a short time, but his status as a tribal leader, with a large household, flocks and herds, meant that he did not go unnoticed. Moreover his reputation as a military leader had gone ahead of him, and in the world of his day he may well have had princely status.[23] Such families entered into solemn agreements promising mutual support, and often cemented such treaties by intermarriage. But Abraham was at a disadvantage in this respect, having no daughters.

After Abimelech had taken Sarah into his harem God intervened to protect her (as he surely would have protected Abraham), and warned Abimelech that Sarah was already another man's wife. The ancient world made sure that a husband's rights were thoroughly protected by law; that Abraham should jeopardize his rights indicates the intensity of his torment. Abimelech needed no convincing that he had come close to death in taking *a man's wife*, though he had done so in all innocence. The incident provides an insight into the customary morality of the day, and sheds light on God's disclosure of his character to a man who was not within the covenant. Even Abimelech pleads the justice of God when he asks,

[23] See D.J. Wiseman, 'Abraham in History and Tradition Part II: Abraham the Prince', *Bibliotheca Sacra* 135 (1977), pp. 228–237.

'*Lord. wilt thou slay an innocent people?*' As the dream continues God teaches him to recognize the restraining hand of God in his life: '*it was I who kept you from sinning against me*', and instructs him on pain of death to put right the wrong by returning Sarah to Abraham. Mercifully in this case restitution was straightforward. But more than that was needed, because only by a public penalty would the matter be finally settled. That is why Abimelech summoned Abraham to court before witnesses (8–9), made his accusation and gave Abraham the opportunity to defend himself.

Though Abraham was to blame, and both Abraham and Sarah were guilty of conspiring to deceive, Abimelech was technically in the wrong and acknowledged the fact by making reparations both to Abraham and to Sarah. This brought the case to a conclusion, so that in future Abraham could consider himself entitled to stay in Abimelech's territory if he so wished, and Sarah was vindicated publicly, and declared free of blame; her reputation was untarnished.

Abimelech had been told that Abraham was *a prophet* (7; Heb. *nābî'*), and the incident ends with Abraham exercising one of the functions of a prophet – praying for others. Abimelech feared the Lord's words, '*you are a dead man*' (3), and Abraham's part in the reconciliation was to intercede to the end that God would remove the curse of barrenness from Abimelech's household. It was ironical that Abraham should have to pray such a prayer on behalf of Abimelech, in view of the fact that he had been praying over decades for an end to Sarah's barrenness. But 'the Lord turned the captivity of Job, when he prayed for his friends' (Jb. 42:10, AV), and Abraham was soon to see the answer to his prayers for a son. His prayer was 'unanswered' only because God's time had not yet come, not because of any inability on the Lord's part to remove barrenness, as the answered prayer for Abimelech demonstrated.

Part 2
ISAAC
(Genesis 21:1 – 28:9)

Genesis 21:1–7

The promised son is born

The Lord visited Sarah as he had said, and the Lord did to Sarah as he had promised. ²And Sarah conceived, and bore Abraham a son in his old age at the time of which God had spoken to him. ³Abraham called the name of his son who was born to him, whom Sarah bore him, Isaac. ⁴And Abraham circumcised his son Isaac when he was eight days old, as God had commanded him. ⁵Abraham was a hundred years old when his son Isaac was born to him. ⁶And Sarah said, 'God has made laughter for me; every one who hears will laugh over me.' ⁷And she said, 'Who would have said to Abraham that Sarah would suckle children? Yet I have borne him a son in his old age.'

In every detail the promise of the Lord was fulfilled, and special mention is made of its timing. Though faith had been severely tested over more than twenty years, during which the fulfilment of the promise seemed progressively less likely, the Lord stood by his word. At the right time everything worked out with quiet precision, and *Sarah ... bore Abraham a son ... at the time of which God had spoken to him.* God does keep his promises. A new era had begun in the outworking of God's purpose for the world, and from this time on the narrative directs attention towards Isaac, as did his parents and the people round about.

Abraham for his part knew the duties he had to fulfil towards the child. His name had been God-given (17:19), and the naming ceremony recalled the incident the previous year when the Lord had appeared to Abraham and had pronounced upon the part his son would play in the covenant (17:19). In accordance with the command of God then given, Abraham circumcised his son. As for Sarah, the impossible had happened. Her happiness knew no bounds, and the congratulations of her neighbours brought them in to share in the God-given laughter. Nothing can give such deep, lasting satisfaction as the faithfulness of God, demonstrated in the fulfilment of his promises, especially, perhaps, after a long time of expectant waiting. When delay seems interminable, there is encouragement here to persevere. 'If it seem slow, wait for it; it will surely come' (Hab. 2:3).

Genesis 21:8–21

The rift between Ishmael and Isaac

And the child grew, and was weaned; and Abraham made a great feast on the day that Isaac was weaned. [9]*But Sarah saw the son of Hagar the Egyptian, whom she had borne to Abraham, playing with her son Isaac.* [10]*So she said to Abraham, 'Cast out this slave woman with her son; for the son of this slave woman shall not be heir with my son Isaac.'* [11]*And the thing was very displeasing to Abraham on account of his son.* [12]*But God said to Abraham, 'Be not displeased because of the lad and because of your slave woman; whatever Sarah says to you, do as she tells you, for through Isaac shall your descendants be named.* [13]*And I will make a nation of the son of the slave woman also, because he is your offspring.'* [14]*So Abraham rose early in the morning, and took bread and a skin of water, and gave it to Hagar, putting it on her shoulder, along with the child, and sent her away. And she departed, and wandered in the wilderness of Beer-sheba.*

[15]*When the water in the skin was gone, she cast the child under one of the bushes.* [16]*Then she went, and sat down over against him a good way off, about the distance of a bowshot; for she said, 'Let me not look upon the death of the child.' And as she sat over against him, the child lifted up his voice and wept.* [17]*And God heard the voice of the lad; and the angel of God called to Hagar from heaven, and said to her, 'What troubles you, Hagar? Fear not; for God has heard the voice of the lad where he is.* [18]*Arise, lift up the lad, and hold him fast with your hand; for I will make him a great nation.'* [19]*Then God opened her eyes, and she saw a well of water; and she*

went, and filled the skin with water, and gave the lad a drink. [20]*And God was with the lad, and he grew up; he lived in the wilderness, and became an expert with the bow.* [21]*He lived in the wilderness of Paran; and his mother took a wife for him from the land of Egypt.*

Isaac may have been as much as three years old by the time of his weaning, when it was customary to hold a feast of rejoicing for healthy growth and transition from infancy to childhood. Such occasions can turn sour, and, with Isaac the centre of festivities, it was, perhaps, predictable that Ishmael, who for fourteen years had been the only child, should resent Isaac's limelight. It is not quite clear what was going on between Ishmael and Isaac. The Hebrew reads *mᵉṣaḥēq*, translated 'mocking' (AV, RV), and 'playing' (RV mg., RSV). The verb puns on the name Isaac, and means in this context 'poking fun' (at Isaac, understood). It was too much for Sarah to see *the son of Hagar the Egyptian* taking advantage of her little boy, hence her outburst to her husband, ordering him to get rid of the slave-woman and her son. Sarah's words, though spoken in anger, happened to accord with God's purpose, and were for that reason upheld. It was wise that the two sons should be separated, just as it had been wise for Abraham and Lot to go their separate ways (13:2–12), and so Abraham was instructed, *'whatever Sarah says to you, do as she tells you'*. The Lord has a word for us even in our severest dilemmas. Isaac's line was God's chosen instrument because he was the child of the promise, a theme which Paul was to use as an allegory (Gal. 4:21–31), contrasting salvation by human effort with salvation by faith. The two are incompatible.

The fact that God had not chosen Ishmael did not, however, imply that God had no concern for him. This is made abundantly plain, first by the divine promise that God will make a nation of the son of the slave-woman also, because he is Abraham's son. It is reinforced by God's care of Hagar, appearing to her as he had done on the previous occasion (16:17-14), and saving the life of her son. For Abraham the separation had the bitter pain associated with a divorce. He would see neither Hagar nor Ishmael again. Nor could he make adequate provision for them, but what Abraham could not do God ensured for them both.

It was no easy experience for the unsupported mother, who had used up all her resources and who thought the end had come, but it was in her despair that God revealed himself to her, assured her that he still knew all about her sufferings – and had heard Ishmael's tears and prayers. The teenager cried out to God and was saved from death. More than that, he was assured of a future. His mother's support, water to drink, and God's presence with the lad gave him renewed health and security, even for life in the wilderness, and eventually he married a wife from Egypt. The story of Ishmael is finished for the present so that full attention may be given to Isaac, but Ishmael is not outside the scope of God's purposes, though his destiny is different from that of Isaac. As the writer says, *God was with the lad.*

Hagar's life had been full of trouble, and it was not of her making. It all stemmed from Abraham's lapse of faith in decamping to Egypt, and from his later disobedience. Does our disobedience ever fail to damage and sadden the life of someone else? And does the Lord ever fail to be gracious to those we have hurt?

Genesis 21:22–34

A border dispute

At that time Abimelech and Phicol the commander of his army said to Abraham, 'God is with you in all that you do; 23now therefore swear to me here by God that you will not deal falsely with me or with my offspring or with my posterity, but as I have dealt loyally with you, you will deal with me and with the land where you have sojourned.' 24And Abraham said, 'I will swear.'

25When Abraham complained to Abimelech about a well of water which Abimelech's servants had seized, 26Abimelech said, 'I do not know who has done this thing; you did not tell me, and I have not heard of it until today.' 27So Abraham took sheep and oxen and gave them to Abimelech, and the two men made a covenant. 28Abraham set seven ewe lambs of the flock apart. 29And Abimelech said to Abraham, 'What is the meaning of these seven ewe lambs which you have set apart?' 30He said, 'These seven ewe lambs you will take from my hand, that you may be a witness for me that I dug this well.' 31Therefore that place was called Beer-sheba; because there both of them swore an oath. 32So they made a covenant at Beer-sheba. Then Abimelech and Phicol the commander of his army rose up and returned to the land of the Philistines. 33Abraham planted a tamarisk tree in Beer-sheba, and called there on the name of the Lord, the Everlasting God. 34And Abraham sojourned many days in the land of the Philistines.

This further subject, which will crop up again (chapter 26), is

87

included in the narrative at this point. Abraham lived so close to the wide open spaces of the desert that the western border of his territory was the only one that needed to be defined or defended. In this connection Abimelech, accompanied by his army chief, Phicol, made a diplomatic journey to make a formal treaty with Abraham. Building on the fact that Abraham had received hospitality from Abimelech, he could expect a favourable reception, and a promise of loyalty, but the agreement was no doubt prompted by the observation that Abraham was prospering: '*God is with you in all that you do*', and when more land was needed Abraham would naturally look towards the more fertile area on the coastal plain. Abraham was happy to enter into an agreement, but he took the opportunity to mention a grievance that had arisen over possession of a well, which Abraham had dug and therefore had a right to use.

Though he was the aggrieved party, Abraham provided the animals for the covenant ceremony (he was the one with animals to hand), but he also made a gift of *seven ewe lambs* to secure the well for himself and his descendants. It became known, therefore, as 'the well of seven' or 'the well of the oath', Beer-sheba, and a very deep and ancient well can be seen today in the excavation of a site close to modern Beersheba, just outside the city wall. Though the evidence that this may be the well of Abraham falls short of proof, and the text makes no mention of a city in his day, the well is a symbol, reminiscent of this story.

Abraham's *tamarisk tree* both provided shade and reinforced his claim to the site. More telling still was his worship of the Lord, *the Everlasting God*, who had made him the gift of the land. Taking advantage of the covenant with Abimelech, he felt free to move into his neighbour's land, known later as *the land of the Philistines*. In the last analysis this belonged to him too as part of the divine gift of land. The name *Everlasting God* (Heb. '*El 'Olām*) is used only here in Genesis. Did Abraham ponder over the oath which he and Abimelech had just sworn, and suddenly see that Yahweh is able to superintend an oath into perpetuity because he is the eternal God?[1] By the same token the Lord's word continues to apply to us and to our children after us, and to all generations (Gn. 17:9).

---

[1] *Cf.* J.A. Motyer. *The Revelation of the Divine Name*, p. 26.

Genesis 22:1–24

Proved and tested

*After these things God tested Abraham, and said to him, 'Abraham!' And
he said, 'Here am I.'* ^{2}*He said, 'Take your son, your only son Isaac, whom
you love, and go to the land of Moriah, and offer him there as a burnt
offering upon one of the mountains of which I shall tell you.'* ^{3}*So Abraham
rose early in the morning, saddled his ass, and took two of his young men
with him, and his son Isaac; and he cut the wood for the burnt offering, and
arose and went to the place of which God had told him.* ^{4}*On the third day
Abraham lifted up his eyes and saw the place afar off.* ^{5}*Then Abraham said
to his young men, 'Stay here with the ass; I and the lad will go yonder and
worship, and come again to you.'* ^{6}*And Abraham took the wood of the burnt
offering, and laid it on Isaac his son; and he took in his hand the fire and
the knife. So they went both of them together.* ^{7}*And Isaac said to his father
Abraham, 'My father!' And he said, 'Here am I, my son.' He said,
'Behold, the fire and the wood; but where is the lamb for a burnt offering?'*
^{8}*Abraham said, 'God will provide himself the lamb for a burnt offering, my
son.' So they went both of them together.*

^{9}*When they came to the place of which God had told him, Abraham built
an altar there, and laid the wood in order, and bound Isaac his son, and
laid him on the altar, upon the wood.* ^{10}*Then Abraham put forth his hand,
and took the knife to slay his son.* ^{11}*But the angel of the Lord called to him
from heaven, and said, 'Abraham, Abraham!' And he said, 'Here am I.'*
^{12}*He said, 'Do not lay your hand on the lad or do anything to him; for now
I know that you fear God, seeing you have not withheld your son, your only
son, from me.'* ^{13}*And Abraham lifted up his eyes and looked, and behold,
behind him was a ram, caught in a thicket by his horns; and Abraham went
and took the ram, and offered it up as a burnt offering instead of his son.*
^{14}*So Abraham called the name of that place The Lord will provide; as it is
said to this day, 'On the mountain of the Lord it shall be provided.'*

^{15}*And the angel of the Lord called to Abraham a second time from
heaven,* ^{16}*and said, 'By myself I have sworn, says the Lord, because you
have done this, and have not withheld your son, your only son,* ^{17}*I will
indeed bless you, and I will multiply your descendants as the stars of heaven
and as the sand which is on the seashore. And your descendants shall possess
the gate of their enemies,* ^{18}*and by your descendants shall all the nations of
the earth bless themselves, because you have obeyed my voice.'* ^{19}*So Abraham
returned to his young men, and they arose and went together to Beer-sheba;
and Abraham dwelt at Beer-sheba. ...*

Everyone who lives within earshot of the Filton area of Bristol is aware of the testing of aircraft engines. The whirring roar indicates that these powerful machines are being subjected to unusually severe conditions in order to be sure that, whatever the strains put upon them, they are thoroughly airworthy. People may subject themselves to extreme conditions in order to prove their capabilities, and Scripture reveals that testing is part of God's education of his children so that they may come to maturity (Jas. 1:2–4).

Abraham had had his patience tested almost beyond endurance, but now that Isaac, in late boyhood, is companionable, and happy to accompany his father on an expedition, the real test comes. *God tested Abraham* by demands that went clean contrary both to human reason and to the divine promise. The shock was not unlike that felt by the modern airline passenger when the reverse thrust of the engines is used to bring the plane to a halt. God's promises appeared to be put into reverse gear, after all the years of looking forward to the birth of Isaac. Yet it was Abraham's steadfast faith under great testing that made him into the outstanding example he became of the man of faith (Jas. 2:21–24).

It was a personal test for Abraham, who was called by name. It was also a lonely test, for God's command was not one to share with the mother of an only son. Abraham therefore bore the full force of the instruction to offer up as a burnt offering '*your son, your only son Isaac, whom you love*'. The threefold description rules out any possibility of misunderstanding. Abraham stifles all questions and comments, and simply does as he is told. It is about 70 kilometres (45 miles) from Beersheba to Mount Moriah, if the traditional identification of Mount Moriah with the Jerusalem temple site is correct. Even with an early start it would indeed be *the third day* before their destination came in sight. Abraham sustained himself by counting on the Lord's statement, 'through Isaac shall your descendants be named' (21:12), believing 'that God was able to raise men even from the dead' (Heb. 11:19).

Worship was normally accompanied by the sacrifice of an animal, so when Abraham told his servants that he and the lad would go to worship while they looked after the ass, there was nothing remarkable in his statement. To us, however, who know what was at stake, having been let into the secret of God's command, Abraham's words here reveal faith's certainty: '*I and the lad will go … we will worship … we will come back*' (NIV captures the emphasis of the Hebrew verb forms). Already the testing has brought Abraham's faith to full expression, and having put that faith into words, he will expect to see the Lord uphold his testimony, and by some means bring the two of them back to their base.

As Abraham and Isaac went up the mountain together, Isaac asked the perfectly natural question, *'Where is the lamb for a burnt offering?'* This made a painful moment all the more poignant for his father, who spoke more truly than he realized when he answered, *'God will provide himself the lamb for a burnt offering.'* The name of the place, *Jehovah-jireh*, meaning 'the Lord will provide', became proverbial. Since the Lord had commanded this sacrifice, it was reasonable to suppose that the Lord would see the need (the Hebrew verb *yir'eh* literally means 'see') and meet it, but to answer thus is easier with hindsight than, as in the case of Abraham, without any precedent.

Isaac is often said to fill a passive role in the story. He is allowed little scope by his protective father, but he must have shared his father's faith to the extent of co-operating with him. There was a ritual to perform, once the stone altar was built, that involved arranging the wood in order and binding the limbs of the sacrificial victim. At this point the youth could have escaped from his aged father's grasp and fled, but he did not do so. Instead, he submitted, and heard for himself the voice of the Lord intervening to ensure his release, and fulfil the expectation his father had voiced. There, close by them, was *a ram, caught in a thicket by his horns*. His father, as usual, had been right; the Lord did provide; the ram was released from its predicament, Isaac was released from the altar, and he experienced the wonder of substitutionary salvation. No-one had to tell Abraham to substitute the animal for his son; the principle of substitution was so well established as to be taken for granted.

For Abraham the test was over. He had proved beyond doubt that he feared God, because he had not withheld his only son from him (12), and now he received him back from God's hand, doubly precious as a result (*cf.* Heb. 11:19). But that was not all. *The angel of the Lord called a second time* (15), for the Lord reiterated his blessing on Abraham's descendants and promised them victory over their enemies. Generations to come were to enter into blessing because of the obedient trust of Abraham. It was deeply reassuring, but no reaction from Abraham is recorded. The experience was too deep for words.

Commentators tell us that the purpose of the story was to teach that human sacrifice was misguided, and so all Israel knew that God did not want 'the fruit of my body for the sin of my soul' (Mi. 6:7). And yet, in the end, only a human sacrifice would atone for sin. The ram was unmistakably substituted for Isaac, and in the prescribed sacrifices of a later age the substitutionary idea was most certainly present. The words of Abraham, *'God will provide himself a lamb,'* are prophetic, and John the Baptist had evidently meditated on them when he said, 'Behold, the Lamb of God!' (Jn. 1:29, 36). He may also have had in mind the Passover lamb, and the lamb led to the slaughter (Is. 53:7), for these are the outstanding occasions in the Old Testament when the word 'lamb' is used.

Another significant word in the narrative is 'your *only* son' (12, 16), which the LXX translated as 'beloved' (Gk. *agapētos*), and which recurs at the baptism of Jesus, 'This is my beloved Son' (Mt. 3:17) and at the transfiguration (Mt. 17:5). The beloved Son was also the 'only' or unique Son, for whom there could never be a substitute.

The name of the place, *Jehovah-jireh* (AV, RV), has become part of the church's heritage, particularly through the use made of it by George Müller and Hudson Taylor. For them God's provision included not only the spiritual resources but also such tangible gifts as buildings and daily bread for hundreds of people committed to their care. So sure was George Müller of the call of God to the work of looking after orphans, and in the case of Hudson Taylor of extending the church of God in China to the inland provinces, that they staked everything on the promise of God, *the Lord will provide*. On the principle that the greater includes the lesser, God, they believed, would provide not only the Lamb but every necessity for the fulfilment of his work. Paul's conviction summed it up: 'He who did not spare his own Son but gave him up for us all, will he not also give us all things with him?' (Rom. 8:32). Like Abraham these men were obliged to rely on the Lord, because there was no human source of supply committed to financing them. They acknowledged that they had to do God's work in God's way if they were to receive God's supplies; the way of faith was no easy option, any more than it had been for Abraham, and in the face of dilemmas and tests it demanded not passive submission but a conscious bending of the will to accept the sacrificial cords and the raised knife. But they saw God's provision, and their work goes on.

The Genesis record of Abraham's testing, then, is rather like the first drawing of a great artist, who has in mind a master work. The pencil sketch is perfect in its own right, yet the finished painting far surpasses the original drawing in which the same hand can be seen to have been at work. The way of faith, tested by 'fire', continues to reveal the genuineness of God's servants, and to bring glory to him (1 Pet. 1:6–7).

Genesis 23:1–20

The funeral of a princess

Sarah lived a hundred and twenty-seven years; these were the years of the life of Sarah. ²And Sarah died at Kiriath-arba (that is, Hebron) in the land of Canaan; and Abraham went in to mourn for Sarah and to weep for her. ³And Abraham rose up from before his dead, and said to the Hittites, ⁴'I am a stranger and a sojourner among you; give me property among you for a burying place, that I may bury my dead out of my sight.' ⁵The Hittites answered Abraham, ⁶'Hear us, my lord; you are a mighty prince among us. Bury your dead in the choicest of our sepulchres; none of us will withhold from you his sepulchre, or hinder you from burying your dead.' ⁷Abraham rose and bowed to the Hittites, the people of the land. ⁸And he said to them, 'If you are willing that I should bury my dead out of my sight, hear me, and entreat for me Ephron the son of Zohar, ⁹that he may give me the cave of Machpelah, which he owns; it is at the end of his field. For the full price let him give it to me in your presence as a possession for a burying place.' ¹⁰Now Ephron was sitting among the Hittites; and Ephron the Hittite answered Abraham in the hearing of the Hittites, of all who went in at the gate of his city, ¹¹'No, my lord, hear me; I give you the field, and I give you the cave that is in it; in the presence of the sons of my people, I give it to you; bury your dead.' ¹²Then Abraham bowed down before the people of the land. ¹³And he said to Ephron in the hearing of the people of the land, 'But if you will, hear me; I will give the price of the field; accept it from me, that I may bury my dead there.' ¹⁴Ephron answered Abraham, ¹⁵'My lord, listen to me: a piece of land worth four hundred shekels of silver, what is that between you and me? Bury your dead.' ¹⁶Abraham agreed with Ephron; and Abraham weighed out for Ephron the silver which he had named in the hearing of the Hittites, four hundred shekels of silver, according to the weights current among the merchants.

¹⁷So the field of Ephron in Machpelah, which was to the east of Mamre, the field with the cave which was in it and all the trees that were in the field, throughout its whole area, was made over ¹⁸to Abraham as a possession in the presence of the Hittites, before all who went in at the gate of his city. ¹⁹After this, Abraham buried Sarah his wife in the cave of the field of Machpelah east of Mamre (that is, Hebron) in the land of Canaan.

[20]The field and the cave that is in it were made over to Abraham as a possession for a burying place by the Hittites.

The death of Sarah in Hebron at the age of 127 marked the end of an era for Abraham and for Isaac, but the narrative dwells, not on personal bereavement, but on the funeral arrangements. Others in Abraham's household must have died and been buried, but Sarah's grave must be known, recognized and revered. This could be assured only if Abraham bought the land, owned the title deeds and established a family tomb for posterity.

His negotiations with the Hittites are depicted with all their eastern courtesy and local colour. The Hittites were themselves far from their homeland in Anatolia (modern Turkey), but their empire was extensive by the eighteenth century BC, and enterprising groups from that region may have migrated and settled centuries before that, though little information is available. In this chapter of Genesis they apparently own the land as 'natives'. They had evidently been assimilated into the population because their names are Semitic, and in the continuing story they prove to be settled and established members of local communities (26:34; 27:46; 28:1; 36:2). By comparison with these Hittites Abraham was at a disadvantage, being merely *a stranger and a sojourner* among them. He was in a weak bargaining position, familiar to anyone who has had to find a home in a foreign land, or appeal to local authorities on grounds of special need.

The Hittite reply, '*You are a mighty prince among us*', should be taken seriously. By right of victory in battle Abraham had established his authority over the lands captured by the five kings (chapter 14), and had put the local chieftains in his debt by securing their release. The population thus made beholden to him was to the east of Hebron, but he had become known from Dan to Beersheba and even to the north of Damascus (14:14–15). His wealth, the size of his household, and his integrity made him a desirable ally, whose effective help could be depended upon in case of attack in battle. No wonder the Hittites acknowledged that he was a leader to be reckoned with, a mighty prince, who was entitled to have the best place in their cemetery in accordance with his status: '*Bury your dead in the choicest of our sepulchres*' (6).

The clue was picked up by Abraham. The cave he had in mind was not situated among the sepulchres of the Hittites, but at one end of the field belonging to Ephron, where there was a cave known as the cave of Machpelah, meaning 'the double cave'. This Abraham was prepared to buy for the full price, because he needed a grave that was distinct from those of his neighbours. Mention of *the gate of his city* (10) implies that there was already a walled city on the site, not far from the cave of Machpelah. This city has not so far been identified, and its site may occupy part of the modern city of Hebron, where the mosque, which is a complete Herodian edifice and so goes back to pre-Islamic times, claims to mark the tombs of Abraham and his family. The site is almost certainly authentic. [2]

Citizens passing in and out of the gate as well as the elders were witnesses of the legal transaction between Ephron and Abraham. There was no hurry. Ephron offered the cave as a free gift, out of deference for Abraham's grief: *'bury your dead'*. Abraham insists that he intends to pay for the plot, and Ephron, still insisting that the land is a gift, slips in his assessment of its monetary worth. Each conformed to an expected pattern of diplomatic bargaining, but Abraham, contrary to custom, weighed out silver to the full value of the asking price, disdaining the thought of haggling on so solemn an occasion. *Four hundred shekels of silver* sounds an exorbitant price for a cave, in view of the twenty shekels paid by the Midianites for Joseph (37:28). Ephron did well out of the deal, and probably enjoyed telling generations to come how naive Abraham was over money. If so, the identity of Sarah's grave would be assured as the story of its purchase was repeated.

Though Abraham had asked only for the cave, Ephron refused to separate the cave from the field in which it was situated (11), so the field with its cave, *to the east of Mamre, and all the trees that were in the field* were legally made over to Abraham, the Hittite community being official witnesses of the transaction. Sarah, Abraham's wife, was given an honoured burial, and, by implication, her son Isaac was proclaimed to be Abraham's heir.

Genesis 24:1–67

Finding a wife for Isaac

Now Abraham was old, well advanced in years; and the Lord had blessed Abraham in all things. ²And Abraham said to his servant, the oldest of his house, who had charge of all that he had, 'Put your hand under my thigh, ³and I will make you swear by the Lord, the God of heaven and of the earth,

---

[2] See, for example, 'Patriarchal Burial Site Explored', *BAR* XI, 3 (1985).

that you will not take a wife for my son from the daughters of the Canaanites, among whom I dwell, [4]but will go to my country and to my kindred, and take a wife for my son Isaac.' [5]The servant said to him, 'Perhaps the woman may not be willing to follow me to this land; must I then take your son back to the land from which you came?' [6]Abraham said to him, 'See to it that you do not take my son back there. [7]The Lord, the God of heaven, who took me from my father's house and from the land of my birth, and who spoke to me and swore to me, "To your descendants I will give this land," he will send his angel before you, and you shall take a wife for my son from there. [8]But if the woman is not willing to follow you, then you will be free from this oath of mine; only you must not take my son back there.' [9]So the servant put his hand under the thigh of Abraham his master, and swore to him concerning this matter.

[10]Then the servant took ten of his master's camels and departed, taking all sorts of choice gifts from his master; and he arose, and went to Mesopotamia, to the city of Nahor. [11]And he made the camels kneel down outside the city by the well of water at the time of evening, the time when women go out to draw water. [12]And he said, 'O Lord, God of my master Abraham, grant me success today, I pray thee, and show steadfast love to my master Abraham. [13]Behold, I am standing by the spring of water, and the daughters of the men of the city are coming out to draw water. [14]Let the maiden to whom I shall say, "Pray let down your jar that I may drink," and who shall say, "Drink, and I will water your camels" — let her be the one whom thou hast appointed for thy servant Isaac. By this I shall know that thou hast shown steadfast love to my master.'

[15]Before he had done speaking, behold, Rebekah, who was born to Bethuel the son of Milcah, the wife of Nahor, Abraham's brother, came out with her water jar upon her shoulder. [16]The maiden was very fair to look upon, a virgin, whom no man had known. She went down to the spring, and filled her jar, and came up. [17]Then the servant ran to meet her, and said, 'Pray give me a little water to drink from your jar.' [18]She said, 'Drink, my lord'; and she quickly let down her jar upon her hand, and gave him a drink. [19]When she had finished giving him a drink, she said, 'I will draw for your camels also, until they have done drinking.' [20]So she quickly emptied her jar into the trough and ran again to the well to draw, and she drew for all his camels. [21]The man gazed at her in silence to learn whether the Lord had prospered his journey or not.

[22]When the camels had done drinking, the man took a gold ring weighing a half shekel, and two bracelets for her arms weighing ten gold shekels, [23]and said, 'Tell me whose daughter you are. Is there room in your father's house for us to lodge in?' [24]She said to him, 'I am the daughter of Bethuel

the son of Milcah, whom she bore to Nahor.' ²⁵She added, 'We have both
straw and provender enough, and room to lodge in.' ²⁶The man bowed his
head and worshipped the Lord, ²⁷and said, 'Blessed be the Lord, the God of
my master Abraham, who has not forsaken his steadfast love and his
faithfulness toward my master. As for me, the Lord has led me in the way to
the house of my master's kinsmen.'

    ²⁸Then the maiden ran and told her mother's household about these
things. ²⁹Rebekah had a brother whose name was Laban; and Laban ran
out to the man, to the spring. ³⁰When he saw the ring, and the bracelets on
his sister's arms, and when he heard the words of Rebekah his sister, 'Thus
the man spoke to me,' he went to the man; and behold, he was standing by
the camels at the spring. ³¹He said, 'Come in, O blessed of the Lord; why do
you stand outside? For I have prepared the house and a place for the camels.'
³²So the man came into the house; and Laban ungirded the camels, and gave
him straw and provender for the camels, and water to wash his feet and the
feet of the men who were with him. ³³Then food was set before him to eat; but
he said, 'I will not eat until I have told my errand.' He said, 'Speak on.'

    ³⁴So he said, 'I am Abraham's servant. ³⁵The Lord has greatly blessed
my master, and he has become great; he has given him flocks and herds,
silver and gold, menservants and maidservants, camels and asses. ³⁶And
Sarah my master's wife bore a son to my master when she was old; and to
him he has given all that he has. ³⁷My master made me swear, saying,
"You shall not take a wife for my son from the daughters of the Canaanites,
in whose land I dwell; ³⁸but you shall go to my father's house and to my
kindred, and take a wife for my son." ³⁹I said to my master, "Perhaps the
woman will not follow me." ⁴⁰But he said to me, "The Lord, before whom I
walk, will send his angel with you and prosper your way; and you shall
take a wife for my son from my kindred and from my father's house; ⁴¹then
you will be free from my oath, when you come to my kindred; and if they will
not give her to you, you will be free from my oath."

    ⁴²'I came today to the spring, and said, "O Lord, the God of my master
Abraham, if now thou wilt prosper the way which I go, ⁴³behold, I am
standing by the spring of water; let the young woman who comes out to draw,
to whom I shall say, 'Pray give me a little water from your jar to drink,'
⁴⁴and who will say to me, 'Drink, and I will draw for your camels also,'
let her be the woman whom the Lord has appointed for my master's son."

    ⁴⁵'Before I had done speaking in my heart, behold, Rebekah came out
with her water jar on her shoulder; and she went down to the spring, and
drew. I said to her, "Pray let me drink." ⁴⁶She quickly let down her jar
from her shoulder, and said, "Drink, and I will give your camels drink
also." So I drank, and she gave the camels drink also. ⁴⁷Then I asked her,

"Whose daughter are you?" She said, "The daughter of Bethuel, Nahor's son, whom Milcah bore to him." So I put the ring on her nose, and the bracelets on her arms. [48]*Then I bowed my head and worshipped the Lord, and blessed the Lord, the God of my master Abraham, who had led me by the right way to take the daughter of my master's kinsman for his son.* [49]*Now then, if you will deal loyally and truly with my master, tell me; and if not, tell me; that I may turn to the right hand or to the left.'*

[50]*Then Laban and Bethuel answered, 'The thing comes from the Lord; we cannot speak to you bad or good.* [51]*Behold, Rebekah is before you, take her and go, and let her be the wife of your master's son, as the Lord has spoken.'*

[52]*When Abraham's servant heard their words, he bowed himself to the earth before the Lord.* [53]*And the servant brought forth jewelry of silver and of gold, and raiment, and gave them to Rebekah; he also gave to her brother and to her mother costly ornaments.* [54]*And he and the men who were with him ate and drank, and they spent the night there. When they arose in the morning, he said, 'Send me back to my master.'* [55]*Her brother and her mother said, 'Let the maiden remain with us a while, at least ten days; after that she may go.'* [56]*But he said to them, 'Do not delay me, since the Lord has prospered my way; let me go that I may go to my master.'* [57]*They said, 'We will call the maiden, and ask her.'* [58]*And they called Rebekah, and said to her, 'Will you go with this man?' She said, 'I will go.'* [59]*So they sent away Rebekah their sister and her nurse, and Abraham's servant and his men.* [60]*And they blessed Rebekah, and said to her, 'Our sister, be the mother of thousands of ten thousands; and may your descendants possess the gate of those who hate them!'* [61]*Then Rebekah and her maids arose, and rode upon the camels and followed the man; thus the servant took Rebekah, and went his way.*

[62]*Now Isaac had come from Beer-lahai-roi, and was dwelling in the Negeb.* [63]*And Isaac went out to meditate in the field in the evening; and he lifted up his eyes and looked, and behold, there were camels coming.* [64]*And Rebekah lifted up her eyes, and when she saw Isaac, she alighted from the camel,* [65]*and said to the servant, 'Who is the man yonder, walking in the field to meet us?' The servant said, 'It is my master.' So she took her veil and covered herself.* [66]*And the servant told Isaac all the things that he had done.* [67]*Then Isaac brought her into the tent, and took Rebekah, and she became his wife; and he loved her. So Isaac was comforted after his mother's death.*

There can be little doubt that there was an unusually close bond between Sarah and her only son. In the nature of the case this was to be expected, but the writer tells us as much in the last words of this story. So long as Sarah was there to love and cherish him, Isaac felt no need of a wife, but after her death his sense of loss was very great. Indeed, the story of a bride for Isaac comes as a well-prepared climax, members of the Nahor branch of the family having been listed at the end of chapter 22.

If Sarah had fussed over Isaac, Abraham protected him from decision making and allowed him no initiative in the choice of a wife. Many another special son and heir has been similarly restricted. Isaac was not free to marry a local Canaanite girl, nor was he to travel abroad in search of a wife. Haran was specifically forbidden territory. Perhaps Abraham feared that Isaac might not return; or maybe travellers had told him enough about the family there to alert Abraham that Laban was a slippery customer, not to be trusted with other-worldly Isaac. Yet Abraham had travelled far and wide, and Jacob was to stay for twenty years in Haran, but Isaac was protected and provided for. Since this had been the case all his life, and since he felt he had no option, Isaac accepted it all with good grace. The matter was, after all, in the hands of the Lord God of his father.

For Abraham's senior retainer, responsible for all his property, this commission to find a wife for Isaac may well have seemed the most problematic of his life. The family from which the bride would be chosen was already settled (*cf.* 22:20-24), but it was possible that no woman would be willing to travel into the unknown to marry a man she had never met. Abraham had faced that real possibility, but as he looked back over the events of his own life he was encouraged to believe that the same Lord who had led him, spoken to him and sworn on oath to him to give him descendants, would send his angel before his servant. The servant, however, might not share Abraham's conviction, so Abraham assured him that he would not be held liable if he came back empty-handed! The solemn oath indicated how deadly serious Abraham was in all he asked of his retainer; on the success of this enterprise depended the separateness of the people of God, a necessary condition for developing a counter-culture that would reflect their walk with God.

The elderly retainer set out on his adventure, taking with him servants, ten camels, and choice gifts, his destination some 400 miles to the north. For Rebekah the evening walk to the well outside the city of Nahor was part of the daily routine. There was no reason why this particular evening should be in any way out of the ordinary; indeed, like most teenagers, she may well have been complaining that life was boring, and that nothing ever happened there. Travellers who rested at the well took little notice of her; they were on the caravan route, and there were inns to take care of their needs. This evening, however, no sooner had she drawn up her water-pot from the well than a stranger came up to her to ask for a drink. Why did he choose her out of all the women fetching their water-supplies? Little did she know that her ready response and her willingness to draw water also for the thirsty camels corresponded to the prayer of this elderly man, who steadily watched her as she fulfilled her laborious task. He needed to know *whether the Lord had prospered his journey or not*, and was sufficiently reassured to produce the gold ring and bracelets to present to Rebekah. Here was a girl of unusual spontaneity and helpfulness, with a capacity for the work of a household.

The prayer of Abraham's retainer (12–14) is brief and to the point. He addresses the Lord as Abraham's God rather than his own, but then he is on Abraham's business, and he pleads for the Lord's steadfast love to be shown to the one with whom the Lord has entered into covenant. The fulfilment of his suggested 'sign' provided tangible evidence that his prayer for guidance had not only been heard but answered. Even the kneeling camels worshipped!

It was not until he had handed over the costly jewellery that the girl revealed her identity. She was from the one family in the area related to Abraham, and the servant was not slow to recognize that this meeting was no coincidence. He had found not only a potential wife for his master's son, but also a bed for the night and loving hospitality in a welcoming home, where even the camels could be fed and stabled. With so many confirmations that his prayer had been given an abundant answer, the servant bowed his head and worshipped the Lord, acknowledging the Lord's continuing kindness and faithfulness to Abraham, and incidentally to himself. Now he knew for sure that the Lord had guided him in his journey and had led him specifically to this place. His amazement is expressed in the emphatic 'As for me, the Lord has led me' (of all people!). No such experience had come his way before, and there is something especially wonderful about the first experience of answered prayer, confirming our early steps of faith as nothing else could.

Little indications of character mark the narrative here. Rebekah is quick in the uptake, energetic and practical. Though Bethuel, Abraham's nephew, is still living (50), it is master Laban, Rebekah's brother, who gets wind of the traveller's arrival, sees at a glance the worth of the ring and bracelets that Rebekah is wearing, and decides that this is a visitor worth cultivating. He even takes the path to the well so that he may personally invite the traveller and his retinue to accept his hospitality. No effort is spared in providing for their every need, and Laban himself attends to the camels, his energies triggered by signs of wealth. The motivation of Abraham's servant is quite different. Hungry as he is after a day on the road, precedence must be given to matters more pressing than food. He knows his priorities. He will not eat until he has told his errand.

The narration of all the relevant details, though they are already known to the reader, is full of interest in the light of God's unfolding providence. Prominent at each stage of the story is the theme of the Lord's blessing of Abraham, giving him wealth, and above all a son. Abraham's assurance that the Lord's angel would prosper his servant on his journey puts the meeting with Rebekah and her family into a setting which all present recognize to be of the Lord's ordering. That is why Laban and Bethuel (the son is named before his father) concluded that there was nothing more to be said. Rebekah must go, and become the wife of Abraham's son, *as the Lord has spoken*. In this instance he had spoken, not in words, but in his overruling providence. Rebekah had been sufficiently involved to have been able to observe this divine guidance, and, though she was not consulted, she was evidently delighted with the turn events were taking.

The success of his mission gave the servant a further cause for thanksgiving to God before he presented more gifts to the bride, and to her mother and brother, to confirm the agreement. The consent of Rebekah the next morning concerned only whether she was prepared to leave immediately; that she should leave her family for Canaan was never in question. It was a journey of no return. Since her calling was to become Isaac's wife and the mother of 'thousands of ten thousands', what was to be gained by staying at home a few more days when the adventure could begin at once? Responding to the God whom she was learning to know and worship, she set off gladly, accompanied by her maids, for a new land.

For Isaac it was a matter of patient waiting until his father's ambassador returned. Mention of Beer-lahai-roi (*cf.* 16:14) and the Negeb indicates that he was living in the desert region to the south-west of Beersheba, so Rebekah's journey was an extra long one, but the clear air and the wide open views permitted distant vision of approaching caravans, and one evening his hopes were fulfilled; the messenger had returned. Rebekah, alert and expectant, reacted immediately on catching sight of Isaac, and veiled herself. It is interesting that she did not travel veiled, but custom dictated that as a bride-to-be she needed a veil in the presence of her future husband, until the marriage took place, possibly the same evening.

There are two indications of Isaac's aspirations for his home-life; he *brought her into the tent of his mother Sarah* (67, NIV; *cf.* RSV mg.), so symbolizing the role that he expected Rebekah to play, and he *was comforted after his mother's death*, three years before.[3] During all his thirty-seven years until the death of Sarah, Isaac had been her one and only son, doted on and protected, hence his extreme sense of loss when she died. Rebekah was expected to take her place, which would mean caring for her husband as his mother had done. At the same time she was comforted in this isolated place where she knew no-one; for Isaac loved his wife. Thus each found love and security in the other, and they shared the deep undergirding of the knowledge that the Lord God of Abraham had brought them together. If they were ever tempted to doubt that, they could recall the marvellous providence that took Abraham's servant straight to Rebekah, and the prayer and praise that had surrounded the whole venture, all of which betokened the unmistakable guidance of God. Though they had not met before, Isaac and Rebekah grew to love one another; though they had not chosen one another, their marriage was on a sure footing.

Genesis 25:1–18

Related tribes and the death of Abraham

... *[7]These are the days of the years of Abraham's life, a hundred and seventy-five years. [8]Abraham breathed his last and died in a good old age, an old man and full of years, and was gathered to his people. [9]Isaac and Ishmael his sons buried him in the cave of Machpelah, in the field of Ephron the son of Zohar the Hittite, east of Mamre, [10]the field which Abraham purchased from the Hittites. There Abraham was buried, with Sarah his wife. [11]After the death of Abraham God blessed Isaac his son. And Isaac dwelt at Beer-lahai-roi ...*

Wide open spaces and too sparse a population created a need for

[3] Isaac was forty years old when he married Rebekah (25:20), and he had been thirty-seven when his mother died (*cf.* 23:1 with 17:17).

large families (*cf.* 'fill the earth and subdue it', Gn. 1:28). Abraham's concubines had not been relevant to the narrative and therefore had not so far been mentioned, but some of the children of Keturah, another wife of Abraham, will feature in the history, so they are listed as in family annals. The descendants of Ishmael are also accounted for and left on one side so that the narrator can give full attention to his main theme, which is still centred for the moment on Isaac. Though Keturah and Hagar are mentioned after the death of Sarah, we are not necessarily to infer that Keturah, any more than Hagar, became a member of the household only after the death of Sarah. The six sons of Keturah and the twelve sons of Ishmael became the ancestors of peoples who lived on the eastern borders of Israel's territory, 'over against them', as the Hebrew idiom puts it, in more ways than one (*cf.* p. 59). The picture of Abraham as the father of nations is thus enlarged and defined. With a note that Abraham provided adequately for these sons the writer dismisses them in a few verses. In the salvation history Isaac, the child of Sarah, is the one to be reckoned with.

The death of Abraham and his burial in the cave of Machpelah is recorded between the genealogies of the two lesser wives. Abraham was blessed even in the circumstances of his death. He knew 'length of days', died in a good old age, and had an honourable burial, with both Isaac and Ishmael present to pay their last respects. He is described as *gathered to his people*, a beautiful idiom, which lays stress on the resumption of fellowship with loved ones after death, and provides a prospect of community after the loneliness associated with death. The phrase must have meant more than burial in the family tomb, because so far only Sarah's body lay there, and, in the light of the New Testament, resurrection opens the prospect of fellowship with all who are in Christ, and with all the company of heaven. There will be no loneliness when, along with Abraham and all who share his faith, we worship the eternal God.

Genesis 25:19–34

Sons for Isaac and Rebekah

These are the descendants of Isaac, Abraham's son: Abraham was the father of Isaac, [20]*and Isaac was forty years old when he took to wife Rebekah, the daughter of Bethuel the Aramean of Paddan-aram, the sister of Laban the Aramean.* [21]*And Isaac prayed to the Lord for his wife, because she was*

103

barren; and the Lord granted his prayer, and Rebekah his wife conceived.
²²The children struggled together within her; and she said, 'If it is thus,
why do I live?' So she went to inquire of the Lord. ²³And the Lord said to
her,

> *'Two nations are in your womb,*
> *and two peoples, born of you, shall be divided;*
> *the one shall be stronger than the other,*
> *the elder shall serve the younger.'*

²⁴When her days to be delivered were fulfilled, behold, there were twins in
her womb. ²⁵The first came forth red, all his body like a hairy mantle; so
they called his name Esau. ²⁶Afterward his brother came forth, and his
hand had taken hold of Esau's heel; so his name was called Jacob. Isaac was
sixty years old when she bore them.

²⁷When the boys grew up, Esau was a skilful hunter, a man of the field,
while Jacob was a quiet man, dwelling in tents. ²⁸Isaac loved Esau, because
he ate of his game; but Rebekah loved Jacob.

²⁹Once when Jacob was boiling pottage, Esau came in from the field, and
he was famished. ³⁰And Esau said to Jacob, 'Let me eat some of that red
pottage, for I am famished!' (Therefore his name was called Edom.) ³¹Jacob
said, 'First sell me your birthright.' ³²Esau said, 'I am about to die; of
what use is a birthright to me?' ³³Jacob said, 'Swear to me first.' So he
swore to him, and sold his birthright to Jacob. ³⁴Then Jacob gave Esau
bread and pottage of lentils, and he ate and drank, and rose and went his
way. Thus Esau despised his birthright.

Far from increasing to thousands upon thousands (24:60), Rebekah
saw many an anniversary of her marriage go by without any sign of a
child. *Isaac prayed for his wife* is surely an understatement,
representing years of persistent intercession. As for Abraham and
Sarah, so for Isaac and Rebekah; to be the recipient of God's
promises did not mean that everything would be plain sailing. The
reverse proved to be nearer to the truth, for the children of the
covenant promise were born only after much prayer, as a direct gift
from God. It is no vain thing to trust the Lord, but faith involves
being shut up to God's way and God's time, and demands much
patience. This lesson, taught so early on in the scriptural lesson
book, needs to be presented to young Christians in a forceful way to
prepare them for the tests that are sure to come before long, and
could unsettle them, as indeed they unsettle many who are further
along the way. The writer of Psalm 89, for example, was a person of
mature faith, but he could not resolve the tension between the

covenant promises of God and the destruction of the royal throne of Judah, which the Lord had decreed should last 'for ever'. He and his contemporaries could not possibly live to see how the word of God was to be fulfilled in 'the greater than David', the Lord Jesus Christ. They had to hold on in faith; every believer has to learn to do that.

Isaac and Rebekah could be certain that they were praying in line with the Lord's will when they prayed for a son, but they still needed much faith and patience, because the very certainty tends towards an impatient striving after the fulfilment of the promise. Even when, after nineteen years of marriage, Rebekah found herself pregnant, her problems were not over, for she was troubled by violent movement within her. What could it mean? Taught by long years of sharing Isaac's faith, *she went to inquire of the Lord*, possibly at one of the places where the Lord had spoken to Abraham, and in reply she received a short but telling oracle in poetic form. The Lord finds many different ways of conveying his word, and on this occasion may have used a prophet who was also able to compose memorable verse. As if it were a small thing to hear that she was to have twins, Rebekah was also permitted to look ahead to the destiny of the two boys who were to be born. Rebekah would indeed be the mother, not merely of thousands but of nations. Already the children were struggling for supremacy, and eventually the elder would serve the younger (23).[4]

When the babies were born the differences in their appearance were so striking as to be noted as significant. The elder, red and well endowed with hair, was called *Esau*, which sounds a little like the Hebrew word for 'hairy'. The second-born became noted for an aggressive, self-seeking attitude, typified by his birth with an arm outstretched to clutch the heel of his brother. His name *Jacob*, meaning 'he deceives' or 'supplants', proved to be no misnomer as his life unfolded, and the first to suffer was his brother Esau.[5]

[4] An unusual word, *raḇ*, is used here for 'elder', and it occurs only here in this sense. *Cf.* M.J. Selman, 'Comparative Customs and the Patriarchal Age', *EOPN*, p. 126. 'The cognate Akkadian word, *rabû*, is also used by itself of the eldest son, but so far has turned up only in tablets of the mid-second millennium ... it appears that this biblical datum has some chronological significance.' It would support a second rather than a first millennium date of writing.

[5] The name Jacob has been found in cuneiform and Egyptian texts dating from the early second millennium, in a form which meant 'may God protect'. The Hebrew for 'heel' and 'to take by the heel' or 'supplant' have the same consonants, and therefore lend themselves to puns on the already current name, Jacob. In a curious way various nuances of his life were thus foreshadowed. He took his brother by the heel before they were born; he supplanted him twice; and yet the hand of God protected Jacob, while at the same time taking him through trial and danger to chasten him.

The fact is that neither boy looked promising material for becoming an heir to the covenant promises. Esau, the hunter, lived for immediate pleasures and let the future take care of itself. Jacob was ruthless in his scheming to outwit his brother, who, as the elder of the two, was in a specially privileged position. He had the *birthright*, which meant that he was entitled to inherit more than the younger, and had a special status as compared with any other children. The fact that Isaac favoured Esau reinforced this cultural practice, widespread in the ancient Near East.[6] Jacob sensed that he could get the better of both his father and Esau by playing on Esau's weakness for a good meal at any cost, especially when he was dying of hunger! Jacob, the opportunist, recognized the moment, and had his appetizing dish ready. Esau fell into the trap and demanded some of 'that red stuff'. Red was his colour (25) in more ways than one, hence his nickname *Edom*, which meant 'red'.

Jacob's demand for the birthright was no boyish prank that parental authority could reverse, for the transaction was sealed with an oath, and oaths were binding. Esau knew it, but chose to disregard the consequences, so despising his birthright. His couldn't-care-less attitude disqualified him, and became a warning to others (Heb. 12:16–17) who might equally flippantly forfeit their spiritual heritage. Esau's oath could not be revoked because it was legally binding, and though the door of salvation stands open to welcome those who truly repent, and long to inherit the status Christ died to bestow (Mt. 5:3–10), it is possible, even so, to forfeit spiritual privilege by despising God's promises and by stubbornly rejecting God's way till the door shuts.

Nor was Jacob guiltless. For the moment there is no comment on his ruthlessness, but throughout his life he was to have reason to remember his warped relationship with his brother as he became the victim of the scheming of others, The measure he gave was the measure he got (*cf*. Mt. 7:2), and it was an effective way of learning to know himself. Thus it came about that the 'chosen people' looked back to an ancestor who, far from being a model hero, was first introduced as an unattractive man, sharp in the uptake to take advantage of his brother. The corollary is that, since the Lord was able to transform and use Jacob, he can do the same for others. This is one of the distinctive messages of the Bible.

For the moment, however, Isaac is still the centre of the narrative.

---

[6] *EOPN*, p. 126. *Cf*. Dt. 21:15–17, where in a particular situation a double portion is to be given to the first-born.

Genesis 26:1–35

The Lord appears to Isaac

Now there was a famine in the land, besides the former famine that was in the days of Abraham. And Isaac went to Gerar, to Abimelech king of the Philistines. ²And the Lord appeared to him, and said, 'Do not go down to Egypt; dwell in the land of which I shall tell you. ³Sojourn in this land, and I will be with you, and will bless you; for to you and to your descendants I will give all these lands, and I will fulfil the oath which I swore to Abraham your father. ⁴I will multiply your descendants as the stars of heaven, and will give to your descendants all these lands; and by your descendants all the nations of the earth shall bless themselves: ⁵because Abraham obeyed my voice and kept my charge, my commandments, my statutes, and my laws.'

⁶So Isaac dwelt in Gerar. ⁷When the men of the place asked him about his wife, he said, 'She is my sister'; for he feared to say, 'My wife,' thinking, 'lest the men of the place should kill me for the sake of Rebekah'; because she was fair to look upon. ⁸When he had been there a long time, Abimelech king of the Philistines looked out of a window and saw Isaac fondling Rebekah his wife. ⁹So Abimelech called Isaac, and said, 'Behold, she is your wife; how then could you say, "She is my sister"?' Isaac said to him, 'Because I thought, "Lest I die because of her."' ¹⁰Abimelech said, 'What is this you have done to us? One of the people might easily have lain with your wife, and you would have brought guilt upon us.' ¹¹So Abimelech warned all the people, saying, 'Whoever touches this man or his wife shall be put to death.'

¹²And Isaac sowed in that land, and reaped in the same year a hundredfold. The Lord blessed him, ¹³and the man became rich, and gained more and more until he became very wealthy. ¹⁴He had possessions of flocks and herds, and a great household, so that the Philistines envied him. ¹⁵(Now the Philistines had stopped and filled with earth all the wells which his father's servants had dug in the days of Abraham his father.) ¹⁶And Abimelech said to Isaac, 'Go away from us; for you are much mightier than we.'

¹⁷So Isaac departed from there, and encamped in the valley of Gerar and dwelt there. ¹⁸And Isaac dug again the wells of water which had been dug in the days of Abraham his father; for the Philistines had stopped them after the death of Abraham; and he gave them the names which his father had given them. ¹⁹But when Isaac's servants dug in the valley and found there a well of springing water, ²⁰the herdsmen of Gerar quarrelled with Isaac's herdsmen, saying, 'The water is ours.' So he called the name of the well

Esek, because they contended with him. ²¹*Then they dug another well, and they quarrelled over that also; so he called its name Sitnah.* ²²*And he moved from there and dug another well, and over that they did not quarrel; so he called its name Rehoboth, saying, 'For now the Lord has made room for us, and we shall be fruitful in the land.'*

²³*From there he went up to Beer-sheba.* ²⁴*And the Lord appeared to him the same night and said, 'I am the God of Abraham your father; fear not, for I am with you and will bless you and multiply your descendants for my servant Abraham's sake.'* ²⁵*So he built an altar there and called upon the name of the Lord, and pitched his tent there. And there Isaac's servants dug a well.*

²⁶*Then Abimelech went to him from Gerar with Ahuzzath his adviser and Phicol the commander of his army.* ²⁷*Isaac said to them, 'Why have you come to me, seeing that you hate me and have sent me away from you?'* ²⁸*They said, 'We see plainly that the Lord is with you; so we say, let there be an oath between you and us, and let us make a covenant with you,* ²⁹*that you will do us no harm, just as we have not touched you and have done to you nothing but good and have sent you away in peace. You are now the blessed of the Lord.'* ³⁰*So he made them a feast, and they ate and drank.* ³¹*In the morning they rose early and took oath with one another; and Isaac set them on their way, and they departed from him in peace.* ³²*That same day Isaac's servants came and told him about the well which they had dug, and said to him, 'We have found water.'* ³³*He called it Shibah; therefore the name of the city is Beer-sheba to this day.*

³⁴*When Esau was forty years old, he took to wife Judith the daughter of Beeri the Hittite, and Basemath the daughter of Elon the Hittite;* ³⁵*and they made life bitter for Isaac and Rebekah.*

This chapter is the only one devoted entirely to Isaac, whose story is not only shorter but also less spectacular than that of either Abraham or Jacob. In many ways he is the bridge between the two, recapitulating the lessons learnt by Abraham, and passing on to his sons all that God had so far revealed of the family's destiny and of God himself. His life was a time of consolidation, and there was no necessity for him to travel as his father had done beyond the boundaries of Canaan.

The one adventure of Isaac's life was occasioned by a famine in the always precarious Negeb region. When food became scarce he had the choice, which had earlier faced Abraham, of making either for Egypt, irrigated by the Nile, or for the coast of Canaan, with its higher rainfall. Isaac made for the nearer of the two, and at this time of trouble and perplexity the Lord appeared to him. First the Lord confirmed that Isaac had been right not to go to Egypt. Gerar was where the Lord would be with him to bless him, and, moreover, this territory, which others owned and ruled, would one day be given to his descendants, a promise which began to be fulfilled in the time of David (2 Sa. 5:25; 8:1), when he defeated the Philistines, hundreds of years later.[7] The promise made to Abraham is being reiterated to Isaac; his descendants will be innumerable, and through them blessing will come to all the nations of the earth, *because Abraham obeyed* in every detail the charge God gave him. The implication is that Isaac must be equally careful to ensure, by his perfect obedience, transmission of the heritage for generations to come. Since no mention is made here of any sons, it is likely that Esau and Jacob had not yet been born. Isaac, like his father, had his faith enlarged by testing, and he demonstrated his faith by his readiness to do God's bidding. The commandments, statutes and laws of God had not yet been spelt out, and 'where there is no law there is no transgression' (Rom. 4:15). Maybe that is why we do not hear of Abraham repenting. Such was Abraham's understanding of his Lord that he had an intuitive sense of what was right, and in his actions followed it. His faults were overlooked and his lapses were forgotten, but once the law was given disobedience could not be overlooked.

One such lapse was about to be repeated in Isaac's experience. The ruler in Gerar is still called Abimelech (*cf.* 20:2ff.), perhaps because it was the family name or the traditional throne name. It meant '[God] the king is my father'. In this incident, unlike the occasion when Abram passed off Sarai as his sister (12:11–16), no-one attempted to marry Rebekah, though Isaac passed her off as his sister.[8] What is striking is the high standard of morality in Gerar, and the severity of the punishment decreed there for taking another man's wife. Nothing less than the death penalty was exacted: '*Whoever touches this man or his wife shall be put to death*', such was the

---

[7] The site of Gerar has not been identified, though surface finds at several places in the wadi Gaza indicate possible settlements of the period. See J. J. Bimson, 'Archaeological Data and the Dating of the Patriarchs', *EOPN*, pp. 74–75.

[8] These two wife-sister passages, together with Gn. 20, are frequently dismissed as 'doublets' of one story, the two concerned with Abraham being regarded as coming from different documentary sources. Yet the details are quite distinctive in the three narratives, and there is no evidence for regarding them as doublets. The fact that marriage to a half-sister was to be prohibited in the law (Lv. 18:9, 11; 20:17; Dt. 27:22) is sufficient to account for the absence of any mention of such a relationship later than the book of Genesis.

guilt associated with infringing the marriage laws (10). Even the Philistines could on occasions put God's people to shame.

Having once moved over to Gerar, Isaac stayed *a long time* (8), farmed there and grew rich. The local population resented his success, and he was asked to leave. He had outstayed his welcome. But he did not go far, preferring to make use of wells which his father had had dug when he came this way. It was not that Isaac was using water which others needed, for the wells were filled in until he reopened them, but that the Philistines claimed all the resources of the land as their own, even if they did not intend to use them. Isaac withdrew gradually, leaving behind wells whose names recalled his quarrels with the neighbours, and finally returned to Beersheba, where he received his only other revelation from the Lord. It was a reassurance that he was in the line of God's will and therefore of his blessing. In response to the Lord's initiative, Isaac *built an altar, called on the name of the Lord, and pitched his tent* (25). There is some support here for the suggestion that the tent was intended for worship, as Professor Wiseman argues (*cf.* the same combination of actions in 12:7–8; 13:4, 18, *etc.*).[9] No pattern of worship had as yet been prescribed, but worship was part of life among the peoples around, and those who received God's word could do no less than provide for the ongoing worship of their covenant Lord. Indeed worship was their first thought. They heard and received the word of the Lord, and gave themselves in adoration and worship, pledging their obedience. Similarly those who have had the riches of grace lavished upon them in Christ must fulfil their destiny to worship to the praise of his glory (Eph. 1:12). Their worship will continue on into eternity (Rev. 22:3).

The Abimelech incident had left an open sore which could have given rise to an ongoing vendetta. The previous agreement with Abraham (21:22–24) had been put under strain and was in urgent need of renewal. It is to the credit of Abimelech that in each case the peace initiative was taken by him, perhaps because he feared the consequences of an attack by those who were 'blessed of the Lord'. The different viewpoints of the two sides are openly stated. Isaac is aware of hatred, while Abimelech speaks only of having done good. Isaac, however, is conciliatory, and the feast he makes is part of the reconciliation, which was sealed the next day by reciprocal oaths. This was a covenant between equals, a recognized way of

---

[9] Donald J. Wiseman, 'Abraham in History and Tradition' I, *Bibliotheca Sacra* 134 (1977), pp. 125–126.

establishing alliances, and the same word (Heb. *b'rît*, verse 28) is used for this alliance as is used for God's covenant with his people, though in the divine covenant both the initiative and the terms came from the Lord.

An adequate water-supply was still a major concern, hence the joyous report of Isaac's servants that they had struck water and established another well (*cf.* 21:25–31). The name *Beer-sheba* was a pun on the number 'seven' (of which *Shibah* was a variant) and the verb 'to swear'. Whether the 'seven' was a reference to Abraham's seven lambs (21:28), or whether there were altogether seven wells at Beersheba, is not clear. In this chapter the emphasis is on the oath. For the second time Beersheba had been the site of an agreement, of which its name would for ever be a reminder.

Genesis 27:1 – 28:9

Isaac and the blessing

When Isaac was old and his eyes were dim so that he could not see, he called Esau his older son, and said to him, 'My son'; and he answered, 'Here I am.' ²He said, 'Behold, I am old; I do not know the day of my death. ³Now then, take your weapons, your quiver and your bow, and go out to the field, and hunt game for me, ⁴and prepare for me savoury food, such as I love, and bring it to me that I may eat; that I may bless you before I die.'

⁵Now Rebekah was listening when Isaac spoke to his son Esau. So when Esau went to the field to hunt for game and bring it, ⁶Rebekah said to her son Jacob, 'I heard your father speak to your brother Esau, ⁷"Bring me game, and prepare for me savoury food, that I may eat it, and bless you before the Lord before I die." ⁸Now therefore, my son, obey my word as I command you. ⁹Go to the flock, and fetch me two good kids, that I may prepare from them savoury food for your father, such as he loves; ¹⁰and you shall bring it to your father to eat, so that he may bless you before he dies.'

¹¹But Jacob said to Rebekah his mother, 'Behold, my brother Esau is a hairy man, and I am a smooth man. ¹²Perhaps my father will feel me, and I shall seem to be mocking him, and bring a curse upon myself and not a blessing.' ¹³His mother said to him, 'Upon me be your curse, my son; only obey my word, and go, fetch them to me.' ¹⁴So he went and took them and brought them to his mother; and his mother prepared savoury food, such as his father loved. ¹⁵Then Rebekah took the best garments of Esau her older son, which were with her in the house, and put them on Jacob her younger son; ¹⁶and the skins of the kids she put upon his hands and upon the smooth

111

part of his neck; [17]*and she gave the savoury food and the bread, which she had prepared, into the hand of her son Jacob.*

[18]*So he went in to his father, and said, 'My father'; and he said, 'Here I am: who are you, my son?'* [19]*Jacob said to his father, 'I am Esau your first-born. I have done as you told me; now sit up and eat of my game, that you may bless me.'* [20]*But Isaac said to his son, 'How is it that you have found it so quickly, my son?' He answered, 'Because the Lord your God granted me success.'* [21]*Then Isaac said to Jacob, 'Come near, that I may feel you, my son, to know whether you are really my son Esau or not.'* [22]*So Jacob went near to Isaac his father, who felt him and said, 'The voice is Jacob's voice, but the hands are the hands of Esau.'* [23]*And he did not recognize him, because his hands were hairy like his brother Esau's hands; so he blessed him.* [24]*He said, 'Are you really my son Esau?' He answered, 'I am.'* [25]*Then he said, 'Bring it to me, that I may eat of my son's game and bless you.' So he brought it to him, and he ate; and he brought him wine, and he drank.* [26]*Then his father Isaac said to him, 'Come near and kiss me, my son.'* [27]*So he came near and kissed him; and he smelled the smell of his garments, and blessed him, and said,*

'See, the smell of my son
is as the smell of a field which the Lord has blessed!
[28]*May God give you of the dew of heaven,*
and of the fatness of the earth, and plenty of grain and wine.
[29]*Let peoples serve you,*
and nations bow down to you.
Be lord over your brothers,
and may your mother's sons bow down to you.
Cursed be every one who curses you,
and blessed be every one who blesses you!'

[30]*As soon as Isaac had finished blessing Jacob, when Jacob had scarcely gone out from the presence of Isaac his father, Esau his brother came in from his hunting.* [31]*He also prepared savoury food, and brought it to his father. And he said to his father, 'Let my father arise, and eat of his son's game, that you may bless me.'* [32]*His father Isaac said to him, 'Who are you?' He answered, 'I am your son, your first-born, Esau.'* [33]*Then Isaac trembled violently, and said, 'Who was it then that hunted game and brought it to me, and I ate it all before you came, and I have blessed him? — yes, and he shall be blessed.'* [34]*When Esau heard the words of his father, he cried out with an exceedingly great and bitter cry, and said to his father, 'Bless me, even me also, O my father!'* [35]*But he said, 'Your brother came with guile, and he has taken away your blessing.'* [36]*Esau said, 'Is he not rightly named Jacob? For he has supplanted me these two times. He took away my*

*birthright; and behold, now he has taken away my blessing.' Then he said,
'Have you not reserved a blessing for me?'* ³⁷*Isaac answered Esau, 'Behold, I
have made him your lord, and all his brothers I have given to him for
servants, and with grain and wine I have sustained him. What then can I
do for you, my son?'* ³⁸*Esau said to his father, 'Have you but one blessing,
my father? Bless me, even me also, O my father.' And Esau lifted up his
voice and wept.*

³⁹*Then Isaac his father answered him:*

> *'Behold, away from the fatness of the earth shall your dwelling be,
> and away from the dew of heaven on high.*

⁴⁰*By your sword you shall live,
  and you shall serve your brother;
but when you break loose
  you shall break his yoke from your neck.'*

⁴¹*Now Esau hated Jacob because of the blessing with which his father had
blessed him, and Esau said to himself, 'The days of mourning for my father
are approaching; then I will kill my brother Jacob.'* ⁴²*But the words of Esau
her older son were told to Rebekah; so she sent and called Jacob her younger
son, and said to him, 'Behold, your brother Esau comforts himself by
planning to kill you.* ⁴³*Now therefore, my son, obey my voice; arise, flee to
Laban my brother in Haran,* ⁴⁴*and stay with him a while, until your
brother's fury turns away;* ⁴⁵*until your brother's anger turns away, and he
forgets what you have done to him; then I will send, and fetch you from
there. Why should I be bereft of you both in one day?'*

⁴⁶*Then Rebekah said to Isaac, 'I am weary of my life because of the
Hittite women. If Jacob marries one of the Hittite women such as these, one of
the women of the land, what good will my life be to me?'* ^{28:1}*Then Isaac
called Jacob and blessed him, and charged him, 'You shall not marry one of
the Canaanite women.* ²*Arise, go to Paddan-aram to the house of Bethuel
your mother's father; and take as wife from there one of the daughters of
Laban your mother's brother.* ³*God Almighty bless you and make you
fruitful and multiply you, that you may become a company of peoples.* ⁴*May
he give the blessing of Abraham to you and to your descendants with you,
that you may take possession of the land of your sojournings which God gave
to Abraham!'* ⁵*Thus Isaac sent Jacob away; and he went to Paddan-aram
to Laban, the son of Bethuel the Aramean, the brother of Rebekah, Jacob's
and Esau's mother.*

⁶*Now Esau saw that Isaac had blessed Jacob and sent him away to
Paddan-aram to take a wife from there, and that as he blessed him he
charged him, 'You shall not marry one of the Canaanite women,'* ⁷*and that
Jacob had obeyed his father and his mother and gone to Paddan-aram.* ⁸*So*

when Esau saw that the Canaanite women did not please Isaac his father, ⁹Esau went to Ishmael and took to wife, besides the wives he had, Mahalath the daughter of Ishmael Abraham's son, the sister of Nebaioth.

Three references to the future of Esau and Jacob converge in this last chapter on the life of Isaac. Before the birth of the twins Rebekah had been told 'the elder shall serve the younger': a prophecy (25:23). There was, secondly, the right of the eldest son to extra property and privilege: the birthright; this Esau had forfeited when he 'sold' it to Jacob (25:29–34). This chapter concerns the solemn word of an aged father to his children, roughly corresponding in our culture to the making of a will: the death-bed blessing. *'Behold, I am old; I do not know the day of my death'* was a death-bed formula, which corresponded to our 'last will and testament'. In view of its importance and because of the uncertainty of life the blessing needed to be given in good time, and Isaac lived for many years after this (35:27–29).

Isaac purposefully set about passing on the blessing in such a way as to achieve his own object. In the first place he called only Esau to the ceremony and deliberately excluded Jacob. Secondly, he endeavoured to keep secret a transaction which relied on witnesses for its legality. Thirdly, he left out of account both the prophecy to Rebekah and Esau's rash sale of his rights. Blind but by no means dying, Isaac took Esau into his confidence and sent him to prepare the feast at which the all-important blessing would become his. In the event he did not succeed in keeping his intention secret because Rebekah, only too aware of her husband's prejudices, kept herself informed of his plans, and set in motion her own counter-plan, involving Jacob in her duplicity.

It is clear that Isaac and Rebekah had lost the love which had bound them together at the beginning of their married life (24:67). Though they remained husband and wife they went their separate ways, each plotting to trick the other so as to achieve their own objectives. The family was thus split in two by the parental dual, for Isaac and Rebekah had become polarized in their attachment to Esau and Jacob respectively, and determined to pass on the blessing to the one they favoured. They may have 'lived faithfully together', as the Book of Common Prayer says of them in the prayer at the exchanging of vows in the marriage service, but they hardly remained 'in perfect love and peace together', nor did they seek the Lord's way forward.

Rebekah's hare-brained scheme ran considerable risk of discovery, but she thought it all out with care, and was prepared to take the consequences if it misfired (13). As it turned out she did bear a considerable curse, for she would never see her dear son Jacob again. As for Esau's famous recipe for game, she could serve tender goat meat in half the time without Isaac even noticing the difference. Disguising Jacob's smooth skin was a little problematic, but the skin of a kid served the purpose and, dressed up in Esau's best clothes, Jacob's transformation was complete. Isaac appears to have been somewhat less than bright in failing to pursue the clues that raised questions in his mind, but, as Derek Kidner observes, 'his palate had long since governed his heart (25:28)'.[10]

Jacob went through with the ruse, though he twice had to tell a direct lie, and once even went so far as to claim the help of the Lord God (20). The meal worked its spell, and the scent of the fields on Esau's garments conjured up an image of 'a field which the Lord has blessed', with its abundance of animals and crops. Though the voice was the voice of Jacob, Isaac proceeded to press on with his cherished plan of establishing the chosen line by pronouncing the fateful blessing and curse. His hands were tied by his own secretive plot, because to have questioned his son's identity by calling a witness would have involved giving the game away.

Jacob thus received the blessing intended for his brother, a potent prayer for prosperous farming, supremacy in the family and in international affairs, ensured by divine blessing on his allies and disaster on his enemies. It was so far-reaching as to leave little of importance for the other brother. That is why the return of Esau is so poignant both for him and for his father, so that all our sympathies are aroused by the cruel deception and the bitter cry of Esau in his disappointment. Despite the trickery of Jacob the blessing remained his, and Esau was relegated to territory on the border of the desert, where farming was impossible and his highest hopes would lie in freedom fighting, and in throwing off his brother's domination. Jacob was to pay dearly for his bid for power. He was in danger of death because of Esau's murderous hatred of him; hence Rebekah's plan to send Jacob to her own family in Haran until it was safe for him to come home again.

As Rebekah put the case to Isaac, however, it was all a question of Jacob's marriage. Esau's Hittite wives (26:34–35) had been a trial to both of them. Any more such daughters-in-law would make life

10 *Genesis*, TOTC, p. 156.

intolerable. It was true and it made a good story, though it was not the whole truth. Isaac saw the point and decided to follow his father's lead by sending Jacob to marry into the family from which Rebekah had come, so Jacob went with his father's good will, and with his prayer that the full blessing of Abraham might be upon him and his descendants. To the blessing inadvertently given to Jacob (27:27–29) was added the promise of the land of Canaan, an especially consoling hope to one who was leaving for a distant place in another land. Rebekah had skilfully steered events in Jacob's best interests, but at considerable cost to herself, for in the event he was away twenty years. When he returned no meeting with her is recorded. Esau for his part took the hint about not marrying Canaanite women, and in an attempt to please his father married a daughter of Ishmael. The significance of the promise entirely escaped him.

The prophetic oracle spoken to Rebekah before the birth of her twins had proved to be remarkably accurate: the elder was going to serve the younger. To an extent she had contrived to bring this about by favouring Jacob and furthering his cause. On the other hand, Isaac played into her hands by trying to pass on in secret the legally binding blessing. Both acted in keeping with their character, as did the two boys. Their destiny did not operate as a blind fate, but was bound up with their personal choices and interests. The stark implications of human choices are inescapable in this incident. A similar contrast between two brothers is found in the Lord's parable of the two sons (Lk. 15:11–32). There also the elder brother felt that he had been hard done by, and there is no indication that he changed his stance, whereas the younger brother realized his need, returned home to ask for mercy and found loving acceptance. Self-righteousness is the most impenetrable barrier of all. It can still happen that people who, by upbringing and training, have been close to the good news of the gospel, yet somehow miss the blessing, as Esau did.

We have no means of knowing how the Lord would have fulfilled the future as it was indicated in the divine oracle. His better purpose was thwarted by human scheming and manipulation, which in turn arose out of marital disharmony. Neither partner was alert to the Lord's leading, because each was taken up with personal self-seeking, which is poles apart from repentance and faith, and the patience which waits for the Lord to work out his way.

Part 3
JACOB
(Genesis 28:10 – 36:43)

Genesis 28:10–22
Jacob's ladder

Jacob left Beer-sheba, and went toward Haran. [11]*And he came to a certain place, and stayed there that night, because the sun had set. Taking one of the stones of the place, he put it under his head and lay down in that place to sleep.* [12]*And he dreamed that there was a ladder set up on the earth, and the top of it reached to heaven; and behold, the angels of God were ascending and descending on it!* [13]*And behold, the Lord stood above it and said, 'I am the Lord, the God of Abraham your father and the God of Isaac; the land on which you lie I will give to you and to your descendants;* [14]*and your descendants shall be like the dust of the earth, and you shall spread abroad to the west and to the east and to the north and to the south; and by you and your descendants shall all the families of the earth bless themselves.* [15]*Behold, I am with you and will keep you wherever you go, and will bring you back to this land; for I will not leave you until I have done that of which I have spoken to you.'* [16]*Then Jacob awoke from his sleep and said, 'Surely the Lord is in this place; and I did not know it.'* [17]*And he was afraid, and said, 'How awesome is this place! This is none other than the house of God, and this is the gate of heaven.'*
[18]*So Jacob rose early in the morning, and he took the stone which he had put under his head and set it up for a pillar and poured oil on the top of it.* [19]*He called the name of that place Bethel; but the name of the city was Luz at the first.* [20]*Then Jacob made a vow, saying, 'If God will be with me,*

and will keep me in this way that I go, and will give me bread to eat and clothing to wear, ²¹so that I come again to my father's house in peace, then the Lord shall be my God, ²²and this stone, which I have set up for a pillar, shall be God's house; and of all that thou givest me I will give the tenth to thee.'

Jacob's lonely journey from the home he loved had already taken him 55 miles north of Beersheba. Night was falling, and he prepared to sleep rough under the stars, intending to be away again at dawn the next day. It was at this low point, when Jacob had no human prop and was most aware of his need of protection and guidance, that the Lord revealed himself to undeserving Jacob.

In the rocky limestone country of the central hills it was natural to use of one of the many stones as a head support, and great boulders towering above him may well have suggested the stairway to bridge the gulf between heaven and earth, which he saw in his dream. On the stairs were angels, going up from where he was and coming down to him. He was not after all alone! But more, the Lord stood beside him,[1] and was speaking to him. Just as Francis Thompson captures the wonder of heaven's nearness in 'the traffic of Jacob's ladder pitched betwixt Heaven and Charing Cross', so we can substitute our own memorable spot, for Jacob's experience has been shared by many others since his day. The message he heard exactly suited his circumstances. He was leaving his father's house, but the God of his fathers was speaking to him. He had no friendly relatives to give him shelter en route, but this same God promised to give him the land. He had no wife as yet, but the promise of numerous descendants presupposed his marriage, and linked him with the covenant made with Abraham. His life took on meaning because it was part of the Lord's ongoing purpose for all generations, but in Jacob's immediate situation he could go on his hazardous journey knowing that he would be protected by the ever-present supervision of the Lord. Moreover he had the promise, *'I will bring you back to this land'*; despite Jacob's deceit, God in grace stood by the promises.

For Jacob this was the outstanding spiritual event of his youth, matched in later years by the unforgettable encounter with the angel at Peniel (32:22–32). From this time on the Lord was not just the

---

[1] The Hebrew preposition can mean 'above it' (as in RSV text) or 'beside him' (as in RSV mg.). Since the Lord is about to speak to Jacob, the latter is preferable, though both ideas could be there, *e.g.* 'bending over him'.

God of his father (27:20) but Jacob's own God, though he was still looking for further reassurances (verse 20). Suddenly wide awake after this vivid dream, he resolved to commemorate the event and mark the sacred spot where earth had touched heaven because God had spoken to him. *'Surely the Lord is in this place; and I did not know it.'* It seemed to his newly aroused spiritual consciousness that there must be something special about this ordinary-looking place; he had stumbled upon *the house of God* and *the gate of heaven*, and it was not comfortable to have a guilty conscience. Nevertheless he had survived the encounter with the living God and had even been reassured. Now his concern was to do the right thing. His fathers would have set up an altar, but he took the stone that had supported his head and set it up on end as a standing stone. This he consecrated by anointing it with oil, a symbolic action which was to be developed later in the setting apart of 'anointed ones' (Heb. Messiahs) for particular ministries.

The ceremony of anointing was private to Jacob, and no plaque commemorated it, but the new name, *Bethel*, meaning 'house of God', would eventually be known and would recall the event for countless generations. For the present Jacob committed himself as fully as he knew how to the Lord who had revealed himself and made promises to him. The terms of his vow sound calculating; indeed, in view of the fact that he had received the express promise of the Lord that he would return to Canaan, Jacob was dull and unresponsive to the loving reassurance of God. Before he would commit himself completely Jacob wanted the circumstantial evidence of the outworking of God's promises in his life. If he could see this he would commit himself to the Lord as his God. 'Unless I see in his hands the print of the nails, and place my finger in the mark of the nails, and place my hand in his side, I will not believe,' said Thomas with the same desire for tangible evidence (Jn. 20:25). Marvellously patient, the Lord meets us where we are. Both Jacob and Thomas had their 'conditions' met, though in the nature of the case Jacob's wait was a long one. On Jacob's side the vow he made was not without its cost. When the Lord became his God Bethel's pillar would become Jacob's shrine for worship, and a tenth of his possessions would be dedicated to the Lord. The practice of giving a *tenth*, or tithe, to the God one worships is very ancient, going back before the law of Moses, and to other Near Eastern peoples (*cf.* 14:20). It is still a useful guide in deciding what would constitute a worthy gift to the God to whom we owe everything.

An earlier generation had proposed to reach heaven by building a 'tower' (Gn. 11:1–9). This is probably the stepped pyramid-like structure known as a ziggurat, with a giant staircase. Be that as it may, the attempt did not succeed. In his own time the Lord would 'come down' and reveal that he was not far away, but close at hand, 'a very present help in trouble' (Ps. 46:1), even to an unscrupulous youth, running away from the brother he had twice robbed. The fact strikes us as shocking, even immoral, until we come to see that we are all in the same desperate plight, unworthy to approach God and unable to save ourselves. Then we begin to marvel at the significance of Jacob's experience, and join to praise 'the God of Bethel', for the God who bothered with him is willing also to bother with us, and make us something we could never otherwise have been.

> Then, with my waking thoughts
> Bright with Thy praise,
> Out of my stony griefs
> Bethel I'll raise:
> So by my woes to be
> Nearer, my God, to Thee,
> Nearer to Thee![2]

Genesis 29:1–30

Marriage in Haran

Then Jacob went on his journey, and came to the land of the people of the east. [2]As he looked, he saw a well in the field, and lo, three flocks of sheep lying beside it; for out of that well the flocks were watered. The stone on the well's mouth was large, [3]and when all the flocks were gathered there, the shepherds would roll the stone from the mouth of the well, and water the sheep, and put the stone back in its place upon the mouth of the well.

[4]Jacob said to them, 'My brothers, where do you come from?' They said, 'We are from Haran.' [5]He said to them, 'Do you know Laban the son of Nahor?' They said, 'We know him.' [6]He said to them, 'Is it well with him?' They said, 'It is well; and see, Rachel his daughter is coming with the sheep!' [7]He said, 'Behold, it is still high day, it is not time for the animals to be gathered together; water the sheep, and go, pasture them.' [8]But they said, 'We cannot until all the flocks are gathered together, and the stone is rolled from the mouth of the well; then we water the sheep.'

[2] From the hymn 'Nearer, my God, to Thee' by Sarah F. Adams (1805-48).

⁹*While he was still speaking with them, Rachel came with her father's sheep: for she kept them.* ¹⁰*Now when Jacob saw Rachel the daughter of Laban his mother's brother, and the sheep of Laban his mother's brother, Jacob went up and rolled the stone from the well's mouth, and watered the flock of Laban his mother's brother.* ¹¹*Then Jacob kissed Rachel, and wept aloud.* ¹²*And Jacob told Rachel that he was her father's kinsman, and that he was Rebekah's son: and she ran and told her father.*

¹³*When Laban heard the tidings of Jacob his sister's son, he ran to meet him, and embraced him and kissed him, and brought him to his house. Jacob told Laban all these things,* ¹⁴*and Laban said to him, 'Surely you are my bone and my flesh!' And he stayed with him a month.*

¹⁵*Then Laban said to Jacob, 'Because you are my kinsman, should you therefore serve me for nothing? Tell me, what shall your wages be?'* ¹⁶*Now Laban had two daughters: the name of the older was Leah, and the name of the younger was Rachel.* ¹⁷*Leah's eyes were weak, but Rachel was beautiful and lovely.* ¹⁸*Jacob loved Rachel; and he said, 'I will serve you seven years for your younger daughter Rachel.'* ¹⁹*Laban said, 'It is better that I give her to you than that I should give her to any other man; stay with me.'* ²⁰*So Jacob served seven years for Rachel, and they seemed to him but a few days because of the love he had for her.*

²¹*Then Jacob said to Laban, 'Give me my wife that I may go in to her, for my time is completed.'* ²²*So Laban gathered together all the men of the place, and made a feast.* ²³*But in the evening he took his daughter Leah and brought her to Jacob: and he went in to her.* ²⁴*(Laban gave his maid Zilpah to his daughter Leah to be her maid.)* ²⁵*And in the morning, behold, it was Leah: and Jacob said to Laban, 'What is this you have done to me? Did I not serve with you for Rachel? Why then have you deceived me?'* ²⁶*Laban said, 'It is not so done in our country, to give the younger before the first-born.* ²⁷*Complete the week of this one, and we will give you the other also in return for serving me another seven years.'* ²⁸*Jacob did so, and completed her week: then Laban gave him his daughter Rachel to wife.* ²⁹*(Laban gave his maid Bilhah to his daughter Rachel to be her maid.)* ³⁰*So Jacob went in to Rachel also, and he loved Rachel more than Leah, and served Laban for another seven years.*

Though he had stood at heaven's gate, Jacob could not stay there. He had to 'lift up his feet', as the Hebrew idiom puts it, and pursue the long slog northwards for days and weeks. Then, one day when he was apparently far from any habitation, the road took him close to a well, surrounded by flocks of sheep. The shepherds were sitting idly around, evidently to Jacob's disgust, for it was still the middle of the day, and not time for knocking off. But this stranger did not know the custom of the place, and was premature in his implied criticism that they were a lazy lot. It was understood that they did not begin to move the stone until all had arrived to lend a hand, and moving towards them with her flock was Rachel, daughter of Laban, for whose home Jacob was heading. Were they having a laugh at her expense and expecting her to move the stone? There is evidence that this task of watering the flock was sometimes done by girls and the younger women (24:20; Ex. 2:16–19). On this particular day Rachel unexpectedly found a champion in the stranger at the well. Not only did he show the men he could set them an example, but he also demonstrated his prowess to the girl he wanted to impress, by removing the stone and drawing all the water needed by her flock of sheep.

Unlike Abraham's servant, who had also met the one he was seeking at a well, Jacob had no gifts to present, but he embraced his little cousin and wept as he disclosed his identity. Forgetting all about her sheep she ran, like Rebekah a generation earlier, to tell her father the news. Laban, eager as ever and no doubt remembering the previous occasion, ran out to meet him, welcome him and receive him as a guest in his house. It would not take Laban long to ascertain that in two important respects Jacob's arrival differed from that of Abraham's servant. He was penniless and he did not seem in any hurry to move on. Jacob, who had already fallen in love with Rachel, had probably hit on the possibility of earning enough to pay for his keep *and* the bride price, which he had no other means of raising. Why had Isaac not thought to provide for this as Abraham had done when he sent for a wife for Isaac? Though he gave his blessing he did not part with any possessions.

Jacob's proposition to work seven years for the hand of Rachel in marriage was more than acceptable to Laban. He could marry off the less attractive Leah to him first and so gain more free labour after the seven years expired. Seven years' service for a wife, according to Gordon Wenham, may well have been the accepted period, and if the bride price was paid in kind some present equal to seven years' wages was expected.[3] Such a sum was a guarantee of serious intention and a check on fleeting attachments, as well as a deterrent to easy divorce. That for seven years Jacob could enjoy the company of Rachel though he did not possess her indicates genuine affection,

[3] B.N. Kaye and G.J. Wenham (eds), *Law, Morality and the Bible* (IVP, 1978), p. 35.

respect and concern for her. She had probably been no more than ten or eleven years old when he first met her. Whereas Esau was characteristically impatient, Jacob could wait for what he wanted, and did not count himself hard done by. Moreover there was a timeless quality about his love, so that seven years *seemed to him but a few days because of the love he had for her* (20). The bond between them was a deep affection that was not tormented by the long wait. It had something of the quality of New Testament *agapē*, that is 'patient and kind ... does not insist on its own way ... endures all things' (1 Cor. 13:4–7). Maybe Jacob saw something of his own mother in her niece, and felt at home in her presence. It was a sound basis for a stable marriage.

Laban, however, was in no hurry to arrange the wedding when the seven years were fulfilled, and Jacob had to make the first move. The customs, so strange to us, provide evidence of marriage in another age and culture. The whole event is male-dominated, for Laban arranges the feast and invites men as guests. We miss any reference to a religious ceremony. Late in the evening, when everyone had wined and dined, her father brought in the bride, duly veiled, no doubt, and presented her to her husband. It was not until the morning that Jacob, totally unsuspecting, discovered that he had been married not to Rachel but to Leah. Laban had dared to play this unscrupulous trick because he was certain that Jacob would never be content without the one on whom he had set his heart, and in this way Laban could bargain for further free service. Laban had his consoling suggestion ready. After the week of Leah's wedding-feast Jacob could marry Rachel, and during the subsequent seven years could work off his debt for her. To marry two sisters during each other's lifetime was later to be forbidden (Lv. 18:18); here in Haran it was evidently allowed, and provided a way of making the best of a bad job.

What the two girls thought of the plan (and of their father) goes unrecorded. How did anyone keep Rachel quiet that night? Their mother did not have the influence with Laban that Rebekah had with Isaac, and consequently Laban pursued his way unhindered, even to providing his daughters with maids from his own household. Jacob for his part had ample opportunity to reflect from the receiving end on the gentle art of deception. The measure he had given to Esau he was now receiving himself, even to the reminder that the first-born had certain rights (26).

Genesis 29:31 – 31:16

The prosperity of Jacob

When the Lord saw that Leah was hated, he opened her womb; but Rachel was barren. ...

30:22Then God remembered Rachel, and God hearkened to her and opened her womb. 23She conceived and bore a son, and said, 'God has taken away my reproach'; 24and she called his name Joseph, saying, 'May the Lord add to me another son!'

25When Rachel had borne Joseph, Jacob said to Laban, 'Send me away, that I may go to my own home and country. 26Give me my wives and my children for whom I have served you, and let me go; for you know the service which I have given you.' 27But Laban said to him, 'If you will allow me to say so, I have learned by divination that the Lord has blessed me because of you; 28name your wages, and I will give it.' 29Jacob said to him, 'You yourself know how I have served you, and how your cattle have fared with me. 30For you had little before I came, and it has increased abundantly; and the Lord has blessed you wherever I turned. But now when shall I provide for my own household also?' 31He said, 'What shall I give you?' Jacob said, 'You shall not give me anything; if you will do this for me, I will again feed your flock and keep it; 32let me pass through all your flock today, removing from it every speckled and spotted sheep and every black lamb, and the spotted and speckled among the goats; and such shall be my wages. 33So my honesty will answer for me later, when you come to look into my wages with you. Every one that is not speckled and spotted among the goats and black among the lambs, if found with me, shall be counted stolen.' 34Laban said, 'Good! Let it be as you have said.' 35But that day Laban removed the he-goats that were striped and spotted, and all the she-goats that were speckled and spotted, every one that had white on it, and every lamb that was black, and put them in charge of his sons; 36and he set a distance of three days' journey between himself and Jacob; and Jacob fed the rest of Laban's flock.

37Then Jacob took fresh rods of poplar and almond and plane, and peeled white streaks in them, exposing the white of the rods. 38He set the rods which he had peeled in front of the flocks in the runnels, that is, the watering troughs, where the flocks came to drink. And since they bred when they came to drink, 39the flocks bred in front of the rods and so the flocks brought forth striped, speckled, and spotted. 40And Jacob separated the lambs, and set the faces of the flocks toward the striped and all the black in the flock of Laban; and he put his own droves apart, and did not put them with Laban's flock. 41Whenever the stronger of the flock were breeding Jacob laid the rods in the runnels before the eyes of the flock, that they might breed among the rods,

124

⁴²but for the feebler of the flock he did not lay them there; so the feebler were Laban's and the stronger Jacob's. ⁴³Thus the man grew exceedingly rich, and had large flocks, maidservants and menservants, and camels and asses.

³¹:¹Now Jacob heard that the sons of Laban were saying, 'Jacob has taken all that was our father's; and from what was our father's he has gained all this wealth.' ²And Jacob saw that Laban did not regard him with favour as before. ³Then the Lord said to Jacob, 'Return to the land of your fathers and to your kindred, and I will be with you.' ⁴So Jacob sent and called Rachel and Leah into the field where his flock was, ⁵and said to them, 'I see that your father does not regard me with favour as he did before. But the God of my father has been with me. ⁶You know that I have served your father with all my strength; ⁷yet your father has cheated me and changed my wages ten times, but God did not permit him to harm me. ⁸If he said, "The spotted shall be your wages," then all the flock bore spotted; and if he said, "The striped shall be your wages," then all the flock bore striped. ⁹Thus God has taken away the cattle of your father, and given them to me. ¹⁰In the mating season of the flock I lifted up my eyes, and saw in a dream that the he-goats which leaped upon the flock were striped, spotted, and mottled. ¹¹Then the angel of God said to me in the dream, "Jacob," and I said, "Here I am!" ¹²And he said, "Lift up your eyes and see, all the goats that leap upon the flock are striped, spotted, and mottled; for I have seen all that Laban is doing to you. ¹³I am the God of Bethel, where you anointed a pillar and made a vow to me. Now arise, go forth from this land, and return to the land of your birth."' ¹⁴Then Rachel and Leah answered him, 'Is there any portion or inheritance left to us in our father's house? ¹⁵Are we not regarded by him as foreigners? For he has sold us, and he has been using up the money given for us. ¹⁶All the property which God has taken away from our father belongs to us and to our children; now then, whatever God has said to you, do.'

In the providence of God Jacob experienced the kind of trickery he had devised for Esau, but at the same time the God who had made promises to him at Bethel was faithful in fulfilling them: descendants, possessions, and the return journey to Canaan all feature in this section.

Though Leah became Jacob's first wife she was not the beloved wife. This she was only too aware of, and even the birth of four sons did little to comfort her. She longed for the affection of her husband, and proclaimed the fact in her comments on the names of her children, whom she saw as gifts from the Lord. *Reuben* (32) means 'See, a son', but to Leah it signified that the Lord had seen her misery and had consoled her with a son; *Simeon* (33), a name formed from the verb 'to hear', implied that the Lord had heard that her husband did not love her; *Levi* (34), 'attached', expressed the hope that now her husband would become attached to her; *Judah* (35), 'praise', meant that she was full of praise to the Lord. All these names were in current use, and they permitted the play on words which expressed Leah's hopes and longings. But even the gift of four sons to Jacob did nothing to endear Leah to her husband.

Rachel enjoyed her husband's affections but bore him no children. Envious of her sister, Rachel in her torment blamed Jacob for her childlessness, while he got angry and, avoiding responsibility, attributed it to God's doing. It is clear in retrospect that there was a pattern in the story of Sarah, Rebekah and Rachel: their childlessness was no accident, but Rachel did not have the maturity of faith to accept that untoward circumstances were part of the Lord's providential working, and to wait his time. It is not an easy lesson to learn and act upon, especially when others around are apparently having no such difficulties.

The only possible move she could make was to offer her slave-girl to Jacob, an early attempt at surrogate motherhood, on the understanding that any child born would count as her own. The practice is well documented, being referred to in literature of Mesopotamia over a long period.[4] She gave Bilhah to Jacob, saying, '*she may bear upon my knees.*' This strange expression occurs in two Hurrian myths in the context of accepting and naming the child, and welcoming him into the family; Rachel meant that she was going to call Bilhah's sons her own. Accordingly *she* gave Bilhah's first-born the name *Dan* (6), 'he judged' (*cf.* Daniel 'God is my judge'), implying that God had vindicated her, and her second son, *Naphtali* (8), 'wrestler', recalling her *mighty wrestlings* with her sister, Leah. Far from idealizing these women, the account depicts a stormy home life.

Leah, not to be outdone, gave her maid to Jacob and by her had two sons, *Gad* (11), 'luck', and *Asher* (13), 'happy'. Rachel, still without a child of her own, asked for some of the *mandrakes*, or 'love fruits', large-leaved weeds with a carrot-like root, that Reuben had brought his mother from the fields, and which were commonly

---

[4] There is an example in the laws of Hammurapi (163), in a tablet from Nuzi (*HSS* 5 67), both second millennium BC, and also in a Nimrud tablet (ND 2307) belonging to the first millennium BC. *Cf.* M.J. Selman, 'The Social Environment of the Patriarchs', *TB* 27 (1976), pp. 127–129.

thought to induce fertility. By handing them over Leah 'hired' Rachel's husband that night, and became the mother of *Issachar* (18), whose name is a play on the word for 'hire'. Not only had she hired Jacob from Rachel, but she saw her new son as her reward for having given Jacob her maid. The sixth son of Leah, *Zebulun* (20), 'endowed' or 'honoured', was followed by the only daughter, *Dinah* (21), who is mentioned in anticipation of her part in the later event in Canaan (chapter 34). Finally Rachel had her longed-for son, whose name was a prayer for a brother, for *Joseph* (24) meant 'he adds'. The prayer was answered, but not before the family was back in Canaan (35:16–20).

It is an involved story, and far from ideal; the pitfalls and humiliations of polygamy argue eloquently against the practice. Still Jacob was totally dependent on Laban, having no stock to call his own, and Jacob decided that the time had come to make the break with his father-in-law, and return home. It was more easily said than done. Though Laban invited Jacob to name his wages, Jacob suspected some mean trick would be devised, so he preferred to work things out in his own way. Laban had become rich at Jacob's expense; now Jacob would look to the Lord to bless his cattle and flocks with increase. By choosing for himself the speckled and spotted animals Jacob was on to a good thing. He did not need to study genetics to observe that for every one-coloured animal there were at least three of the others. Laban knew it too, and removed the animals of his choice before Jacob could get a look in. By pasturing them three days' journey away he was ensuring that no animals would stray back to add to Joseph's tally. Though seemingly outwitted, Jacob made use of an accepted practice intended to cause the birth of piebald animals. At the time when breeding took place it was thought (erroneously) that white patches in the view of the ewes would cause the birth of white-flecked animals.

His success over a period of six years was so remarkable as to cause Laban's sons to comment on Jacob's wealth, and jealousy on Laban's part soured his relationship with Jacob (31:1). Even Laban's daughters had become alienated from their father. Everything was conspiring to convince Jacob that there was no place for him any longer in Haran, including a specific word from the Lord, *'Return to the land of your fathers and to your kindred, and I will be with you'* (3), and a dream in which Jacob learnt that the Lord was causing his prosperity, and urging him to go back to the land of his birth (11–12). Though Jacob readily spoke of what God had done for

127

him, he persisted in his opportunism. He was the same manipulative character as had left Canaan twenty years earlier.

Long experience of their father's meanness predisposed Rachel and Leah to undertake the long journey to Canaan in response to Jacob's guidance. There was nothing to keep them in Haran, and they particularly resented the miserly attitude their father took towards money intended for them, *'For he has sold us, and he has been using up the money given for us'* (15). 'Using up' is in the Hebrew 'eating up', implying greed. Money which they should have received as a dowry had never been given to them, so all that Jacob had acquired in stock seemed to them only just and right as a recompense.[5]

One phase of Jacob's life was coming to an end. It had begun with his ignominious departure from home, brought about by his own effrontery in tricking both his father and his brother. He had fled for his life. It was the more remarkable in the circumstances that he should have had his vivid dream in which the Lord gave him instruction and specific promises, which set him in the line to inherit the covenant with Abraham. Then for twenty years there was no further word from the Lord, only the providential outworking of his promise to keep him. Did Jacob ever wonder whether he had imagined the incident at Bethel? If he did he would recall that he had set up a little memorial to be a reassurance to him, and that, one day, he would return to give thanks there. His tenacity meant that he could hold on to the promise when life was ordinary and humdrum. Neither tribulation nor the cares of the world snatched away the seed of God's word (Mk. 4:16–18). Our twentieth-century generations are especially prone to ask for quick results, whereas in spiritual matters long growth is often called for. Twenty years are not too long to allow the Lord to teach his basic lessons, for he is positively at work in us when he seems to be far away.

Genesis 31:17 – 32:21

Return to Canaan

So Jacob arose, and set his sons and his wives on camels; [18]*and he drove*

---

[5] M.J. Selman, 'Comparative Customs and the Patriarchal Age', *EOPN*, p. 116, comments on the incident, 'the girls' complaint can ... be explained against the background of other texts from the Old Babylonian period, Nuzi, and Elephantine, where on occasion a father would withhold from his daughter a part of the bride payment which was normally handed on as a dowry.'

away all his cattle, all his livestock which he had gained, the cattle in his possession which he had acquired in Paddan-aram, to go to the land of Canaan to his father Isaac. ¹⁹*Laban had gone to shear his sheep, and Rachel stole her father's household gods.* ²⁰*And Jacob outwitted Laban the Aramean, in that he did not tell him that he intended to flee.* ²¹*He fled with all that he had, and arose and crossed the Euphrates, and set his face toward the hill country of Gilead.*

²²*When it was told Laban on the third day that Jacob had fled,* ²³*he took his kinsmen with him and pursued him for seven days and followed close after him into the hill country of Gilead.* ²⁴*But God came to Laban the Aramean in a dream by night, and said to him, 'Take heed that you say not a word to Jacob, either good or bad.'*

²⁵*And Laban overtook Jacob. Now Jacob had pitched his tent in the hill country, and Laban with his kinsmen encamped in the hill country of Gilead.* ²⁶*And Laban said to Jacob, 'What have you done, that you have cheated me, and carried away my daughters like captives of the sword?* ²⁷*Why did you flee secretly, and cheat me, and did not tell me, so that I might have sent you away with mirth and songs, with tambourine and lyre?* ²⁸*And why did you not permit me to kiss my sons and my daughters farewell? Now you have done foolishly.* ²⁹*It is in my power to do you harm; but the God of your father spoke to me last night, saying, "Take heed that you speak to Jacob neither good nor bad."* ³⁰*And now you have gone away because you longed greatly for your father's house, but why did you steal my gods?'* ³¹*Jacob answered Laban, 'Because I was afraid, for I thought that you would take your daughters from me by force.* ³²*Any one with whom you find your gods shall not live. In the presence of our kinsmen point out what I have that is yours, and take it.' Now Jacob did not know that Rachel had stolen them.*

³³*So Laban went into Jacob's tent, and into Leah's tent, and into the tent of the two maidservants, but he did not find them. And he went out of Leah's tent, and entered Rachel's.* ³⁴*Now Rachel had taken the household gods and put them in the camel's saddle, and sat upon them. Laban felt all about the tent, but did not find them.* ³⁵*And she said to her father, 'Let not my lord be angry that I cannot rise before you, for the way of women is upon me.' So he searched, but did not find the household gods.*

³⁶*Then Jacob became angry, and upbraided Laban; Jacob said to Laban, 'What is my offence? What is my sin, that you have hotly pursued me?* ³⁷*Although you have felt through all my goods, what have you found of all your household goods? Set it here before my kinsmen and your kinsmen, that they may decide between us two.* ³⁸*These twenty years I have been with you; your ewes and your she-goats have not miscarried, and I have not eaten the*

rams of your flocks. [39]*That which was torn by wild beasts I did not bring to you; I bore the loss of it myself; of my hand you required it, whether stolen by day or stolen by night.* [40]*Thus I was; by day the heat consumed me, and the cold by night, and my sleep fled from my eyes.* [41]*These twenty years I have been in your house; I served you fourteen years for your two daughters, and six years for your flock, and you have changed my wages ten times.* [42]*If the God of my father, the God of Abraham and the Fear of Isaac, had not been on my side, surely now you would have sent me away empty-handed. God saw my affliction and the labour of my hands, and rebuked you last night.'*

[43]*Then Laban answered and said to Jacob, 'The daughters are my daughters, the children are my children, the flocks are my flocks, and all that you see is mine. But what can I do this day to these my daughters, or to their children whom they have borne?* [44]*Come now, let us make a covenant, you and I; and let it be a witness between you and me.'* [45]*So Jacob took a stone, and set it up as a pillar.* [46]*And Jacob said to his kinsmen, 'Gather stones,' and they took stones, and made a heap; and they ate there by the heap.* [47]*Laban called it Jegar-sahadutha: but Jacob called it Galeed.* [48]*Laban said, 'This heap is a witness between you and me today.' Therefore he named it Galeed,* [49]*and the pillar Mizpah, for he said, 'The Lord watch between you and me, when we are absent one from the other.* [50]*If you ill-treat my daughters, or if you take wives besides my daughters, although no man is with us, remember, God is witness between you and me.'*

[51]*Then Laban said to Jacob, 'See this heap and the pillar, which I have set between you and me.* [52]*This heap is a witness, and the pillar is a witness, that I will not pass over this heap to you, and you will not pass over this heap and this pillar to me, for harm.* [53]*The God of Abraham and the God of Nahor, the God of their father, judge between us.' So Jacob swore by the Fear of his father Isaac,* [54]*and Jacob offered a sacrifice on the mountain and called his kinsmen to eat bread; and they ate bread and tarried all night on the mountain.*

[55]*Early in the morning Laban arose, and kissed his grandchildren and his daughters and blessed them; then he departed and returned home.*

[32:1]*Jacob went on his way and the angels of God met him;* [2]*and when Jacob saw them he said, 'This is God's army!' So he called the name of that place Mahanaim.*

[3]*And Jacob sent messengers before him to Esau his brother in the land of Seir, the country of Edom,* [4]*instructing them, 'Thus you shall say to my lord Esau: Thus says your servant Jacob, "I have sojourned with Laban, and stayed until now;* [5]*and I have oxen, asses, flocks, menservants, and maidservants; and I have sent to tell my lord, in order that I may find favour in your sight."'*

⁶And the messengers returned to Jacob, saying, 'We came to your brother Esau, and he is coming to meet you, and four hundred men with him.' ⁷Then Jacob was greatly afraid and distressed; and he divided the people that were with him, and the flocks and herds and camels, into two companies, ⁸thinking, 'If Esau comes to the one company and destroys it, then the company which is left will escape.'

⁹And Jacob said, 'O God of my father Abraham and God of my father Isaac, O Lord who didst say to me, "Return to your country and to your kindred, and I will do you good," ¹⁰I am not worthy of the least of all the steadfast love and all the faithfulness which thou hast shown to thy servant, for with only my staff I crossed this Jordan; and now I have become two companies. ¹¹Deliver me, I pray thee, from the hand of my brother, from the hand of Esau, for I fear him, lest he come and slay us all, the mothers with the children. ¹²But thou didst say, "I will do you good, and make your descendants as the sand of the sea, which cannot be numbered for multitude."'

¹³So he lodged there that night, and took from what he had with him a present for his brother Esau, ¹⁴two hundred she-goats and twenty he-goats, two hundred ewes and twenty rams, ¹⁵thirty milch camels and their colts, forty cows and ten bulls, twenty she-asses and ten he-asses. ¹⁶These he delivered into the hand of his servants, every drove by itself, and said to his servants, 'Pass on before me, and put a space between drove and drove.' ¹⁷He instructed the foremost, 'When Esau my brother meets you, and asks you, "To whom do you belong? Where are you going? And whose are these before you?" ¹⁸Then you shall say, "They belong to your servant Jacob; they are a present sent to my lord Esau; and moreover he is behind us."' ¹⁹He likewise instructed the second and the third and all who followed the droves, 'You shall say the same thing to Esau when you meet him, ²⁰and you shall say, "Moreover your servant Jacob is behind us."' For he thought, 'I may appease him with the present that goes before me, and afterwards I shall see his face; perhaps he will accept me.' ²¹So the present passed on before him; and he himself lodged that night in the camp.

In his entrenched animosity towards Jacob (31:2) Laban would never willingly have permitted Jacob's departure, which deprived him of children and grandchildren, of right-hand man and of cattle in abundance. Jacob the opportunist accordingly took advantage of Laban's absence for sheep-shearing to put a few days' journey between himself and his father-in-law. His slow-moving caravan needed plenty of time, and could hardly hope to escape Laban's expected pursuit, but the Euphrates river, some 50 miles (or 80 km) west of Haran, was a barrier safely crossed before Laban could overtake them.

Predictable as Jacob's method was, he was cowardly to give Laban the slip after being part of the family for so many years. Moreover, having been given the Lord's express order to return to Canaan, he should have had the faith to expect the Lord to deal with Laban's entrenched attitudes. Laban was not beyond the reach of the living God (24). But Jacob could not bring himself to rely on the faithfulness of God; he preferred his own cunningly devised plans and relied instead on his clever ways, despite the lessons the Lord had been teaching him over the years that such methods brought trouble upon him. He outwitted Laban (20), but he failed to discover how the Lord would have worked for him in blessing.

Jacob's wives and precious children he provided with camels so that they could move at speed if necessary to evade capture. They were also spared the slog of covering the miles on foot. Why Rachel made off with her father's household gods continues to be a puzzling feature of the story. As long ago as 1926 it was argued on the basis of a parallel in the Nuzi texts that possession of teraphim, or household gods, was the entitlement to an inheritance. More recently it has been argued that practices at Nuzi do not necessarily have any bearing on Genesis, and that in the Rachel story her theft of the teraphim is not specifically connected with the theme of inheritance.[6] At the very least she was stealing something of value to her father, hence his forceful accusation against Jacob; Rachel could have taken them to spite her father, but it would have been more sensible for her to benefit herself at the same time. Perhaps these objects had an intrinsic value or meant something to her, but if they did entitle her to an inheritance her action is explained, and Laban's insistence that neither family should raid the other (52) is explained also.

Meanwhile Laban had heard the news that Jacob had walked out on him (22) and, determined not to let him go without a struggle, set out in hot pursuit. His initial anger was modified by the dream in which he received God's warning to take great care in his dealings with Jacob, an intervention which would have greatly cheered Jacob, had he known about it. When Laban caught up with him Jacob heard a succession of accusations, but was spared any attack on his life, such as Laban had evidently planned (29). Jacob's terse reply

[6] M.J. Selman, 'Comparative Customs and the Patriarchal Age', *EOPN*, pp. 93, 101, 110. J. van Seters, *Abraham in History and Tradition* (Yale, 1975), pp. 91–92.

to a series of questions succeeded in putting Laban in the wrong. Unwittingly Jacob's *any one with whom you find your gods shall not live* (32) put Rachel in danger and caused her in a tense moment to take unfair advantage of her father, so that he did not discover where she had hidden the idols. So Jacob became self-righteous and argued that he had been badly done by, pointing out all that he had endured during the years as shepherd of Laban's flocks, the losses he had borne and the sleepless nights he had spent. All his faithful service had been unappreciated, and he had never been able to depend on receiving his carefully negotiated income: *you have changed my wages ten times* (41), for the worse, by implication. Having heard that the Lord had warned Laban not to harm Jacob, Jacob the trickster now turned that disclosure to Laban's disadvantage. Jacob had the God of his fathers on his side and Laban had been in the wrong! He had better be careful and watch his step.

It is fascinating to watch Jacob and Laban, both of whom were past-masters at manipulating people to their own advantage, outdoing one another in the art, and to see each in turn nursing his wounds. Both men paid lip-service to the God of their fathers when to appeal to God was to their personal advantage, but in practice each depended on his wits. Jacob had consistently done so from the day he fled from his home, and he was still confident that *he* could get the better of Laban. He reckoned that he deserved to do so, and now it seemed that the Lord was on his side, protecting him. His confidence and self-justification increased accordingly. He was the very same Jacob who had tricked his brother and his father years before, and had not changed one whit as a result of the Lord's dealings with him.

An agreement

Laban knew he was defeated, though he would not admit the fact. He still claimed the right to keep *his* daughters, *his* grandchildren and *his* stock. No 'giving away' ceremony had made clear at the marriage that this was a right which every father renounced, nor had there been any break with father and mother to enforce it. After all the years the parting was painful in the extreme for Laban, but worst of all was his loss of the affection of his daughters. He even envisaged the possibility of armed hostility from the family in the future. For this reason he proposed that a covenant agreement should bring their hostility to an end.

It was an unambiguous ceremony, indicating that reconciliation had been reached between the two parties. In the first place there was a enduring symbol, by means of which the transaction would be recalled and its terms passed on to succeeding generations. Jacob and Laban both set up a slab of rock, while others fetched stones to form a conspicuous cairn. The names given to the cairn were a pointer to its function as a *witness*, or, as we should say, a memorial.[7] Modern international treaties might be more enduring if they were symbolized in stone and intended for the observance of future generations. But there was a second factor: both Jacob and Laban knew that they had to take God into account. It was he who would keep watch between them when they were apart, and would punish any infringement of the covenant agreement, hence the name *Mizpah* (49), 'watch tower', implying that the Lord stood guard at this memorial stone. Finally the sacrificial meal, offered first to God and then shared by the parties to the covenant, sealed the solemn obligation to respect each other's territory and boundary line. The mountain-top experience lasted all night, and when day dawned Laban was ready to leave. Despite all the outrage and resentment he left a blessing behind him.

Facing Esau

No sooner was one crisis over than another loomed ahead. Sooner or later Jacob would have to face Esau, and he had no reason to expect a loving reception from his brother who had wanted to kill him. It would have been in keeping with Jacob's character to sneak back into Canaan. He could easily have found a route that avoided Esau's territory, Seir, to the south-east of the Dead Sea. But such was the pressure of the past upon his conscience that he could no longer ignore this evidence of guilt. He needed to be reconciled to Esau.

As Jacob and his company resumed their journey Jacob had a supernatural experience which he took as a good omen: *the angels of God met him* (32:1). These 'angels' were evidently in the guise of soldiers, like the army of the Lord of which Elisha was aware when

[7] Whereas the name *Galeed* was Hebrew, *Jegar-sahadutha* was Aramaic for 'heap of witness'. Aramaic was the language of Aram, the country to which Laban belonged. This is the earliest reference in the Bible to this language, which in the first millennium was to become the international language of diplomacy. It occurs in Ezra 4:8 – 6:18 and Daniel 2:4 – 7:28, together with one verse in Jeremiah (10:11). There were many similarities between Hebrew and Aramaic, despite the contrary evidence of this verse. *Cf.* F.F. Bruce, *The Books and the Parchments*, Fourth Edition (Pickering and Inglis, 1984), pp. 39–40.

he prayed that his young servant might also 'see' the horses and chariots of fire round about Elisha (2 Ki. 6:17). Jacob, however, unlike Elisha who depended entirely on the heavenly troops and on the God who directed them, saw them as reinforcements only, supplementing his own stratagem. His name for the place, *Mahanaim* (2), meant 'two camps', as opposed to the one he directed. He accepted without question the assumption that God's troops were going to fight on his side, but he also decided to divide his own group into two companies, so giving himself possibilities of manoeuvre, and the hope that at least one would escape slaughter. Once again he was relying on his own wits rather than on his God, who had directed him and who would therefore keep him.

Encouraged by his vision, Jacob had sent messengers to Esau, giving a minimum of news, and hoping that time had healed his deeply wounded brother. Instead of that, Esau mustered his armed men and was on his way to attack his brother, so precipitating the greatest crisis of Jacob's life. Did he regret that he had attempted to become reconciled to Esau? There was no time to lose, and he quickly turned to prayer as well as to strategy. He was in a tight corner, so it was advisable to pray, though he had in the back of his mind an intriguing scheme that he thought would once again get the better of Esau.

It was a marvellous prayer. Concise as he had to be in his urgency, Jacob nevertheless took time to address God in a full and meaningful way (no slapdash approach or familiarity for him). As he said '*O God of my father Abraham*', he was putting his personal need in the powerful setting of the whole saving purpose of God outlined in the everlasting covenant (Gn. 17:7). The Book of Common Prayer provides excellent examples of approaches to God on the grounds of which requests may appropriately be made. The Easter collect is a good example: 'Almighty God, who through thine only-begotten Son Jesus Christ hast overcome death...', and with that truth in mind we dare to pray that the good desires he gives us we may bring to good effect. By invoking the God of his father Abraham and God of his father Isaac, Jacob was consciously calling to mind what God himself had done in making himself known to the family. Jacob was in the succession, for he too had heard the word of the Lord, telling him to return. When he prays, far from trying to pull himself up by his own bootlaces, Jacob is seeing himself and his problem in relation to the revealed purpose of God, in such a way that a response is to be expected, for God cannot fail to stand by his word.

135

'I am not worthy' is Jacob's first admission of guilt (10), intensified by his awareness of all he had received since he had fled as a penniless youth from his brother's vengeance. He had experienced the Lord's steadfast love and faithfulness, and the realization humbled him. Whereas he had left home on his own, lonely and afraid, he was now *two companies.* Finally Jacob came to the petition that formed the climax of his prayer, *'Deliver me, I pray thee, from the hand of my brother'* (11). Without any insincerity or disguise Jacob admitted his deepest fear, that he would see his children and their mothers put to death. In his fear he recalled the covenant promise again, *'But thou didst say.'* He did not quote exactly the words he had heard at Bethel, but used the reference to the sand upon the seashore from the promise made to Abraham after Isaac had been restored to him (22:17). It would hardly be surprising if Isaac had often quoted these words to his two boys when he was telling them about his escape from death. Moreover, it was a long time since Jacob had seen sand upon the seashore, and the association between the promise and the land of Canaan to which he was going was still strong.

Still full of apprehension despite his prayer, Jacob immediately went on to implement his plan to send a present to Esau. It was a stock farmer's delight: first a sizeable flock of goats, followed after a gap by an equal number of sheep; then camels, then cows, and finally asses, each drove with a proportionate number of males to ensure maximum increase. By the time Esau heard for the fifth time the words, *'They belong to your servant Jacob; they are a present sent to my lord Esau,'* he would find it difficult to resist a smile and maintain his hostility, or so Jacob hoped.

But he was still intensely troubled.

Genesis 32: 22–32

Jacob at Peniel

The same night he arose and took his two wives, his two maids, and his eleven children, and crossed the ford of the Jabbok. ²³He took them and sent them across the stream, and likewise everything that he had. ²⁴And Jacob was left alone; and a man wrestled with him until the breaking of the day. ²⁵When the man saw that he did not prevail against Jacob, he touched the hollow of his thigh; and Jacob's thigh was put out of joint as he wrestled with him. ²⁶Then he said, 'Let me go, for the day is breaking.' But Jacob said, 'I will not let you go, unless you bless me.' ²⁷And he said to him,

'What is your name?' And he said, 'Jacob.' ²⁸*Then he said, 'Your name shall no more be called Jacob, but Israel, for you have striven with God and with men, and have prevailed.'* ²⁹*Then Jacob asked him, 'Tell me, I pray, your name.' But he said, 'Why is it that you ask my name?' And there he blessed him.* ³⁰*So Jacob called the name of the place Peniel, saying, 'For I have seen God face to face, and yet my life is preserved.'* ³¹*The sun rose upon him as he passed Penuel, limping because of his thigh.* ³²*Therefore to this day the Israelites do not eat the sinew of the hip which is upon the hollow of the thigh, because he touched the hollow of Jacob's thigh on the sinew of the hip.*

When everything is at stake a night of prayer is no burden, but rather a life-line. Jacob knew he had to face up to his fears on his own before God, and to that end he sent his wives and children ahead of him across the Jabbok river, though night had already fallen. Since Esau was unlikely to attack at night, Jacob, stripped of all his possessions and prestige, was free to concentrate on the one issue that dominated his thoughts. *Jacob was left alone*, says the text, yet he was not alone. *A man wrestled with him until the breaking of the day*, though there had been no-one about. In such a crisis, when faith is being tested to the hilt, the 'to and fro' of the battle feels very much like wrestling, and it can leave its physical scars. In this literal wrestling-match Jacob refused to accept defeat until it was unavoidable. His opponent 'hit below the belt' and forced him to give in. With his hip out of joint Jacob was totally helpless because of the excruciating pain. All he could do was cling to his opponent for support.

At last Jacob had to admit defeat, and yet he was the opportunist even in his downfall. He would not readily release his opponent on whom he was leaning: *'I will not let you go, unless you bless me.'* This was at last the cry of faith. All Jacob's supposed strength had suddenly ebbed from him and all he could do was to cry for help. Since the greater blesses the lesser, Jacob was requesting a share in the might of the one who had defeated him, in much the same way as a champion may be requested to take up the cause of a promising youngster. Jacob needed the sponsorship of the master, and clung on until he received it.

First he is given a new name (28). From this point on he will be known not only as Jacob but also as *Israel*, 'God strives', to commemorate the night when he fought with God *and prevailed*. Jacob would no doubt have put it differently; it was the night he became a cripple. From this point on he would experience pain and weakness with every step. Though he asked the name of the one who had wounded him, he was not told. His own new name was sufficient proof that he had been confronted by the living God, who proceeded to give him a blessing. That awesome experience became for ever connected with the ravine called *Peniel*, 'the face of God', by Jacob. It amazed him that he should have seen God (not to mention wrestling with him) and remain alive. Since he had not only wrestled with God but prevailed, then it must mean that he was to receive the answer to his prayer for deliverance when Esau attacked. For some unaccountable reason God had appeared, wrestled with him and caused him to give in. If God had forgiven his deception, as it seemed he must have done, Jacob could meet Esau without fear. *The sun rose upon him*, and he was light of heart even though he had a permanent limp. His lifetime's struggle against allowing the God of his fathers to hold the reins of his life had at last come to an end.

From this point on he was a changed man. Esau had seemed to be his most fearsome adversary, whereas he now saw that his own conscience had made a coward of him, and the one who had been hedging him about like a trapper to catch him was God. Once right with God he could face the future. Was not God's army on his side (32:1)?

By any reckoning this incident is fascinating. But has it any meaning for Christians today, and if so, what should it teach us? I remember well being given the example of Jacob the wrestler as a pattern of persevering prayer. It seemed that it should be possible, by hanging on long enough in prayer to God, to obtain answers which were not granted to the half-hearted. That this is true is proved by the teaching of Jesus about the hard-hearted judge and the persistent widow (Lk. 18:1–8). But it would be contrary to biblical teaching, and even to what Jesus says in this passage in Luke, to think that answers to prayer need to be wrested from God, as though he were reluctant to give to those who ask. In fact the passage says less about prayer than about God's search for us. Certainly Jacob was facing a crisis, and for that reason found a place on his own where he could think and pray, but God took the initiative in appearing to him as a wrestling opponent. God was in charge, not Jacob, and that was precisely the point. When it comes to dealings with God, though we may think that we took the initiative, we find that he was there first, loving God that he is, putting into our minds good desires that aroused our discontent and drove us to himself. In Jacob's case it took God twenty years to bring Jacob to this point of surrender on the border of the promised land; the Lord is not in any hurry, crucial as the transaction is. But when his time comes the transformation is complete: it is a transition from death to life, from self-help to faith in the God who cripples Jacob in order to bless him.

In the Old Testament Jacob/Israel, the individual, came to stand for the people of God, called by that name. In the same way as Jacob had needed the transforming power of God, so in every generation did his successors. The name *Jacob* stood for the raw material taken by the Lord to achieve his purposes, while *Israel* called to mind the transforming power which made a new man of Jacob, and which could have done the same for his descendants, had they been willing. The prophet Hosea made free use of the two names in his teaching, and for his generation, soon to be swept into exile, he pleaded,

'So you, by the help of your God, return,
hold fast to love and justice,
and wait continually for your God' (Ho. 12:6).

The Lord appeared without any intermediary to Jacob, as he had done to Abraham and Isaac before him; he intervened directly to strike down Saul of Tarsus, and force him to face up to facts he had been refusing to reckon with. Most of the time, however, both before and after the coming of Jesus, the Lord has worked through his servants who declared the word of the Lord. Though you and I do not 'see the Lord', he still deals with us personally, breaks down our defences, and moves us to return to him in repentance so that we may receive the blessing he has for us.

Genesis 33:1–20

Jacob meets Esau

And Jacob lifted up his eyes and looked, and behold, Esau was coming, and four hundred men with him. So he divided the children among Leah and Rachel and the two maids. ²And he put the maids with their children in front, then Leah with her children, and Rachel and Joseph last of all. ³He himself went on before them, bowing himself to the ground seven times, until he came near to his brother.

⁴But Esau ran to meet him, and embraced him, and fell on his neck and kissed him, and they wept. ⁵And when Esau raised his eyes and saw the

139

women and children, he said, 'Who are these with you?' Jacob said, 'The children whom God has graciously given you servant.' [6]*Then the maids drew near, they and their children, and bowed down;* [7]*Leah likewise and her children drew near and bowed down; and last Joseph and Rachel drew near, and they bowed down.* [8]*Esau said, 'What do you mean by all this company which I met?' Jacob answered, 'To find favour in the sight of my lord.'* [9]*But Esau said, 'I have enough, my brother; keep what you have for yourself.'* [10]*Jacob said, 'No, I pray you, if I have found favour in your sight, then accept my present from my hand; for truly to see your face is like seeing the face of God, with such favour have you received me.* [11]*Accept, I pray you, my gift that is brought to you, because God has dealt graciously with me, and because I have enough.' Thus he urged him, and he took it.*

[12]*Then Esau said, 'Let us journey on our way, and I will go before you.'* [13]*But Jacob said to him, 'My lord knows that the children are frail, and that the flocks and herds giving suck are a care to me; and if they are overdriven for one day, all the flocks will die.* [14]*Let my lord pass on before his servant, and I will lead on slowly, according to the pace of the cattle which are before me and according to the pace of the children, until I come to my lord in Seir.'*

[15]*So Esau said, 'Let me leave with you some of the men who are with me.' But he said, 'What need is there? Let me find favour in the sight of my lord.'* [16]*So Esau returned that day on his way to Seir.* [17]*But Jacob journeyed to Succoth, and built himself a house, and made booths for his cattle; therefore the name of the place is called Succoth.*

[18]*And Jacob came safely to the city of Shechem, which is in the land of Canaan, on his way from Paddan-aram; and he camped before the city.* [19]*And from the sons of Hamor, Shechem's father, he bought for a hundred pieces of money the piece of land on which he had pitched his tent.* [20]*There he erected an altar and called it El-Elohe-Israel.*

Was it to be a reconciliation or a battle? Though he had made his peace with God and had prayed for deliverance, Jacob took the utmost precaution to protect his wives and children, especially Rachel with Joseph. The army that met him was small as armies go, but it was overpowering to a family group, totally without armaments. The change in Jacob, brought about by his Peniel experience of God, is demonstrated by the courageous lead he took in going ahead of the company, prepared to take the brunt of his brother's murderous attack, prostrating himself seven times as he approached and then standing, waiting to see what Esau would do. The lone figure of one who had taken the initiative in seeking to be reconciled to his brother was for the first time putting to the proof the Lord's verdict that he had prevailed.

Jacob did not have to wait long. *Esau ran to meet him, and embraced him, and fell on his neck and kissed him, and they wept* (4). Did Jesus have this first reconciliation in mind when he told of the father's welcome for the lost son (Lk. 15:20)? All the bitter enmity that had separated these two men for twenty years was swept away by the forgiving love that flooded their beings. Barriers of resentment, hatred and fear fell in a moment, and permitted the joy of renewed friendship, introductions to the family and exchange of news. It is just possible that Esau had intended this all along, and that the four hundred men were his armed bodyguard, as much for prestige as for protection. In that case Jacob's generous presents had been unnecessary, and Esau needed to assure himself that Jacob intended him to keep all those animals. It was essential for Jacob's peace of mind that Esau should accept his present as proof of his ongoing friendship; he had thought, 'perhaps he will accept me' (32:20), and he was still suspicious. God had dealt graciously with him at Peniel (the name meant 'the face of God'), and the meeting with Esau had been *like seeing the face of God* (10). It was deliberate flattery, but the two events were interlinked. Esau accepted Jacob's gift, so setting his seal on the reconciliation.

In the elation and relief Jacob was experiencing, it would have been easy to cast caution to the winds, but Jacob had no intention of travelling with Esau. Nor did he accept Esau's offer of an armed escort, claiming that it was not necessary. The fact was that he was travelling to a different destination, though he pretended that he would join Esau in Seir (14). It was important, moreover, not to overestimate their compatibility. So Esau travelled due south, while Jacob moved a few miles towards the Jordan valley, and settled for a while at *Succoth*, meaning 'booths', or 'shelters'. After the strains of the long journey, and in particular the tensions created by Esau's visit, a rest was welcome.

Despite his total capitulation at Peniel Jacob kept his scheming ways, pretending one thing and intending another. He remained the same Jacob as Esau had known years earlier, giving his brother the slip under cover of following gently for the sake of the children and tender animals. Heartening as it would be if defects of character were immediately removed by a conversion experience, evidence from Scripture and from life indicates otherwise. As Article 9 of the Articles of Religion puts it, 'And this infection of nature doth remain, yea in them that are regenerated'.

From Succoth to Shechem was a mere 30 miles (48 km). The route took Jacob's company into Canaan via the traditional crossing-point at Adam (Jos. 3:16), where the Jabbok joins the Jordan, and up into the central hills, with their precipitous cliffs and winding valleys. Only when they came to Shechem was there the possibility of pitching camp, close to the walls of the city, which had evidently been built since the period of Abraham's arrival in Canaan, a century or so earlier.[8] At that time the site had been marked by a sacred oak, and, because the Lord had appeared to Abraham there, he had built his own altar to the Lord and worshipped for the first time in the land of Canaan at Shechem (12:6–7). It was appropriate that Jacob should follow in Abraham's footsteps, but, whereas Abraham owned no land there, Jacob bought the field where he had resolved to commemorate his return to the land of his birth, by building an altar to the Lord. His name for the altar, *El-Elohe-Israel*, meaning 'God is the God of Israel', indicates that he had appreciated the significance of the dark night at the Jabbok, as a result of which his name had been changed. He now consciously and deliberately acknowledged that the Lord was his God, whom he trusted to fulfil all his promises (28:20–22). God's word, not human cunning, had prevailed.

Two generations on from Abraham all the covenanted purposes of God were vested in one man, Jacob, and his sons. Was it possible that from so small and unpromising a beginning the whole world could be significantly changed? In terms of human understanding the proposition was highly unlikely, but there was dynamism in the word of the Lord, and it would not fail. Jesus saw his own ministry in a similar light; it was 'like a grain of mustard seed, ... the smallest of all the seeds on earth; yet when it is sown it grows up and becomes the greatest of all shrubs ...' (Mk. 4:30–32). The quiet, hidden work of God's Spirit goes on through the centuries, embracing succeeding generations, all of which belong in his world-wide outreach and are part of a greater whole, called by Jesus 'the kingdom of God'. Statistics cannot estimate its size, nor reckon its worth.

---

[8] J.J. Bimson, 'Archaeological Data and the Dating of the Patriarchs', *EOPN*, pp. 59–92, argues that Abraham belonged to the period known as Middle Bronze I, and Jacob to MB II. There was a city at Shechem in MB IIA, a period which is now reckoned to have begun about 2000 BC, which was approximately the time of Jacob's birth.

Genesis 34:1–31

Seduction and treachery

Now Dinah the daughter of Leah, whom she had borne to Jacob, went out to visit the women of the land; ²and when Shechem the son of Hamor the Hivite, the prince of the land, saw her, he seized her and lay with her and humbled her. ³And his soul was drawn to Dinah the daughter of Jacob; he loved the maiden and spoke tenderly to her. ⁴So Shechem spoke to his father Hamor, saying, 'Get me this maiden for my wife.' ⁵Now Jacob heard that he had defiled his daughter Dinah; but his sons were with his cattle in the field, so Jacob held his peace until they came. ⁶And Hamor the father of Shechem went out to Jacob to speak with him. ⁷The sons of Jacob came in from the field when they heard of it; and the men were indignant and very angry, because he had wrought folly in Israel by lying with Jacob's daughter, for such a thing ought not to be done.

⁸*But Hamor spoke with them, saying, 'The soul of my son Shechem longs for your daughter; I pray you, give her to him in marriage. ⁹Make marriages with us; give your daughters to us, and take our daughters for yourselves. ¹⁰You shall dwell with us; and the land shall be open to you; dwell and trade in it, and get property in it.' ¹¹Shechem also said to her father and to her brothers, 'Let me find favour in your eyes, and whatever you say to me I will give. ¹²Ask of me ever so much as marriage present and gift, and I will give according as you say to me; only give me the maiden to be my wife.'*

¹³*The sons of Jacob answered Shechem and his father Hamor deceitfully, because he had defiled their sister Dinah. ¹⁴They said to them, 'We cannot do this thing, to give our sister to one who is uncircumcised, for that would be a disgrace to us. ¹⁵Only on this condition will we consent to you: that you will become as we are and every male of you be circumcised. ¹⁶Then we will give our daughters to you, and we will take your daughters to ourselves, and we will dwell with you and become one people. ¹⁷But if you will not listen to us and be circumcised, then we will take our daughter, and we will be gone.'*

¹⁸*Their words pleased Hamor and Hamor's son Shechem. ¹⁹And the young man did not delay to do the thing, because he had delight in Jacob's daughter. Now he was the most honoured of all his family. ²⁰So Hamor and his son Shechem came to the gate of their city and spoke to the men of their city, saying, ²¹'These men are friendly with us; let them dwell in the land and trade in it, for behold, the land is large enough for them; let us take their daughters in marriage, and let us give them our daughters. ²²Only on this condition will the men agree to dwell with us, to become one people: that every male among us be circumcised as they are circumcised. ²³Will not their*

cattle, their property and all their beasts be ours? Only let us agree with them, and they will dwell with us.' ^{24}*And all who went out of the gate of his city hearkened to Hamor and his son Shechem; and every male was circumcised, all who went out of the gate of his city.*

^{25}*On the third day, when they were sore, two of the sons of Jacob, Simeon and Levi, Dinah's brothers, took their swords and came upon the city unawares, and killed all the males.* ^{26}*They slew Hamor and his son Shechem with the sword, and took Dinah out of Shechem's house, and went away.* ^{27}*And the sons of Jacob came upon the slain, and plundered the city, because their sister had been defiled;* ^{28}*they took their flocks and their herds, their asses, and whatever was in the city and in the field;* ^{29}*all their wealth, all their little ones and their wives, all that was in the houses, they captured and made their prey.* ^{30}*Then Jacob said to Simeon and Levi, 'You have brought trouble on me by making me odious to the inhabitants of the land, the Canaanites and the Perizzites; my numbers are few, and if they gather themselves against me and attack me, I shall be destroyed, both I and my household.'* ^{31}*But they said, 'Should he treat our sister as a harlot?'*

This early encounter between Jacob and the inhabitants of Canaan illustrates the kind of difficulty that beset attempts to live amicably alongside people whose standards of conduct were different from those of Abraham's family. It was the young people who were particularly vulnerable.

Some years must have passed since Jacob's arrival in the Shechem region, because Leah's children were now grown up enough to be taking responsibility for the cattle, and to be having their say in family decisions. Jacob had to take the point of view of Leah's sons into account before attempting to take any action concerning the seduction of Dinah, their young sister. In the course of going out to visit some of her girl-friends, she had been noticed by the son of the royal family, Shechem, son of Hamor, ruler of the Hivite inhabitants, who had called his son after the name of the great city in which they lived. No sooner had Shechem set eyes on Dinah than he took advantage of her and seduced her. Though the attraction proved to be more than a passing fancy, and though he evidently won her by his love that 'spoke to her heart', as the Hebrew says, this in no way excused him, even though he was high born. *Such a thing ought not to be done*, says the writer categorically, reflecting as he does so the accepted standards not only of his own day but also of Jacob's time. Legislation would eventually specify punishments and so deter potential offenders (Ex. 22:16–17; Dt. 22:28–29). The crime was seen, not from the point of view of the girl, but as a wrong against her father, who thereby lost his right to make a suitable match for his daughter and also forfeited the bridal gift that should be paid to him.

To do him justice, Shechem had no intention of refusing to make a handsome payment, and he fully intended to make Dinah his wife. He, too, knew what was expected of him by community judgment in these matters, and there was no requirement he could not fulfil. But there had been some arrogance in his assumption that Dinah's father would regard him as a desirable son-in-law, and he had forced the issue for his own self-gratification. He would get his father to straighten the matter up and talk nicely to the family.

When the family conference took place it came to light that more was envisaged than the settlement of this one incident. The marriage between Dinah and Shechem was to mark the permanent alliance between the two peoples, so that they would lose their separate identities and *become one people* (16). There was, of course, an ulterior motive. The residents saw the opportunity to enrich themselves at the expense of these near neighbours (23). Circumcision seemed a small price to pay, and the inhabitants of the city who conferred at the square within the city gate agreed that *all who went out of the gate* (*i.e.* males who had reached puberty and were therefore full citizens) should submit to circumcision.

It was all part of a plot on the part of Simeon and Levi, two of Dinah's full brothers whose burning anger sought revenge; but it was carefully concealed, even from Jacob. While the men of the city were still suffering the effects of the operating-knife, these two brothers killed them all, including Shechem and his father. The women and children were taken, together with all the wealth of the city, as spoils of war, though nothing is said about the fate of the buildings. Evidently Jacob's sons and their households did not move in and occupy the city, though it was to be one of the first places Joshua made for once he and the tribes with him entered Canaan (Jos. 8:30 35; Ebal and Gerizim were mountains that overlooked Shechem). Local memory of the incident may have remained to be handed on over the generations. At the time, Jacob was only too aware of the threat to which his sons had exposed the whole family. Their treachery might bring a concerted attack from neighbouring tribes, who could justify their invasion as a punitive raid and wipe out the people of Jacob's camp.

This incident illustrates the far-reaching effects of so-called private actions. The immediate family is necessarily involved, but where leading members of a community are concerned, the offender is not the only one who has to pay the penalty. One assault on a girl provoked a revenge that wiped out many innocent people and ruined every family in the city. If Jacob had not moved away, the vendetta would have been likely to continue indefinitely. One evil deed thus provokes another, and evil proliferates. It is worth while to conjecture how Jacob might have turned the incident to a less disastrous outcome had he taken the lead himself, in consultation with his sons. Could Dinah not have been permitted to marry Shechem, without any long-term alliance with the Canaanite city being contracted or implied? This is undoubtedly what should have happened, but that would have meant forgiving and overlooking the original wrong, which the Shechemites do not seem to have taken very seriously. It was this casual treatment of their sister that angered Simeon and Levi (31). Family pride had been wounded, and in this situation forgiveness would look like weakness. That is one reason why forgiveness is so costly: it can so easily be misinterpreted, and so devalued.

Genesis 35:1–29

Return to Bethel and Hebron

God said to Jacob, 'Arise, go up to Bethel, and dwell there; and make there an altar to the God who appeared to you when you fled from your brother Esau.' ²So Jacob said to his household and to all who were with him, 'Put away the foreign gods that are among you, and purify yourselves, and change your garments; ³then let us arise and go up to Bethel, that I may make there an altar to the God who answered me in the day of my distress and has been with me wherever I have gone.' ⁴So they gave to Jacob all the foreign gods that they had, and the rings that were in their ears; and Jacob hid them under the oak which was near Shechem.

⁵And as they journeyed, a terror from God fell upon the cities that were round about them, so that they did not pursue the sons of Jacob. ⁶And Jacob came to Luz (that is, Bethel), which is in the land of Canaan, he and all the people who were with him, ⁷and there he built an altar, and called the place El-bethel, because there God had revealed himself to him when he fled from his brother. ⁸And Deborah, Rebekah's nurse, died, and she was buried under an oak below Bethel; so the name of it was called Allon-bacuth.

⁹God appeared to Jacob again, when he came from Paddan-aram, and blessed him. ¹⁰*And God said to him, 'Your name is Jacob; no longer shall your name be called Jacob, but Israel shall be your name.' So his name was called Israel.* ¹¹*And God said to him, 'I am God Almighty: be fruitful and multiply; a nation and a company of nations shall come from you, and kings shall spring from you.* ¹²*The land which I gave to Abraham and Isaac I will give to you, and I will give the land to your descendants after you.'* ¹³*Then God went up from him in the place where he had spoken with him.* ¹⁴*And Jacob set up a pillar in the place where he had spoken with him, a pillar of stone; and he poured out a drink offering on it, and poured oil on it.* ¹⁵*So Jacob called the name of the place where God had spoken with him, Bethel.*

¹⁶*Then they journeyed from Bethel; and when they were still some distance from Ephrath, Rachel travailed, and she had hard labour.* ¹⁷*And when she was in her hard labour, the midwife said to her, 'Fear not; for now you will have another son.'* ¹⁸*And as her soul was departing (for she died), she called his name Ben-oni; but his father called his name Benjamin.* ¹⁹*So Rachel died, and she was buried on the way to Ephrath (that is, Bethlehem),* ²⁰*and Jacob set up a pillar upon her grave; it is the pillar of Rachel's tomb, which is there to this day.* ²¹*Israel journeyed on, and pitched his tent beyond the tower of Eder.*

²²*While Israel dwelt in that land Reuben went and lay with Bilhah his father's concubine; and Israel heard of it.*

Now the sons of Jacob were twelve. ²³*The sons of Leah: Reuben (Jacob's first-born), Simeon, Levi, Judah, Issachar, and Zebulun.* ²⁴*The sons of Rachel: Joseph and Benjamin.* ²⁵*The sons of Bilhah, Rachel's maid: Dan and Naphtali.* ²⁶*The sons of Zilpah, Leah's maid: Gad and Asher. These were the sons of Jacob who were born to him in Paddan-aram.*

²⁷*And Jacob came to his father Isaac at Mamre, or Kiriath-arba (that is, Hebron), where Abraham and Isaac had sojourned.* ²⁸*Now the days of Isaac were a hundred and eighty years.* ²⁹*And Isaac breathed his last; and he died and was gathered to his people, old and full of days; and his sons Esau and Jacob buried him.*

Whereas Shechem had had no previous significance for Jacob, *Bethel* stood for everything that had really mattered. It was the beginning of his walk with God, initiated by the appearance of the living God to him in his dream and encapsulated in the name Bethel, coined by Jacob as his own private name for the sacred spot. When the Lord had appeared to him in Haran he had called himself 'God of Bethel' (31:13) and had reminded Jacob of his vow, made spontaneously in response to the sheer wonder of the event. God had fulfilled Jacob's prayers, providing for him all he needed and bringing him safely through extreme hazards back to Canaan, but Jacob had not attempted to travel south to 'his father's house' (28:20–22), a journey which would have taken him close to Bethel.

At a time when it was dangerous to remain in Shechem, the Lord spoke to Jacob again, expressly telling him to go back to Bethel to live, and to build an altar there in order to worship *the God who appeared to you when you fled from your brother Esau* (1). It was a pointed summons to fulfil his vow, which he had for so long neglected, but which the Lord had not forgotten ('It is better that you should not vow than that you should vow and not pay', Ec. 5:5). The reason for his delay becomes apparent when he orders his household to *'put away the foreign gods that are among you, and purify yourselves'* (2). It comes as a shock to learn that other gods were worshipped by Jacob's entourage with his connivance, though Rachel's theft of her father's household gods should have prepared us, by giving us evidence that the break with popular religion had not been decisively made. There was no doubt in Jacob's mind that commitment to the God of Bethel involved allegiance to him alone, for he was no mere territorial deity, but the God of all the families of the earth (28:14), and therefore the only God. Moreover, Jacob now took the opportunity to testify to the whole family that his God had answered him in the day of his distress and had been with him wherever he had gone (3).

In the light of such faithfulness the whole company saw the need to comply with Jacob's request, and handed over to him the expensive idolatrous objects in their possession, *and Jacob hid them.* Though there may be a hint that he disposed of them in such a way that they could at a later date be recovered by their owners, the verb means 'bury' (*cf.* 'Jacob buried them', NIV). The temptation was great because idolatrous paraphernalia represented popular 'securities'; to give them up was therefore telling proof of a new allegiance. Did Rachel leave her father's teraphim there? The occasion was both a purge and a renewal of faith, in which the whole community was involved, as it had been in the treachery of Simeon and Levi. For good and ill, our lives are bound up in the consequences of other people's choices and decisions, just as other people are affected by those we make.

Reluctance to dispense with idolatrous practices, associated with foreign gods, was a danger to be reckoned with at every stage of Israel's history. Joshua challenged the great assembly at Shechem on the same point after he had led the tribes into Canaan (Jos. 24:15, 20, 23). It was perfectly obvious that there was no god to compare with their God (Jos. 24:15, 17–18), but the people among whom they lived were influential, confident and prosperous. The people of God were at their peak when they resisted the desire to emulate their neighbours and were true to their God.

This was the case as they took the up-hill road to Luz, passing on the way cities which might justifiably have attacked them, but which refrained because *a terror from God fell upon the cities that were round about them* (5). This was the first of several occasions when panic among their enemies enabled Israel to win a victory (*e.g.* Ex. 15:16; Dt. 2:25; Jos. 2:9), or to avoid battle altogether. It was a protection they had done nothing to deserve: 'The Lord will keep you from all evil; he will keep your life' (Ps. 121:7). It enabled Jacob to return in peace to the very spot where God had appeared to him on his flight from Esau, and which he again named *El-Bethel* (7). Not far away, at the foot of the hill, was the grave of Deborah, Rebekah's nurse (24:59). There is nothing to suggest that she had been in Jacob's caravan, and by this time she would have been very old, having left Haran some 140 years earlier (compare 25:20 with 35:28). Her grave would, however, have been of considerable interest to this family, which had come from the same place in Haran as Jacob's wives.

There was, however, another good reason for mentioning Deborah. One conspicuous omission from the narrative is the death of Rebekah, who had taken upon herself the curse of Jacob, when he was hesitating as to whether he would deceive Isaac and rob Esau of the blessing (27:13). The reader does not know how the curse worked out, but notes that Rebekah is absent, and draws his own conclusion from the oblique reference to her. She had evidently died prematurely, before Jacob could be reunited with her. The unnamed nurse who had accompanied Rebekah when she left home now becomes significant in the story, for she enables the author to recollect Rebekah's role without openly moralizing about her.[9]

A new blessing

Jacob's return to the place where God had first blessed him was no disappointment, for *God appeared to Jacob again* (9). By renaming him Israel, God confirmed that he had indeed been the one who had

[9] *Cf.* U. Cassuto, *A Commentary on the Book of Genesis*, II, p. 63.

met him in human form at Peniel, and had wrestled with Jacob. Jacob had asked in vain to know the name of his opponent, but now Jacob is told without asking, *I am God Almighty* (11). This name *El Shaddai* was the one by which the Lord had addressed Abraham, when he reaffirmed his covenant with him, gave him the sign of circumcision and pronounced that Sarah was to bear Isaac (17:1–21). Isaac had used this awesome name in blessing when he had bidden Jacob farewell. Now Jacob hears it from God himself and can know for sure that the words of the covenant blessing will be fulfilled. His family will become *a nation and a company of nations*; kings will spring from him (*cf.* the promise to Sarah, 17:16), and the land is given to him and his descendants. It had already been given to Abraham and Isaac, and Jacob was also meant to live in conscious enjoyment of God's gift, though it was to be hundreds of years before his descendants were to be its acknowledged possessors. Kings and the kingdom of Israel were 800 years or so further into the future, and the prediction of a multitude of nations who were to be blessed in Abraham involved the coming of Jesus and the founding of the church. Such is the scale of prediction in Scripture that it bears little resemblance to the short-term detail of the horoscope. Divine foretelling is on the grand scale and indicates the purpose of human life, for God had his saving plan in mind 'before the foundation of the world' (1 Pet. 1:20). Because of this purpose it was possible for the notion of history, as opposed to chronicles of events, to be perceived, as it was for the first time in the Old Testament (*cf.* Introduction, pp. 11–13).

The ritual of Jacob's first visit to this place was repeated, but whereas in his youth he could give little content to his use of the name God, now in the light of God's dealings with him over the years he knew his faith was secure in the living God, who had chastened him, provided and guided, and would continue to do so, not only in his life but in the generations to come. The name Bethel was also repeated, but it is clear that Jacob did not think of God as localized there in a pillar of stone, as used to be taught in some textbooks. His testimony that God had been with him wherever he had gone (3) shows that his theology was altogether more adequate and exalted.

Jacob's confidence was soon to be tested as he journeyed south on his way to *Ephrath* (16). Rachel, who had prayed for another son to be added to the first (30:24), was about to give birth long before they reached their destination. In her agony of suffering even the birth of a boy failed to bring relief from pain, and in her dying moments she named him accordingly, *Ben-oni*, 'son of my sorrow'. Such a sad name was unsuitable for a child, and Jacob changed it to Benjamin, meaning 'son of (my) right hand'. He did not coin the name, for it was known at Mari (*cf.* pp. 21–22), but it had a double allusion. In the ancient Near East it was customary to look east when taking direction, and so the right hand pointed south. This baby boy was born on a journey south through Canaan, and so was 'a son of the south'. At the same time Jacob wanted to honour Rachel, and by calling her son the 'son of my right hand' Jacob exalted him to the highest place among all his brothers, just as in Psalm 110:1 the Lord gave the most exalted place of all to David's Lord when he said 'Sit at my right hand' (*cf.* Mt. 22:43–45). Jacob's love for Rachel endured, and years later he recalled the desolation he felt at her death (48:7). Too often children whose mothers have died giving them birth are blamed rather than esteemed, but Jacob gave Benjamin a special place in his affections.

Later, when tribal territory was allocated, the border of Benjamin included the place of his birth and of his mother's death (1 Sa. 10:2). Once again Jacob set up a pillar, this time as a memorial to a beloved wife; it endured at least until the time of the narrator, and the site was still a landmark in the lifetime of Jeremiah (Je. 31:15).[10]

Three brief paragraphs conclude this section of the book devoted to Jacob, as distinct from most of the final fourteen chapters where Joseph is the leading character. First a blot on the family record is reported without further comment. Reuben disgraced himself with his father's concubine, Bilhah, and this serious offence came to Jacob's notice. In the list of Jacob's sons which follows Reuben is named in his privileged position as first-born, but when Jacob came to the point of giving his deathbed blessing Reuben did not have the pre-eminence (49:4). This was no arbitrary decision on the part of Jacob, but rather a judicial disinheritance resulting from his grave misdeed. In view of the fact that Simeon and Levi had brought their father into disrepute (34:30), the fourth son, Judah, was next in line to inherit the birthright privileges.[11] He became spokesman for the brothers when they went to Egypt for a second time and offered to

[10] The shrine just north of Bethlehem, which is pointed out to tourists as Rachel's tomb, cannot be authentic. Jeremiah indicates that her tomb was north of Jerusalem, at Ramah.

[11] Examples of disinheritance for serious offences occur outside the Bible. *Cf. EOPN*, p. 126.

become a surety for Benjamin (chapters 43 and 44). In Jacob's deathbed blessing Judah was to be the one before whom his brothers would bow (49:8). Hundreds of years later David of the tribe of Judah was to become king over the whole of Israel, and eventually Jesus the Messiah was to be born into his line. Such far-reaching themes, spanning both Testaments, defy human explanation.

The fate of Bilhah goes unrecorded, but if Reuben was disgraced, so was she. This short statement opens a window on the frustrations and iniquities of a polygamous household, and on the havoc polygamy caused to the divine intention of marriage as two becoming 'one flesh'.

Now the sons of Jacob were twelve, a number that was to be matched by the apostles of Jesus (Mk. 3:14), and was used in Revelation 21:12, 14 to symbolize the complete church of both Old and New Testaments. Whereas Abraham, Isaac and Jacob had been the only *one* in their generations, the promise is now opened out and vested in twelve sons. Though the divine intention was to reach out in blessing to all the families of the earth (12:3), the vehicle of blessing was always relatively small and insignificant.

The death of Isaac was the occasion for a family reunion, Esau and Jacob meeting again at the deathbed of their father. Isaac thus lived to see that, in the providence of God, his two sons had been reconciled, Jacob had been blessed with sons, and both were well provided for. His death was therefore a time for thanksgiving rather than for sadness. Like Abraham (25:8), he was *gathered to his people* (29), part of an ongoing family beyond the grave.[12] Hope of a reunion beyond cheered the loneliness of death.

Genesis 36:1–43

Esau, father of the Edomites

... *⁶Then Esau took his wives, his sons, his daughters, and all the members of his household, his cattle, all his beasts, and all his property which he had acquired in the land of Canaan; and he went into a land away from his brother Jacob. ⁷For their possessions were too great for them to dwell together; the land of their sojournings could not support them because of their cattle. ⁸So Esau dwelt in the hill country of Seir; Esau is Edom....*

---

[12] As Derek Kidner points out, 'The expression *gathered to his people* ... must point, however indistinctly, to the continued existence of the dead.' *Genesis, TOTC*, p. 150.

The Edomites, close relatives and neighbours of Israel, played a part in Israel's story through the centuries, and the rivalry between Esau and Jacob remained a sore point as late as the post-exilic period (Mal. 1:2–5). A chapter like this, consisting almost entirely of otherwise unknown names, may seem at first sight to be an interruption of the story; on further reflection it proves that Esau, though he did not receive the birthright, nevertheless prospered and, while Jacob and his family took refuge and eventually became slaves in Egypt, Esau's clan developed and became organized. It seems likely that family details were recorded, and that written genealogies underlie the information included here. Verses 2–3 differ from 26:34–35 and 28:9, but no attempt was made to bring the accounts into line, probably because archival records were taken over as they stood. By this method Esau's future could be summarized and dismissed before Genesis resumed the account of Jacob's son Joseph, around whose story the events of the whole family turned. By comparison the history of Esau's family was uneventful.

Esau's three wives mentioned in verses 2–5 each came from different racial groups, though they are broadly classed as Canaanite. (Judith, the first in 26:34, is not mentioned.) First now is the daughter of Elon the Hittite, called Basemath in 26:34, but here *Adah*, which may have been Esau's name for her as opposed to that of her Hittite family. Ishmael's daughter also has a new name, *Basemath* (*cf.* 28:9). It was after the birth of his fifth son that he migrated, with his family and all his stock, to the land which later bore the name Edom, south-east of the Dead Sea, consisting largely of high rocky plateau bordering on desert. The words of Isaac, 'away from the fatness of the earth shall your dwelling be, and away from the dew of heaven on high' (27:39), were an apt reference to this inhospitable land. There Esau enjoyed independence, as opposed to the dependent status of Jacob in Egypt, which eventually became slavery for his descendants; but it was those who had been enslaved who experienced the Lord's deliverance, and so became his redeemed people.

By reckoning the grandsons of Esau born to Eliphaz and Reuel, and the sons of Oholibamah (but omitting the son of his concubine), Esau became the father of twelve tribes, like his brother Jacob, and the tribal heads are named (15–19). Little is said about the conquest of the land of Seir, which had been inhabited by Horites (20; *cf.* 14:6), though Zibeon is a Hivite in verse 2. Esau dispossessed the

153

Horites (Dt. 2:12, 22), but evidently married the daughter of one of their chiefs. Zibeon.[13] He was perfectly free to do so.

The land of Edom was organized as a monarchy earlier than was Israel. This is not surprising, because there was in the traditions of Israel a marked opposition to the idea of setting up kings (1 Sa. 8:7; cf. Dt. 17:14–20). The Lord was regarded as king, and had the right to choose his man for the leadership, as happened in the time of the Judges. Yet the kings named here (31–39) resemble the Judges in that there is no hereditary ruler, and no recognized capital city. Instead many different families and cities shared the honour. Bozrah (33) continued an important place, and stood for Edom as Damascus stood for Syria (e.g. Is. 63:1; Am. 1:12). It was probably the capital in later centuries. Now known as Buseirah, it was explored by Nelson Glueck in the 1930s, and many effigies in stone and pottery were found there.[14] Though many of these were no doubt manufactured later than patriarchal times, the triumph of idolatry over the knowledge of God, which Esau had and could have perpetuated, is plain. Despite the struggle of the prophets over the same issue in Israel, excavations have nowhere unearthed a plethora of idols in the territory of Israel or Judah. Esau's defection set a precedent, which later was to lead to identification with the idolatrous religion of the local population. If it had not been for the many forms of divine discipline, which culminated in the Exile, the story would have been of the same sorry decline among Jacob's descendants. It was the mercy of God that refused to 'give them up', and instead worked to produce a people who were capable of receiving his salvation. That is the theme of the rest of the Old Testament.

The book of Job is set in patriarchal times, and the senior among his friends was Eliphaz the Temanite (cf. 11), evidently an Edomite. For this reason the book points to Edom as its probable background. The prophecy of Obadiah is addressed to the Edomites, together with passages in other prophets (Is. 34; 63:1–6; Je. 49:7–22; Ezk. 25:12–14; Am. 1:11–12), so Edom was not left without any witness and could have repented. Their 'bush telegraph' would see that such messages found their destination.

---

[13] Both Horites and Hivites are frequently identified as Hurrians (cf. Peter C. Craigie, 'Ugarit, Canaan, and Israel', TB 34 (1983), p. 159), and some of the names in verses 20–30 have Hurrian parallels. 'The Hurrians were among the principal intermediaries of culture and civilization throughout the Ancient Near East' (Craigie, pp. 157–158).

[14] Nelson Glueck, Deities and Dolphins (Cassell, 1966), p. 231.

Part 4
JOSEPH
(Genesis 37 – 50)

The Jacob narrative has not strictly come to an end, despite the summary (37:1–2a) which dismisses him for the time being. Indeed the patriarch continues as chief in the clan until his death (49:33), but interest turns to his sons, and in particular to Joseph, through whom the whole family became residents in Egypt.

It is a striking feature of the patriarchal narratives that people of different stock, whether in the Tigris-Euphrates valley, Syria, Canaan or Egypt, were able to move freely and live alongside one another, provided that one group did not become outstandingly more numerous so as to become a threat to the others. There is a feeling of space, of welcome for all who came peacefully, and a tolerance of different ways of life. As human groupings became larger and more powerful, nationalistic ambitions tended to become more exclusive of foreigners. This transition took place during the residence of the Israelites in Egypt, with the 'new king over Egypt, who did not know Joseph' (Ex. 1:8). During the first millennium BC nationalism was to develop even more fully with the rise of the great empires of Assyria, Babylon and Persia, giving a totally different 'feel' to relationships between peoples and lands.

The extraordinary way in which Joseph was able to rise to power in Egypt has often been explained by drawing attention to a foreign dynasty, known as the Hyksos or 'shepherd kings', who ruled over Egypt from about 1710 to 1540 BC. These were Semitic chiefs, who came to power at a time of Egyptian weakness and eventually took over the kingship of Egypt, establishing their capital at Avaris, in the east of the delta. In time they replaced Egyptian officials with their own Semitic diplomats, and 'into this background, Joseph ... fits perfectly'.[1] True though that is, the Hyksos period is a little late for the Joseph narrative if Abraham migrated to Canaan about 2092 BC, and Jacob moved his family to Egypt in 1877.[2] There is a discrepancy of nearly two centuries. The book of Genesis does not, however, require a Semitic dynasty in order to explain the rise of Joseph. His convincing interpretation of the Pharaoh's dream was sufficiently impressive to account for the promotion that follows. The nineteenth century BC was the golden age of Egypt's classical literature and a time when Egypt was politically strong. It is to this period that belongs the famous tomb-painting of Semites visiting Egypt which was found at Beni-Hassan, about 140 miles south of the delta, and which shows the visitors paying their respects to the administrator of the eastern desert. The patriarchs were evidently not the only Semitic visitors to Egypt before the Hyksos period. It is easy to underestimate the distances covered on foot by whole families (for there are children in the picture), and what took them so far up the Nile when the capital was at Memphis, over 100 miles further north? The Bible narrative takes for granted trading caravans, plying the trade routes between one country and another and enriching themselves in the process.

From a literary standpoint the Joseph narrative is outstanding for its honesty, clear characterization and theological interest. Joseph is one of the 'good' men of the Old Testament, and yet the mature Joseph comes across without any trace of smug piety. There is universal interest in the childhood struggle for recognition, and deep sympathy for the lad sold to total strangers by jealous brothers. Injustice dogs his steps, and yet he avoids self-pity and patiently endures long imprisonment, until suddenly his vindication transports him from the depths to the heights. Little reference is made to his faith, and yet his character has been matured and his trust in God developed through his trials. Prosperity does not make him proud, and when he confers with his brothers he reveals that he has meditated on the course of his life and has come to see the hand of God controlling even the painful sequence of events resulting from his brothers' malicious intent in selling him. His faith has been the

---

[1] K. A. Kitchen, art 'Egypt', *IBD*, I, p. 420. This article is an excellent source of information, illustrated with photographs and diagrams, concerning Egypt and Israel's history.   [2] *Cf.* Introduction, p. 20.

making of him. There must be some pattern here which could enable us today to come to terms with life's injustice and suffering, in such a way as to avoid resentment and turn evil to good account.

Genesis 37:1–36

Joseph, the favourite son

Jacob dwelt in the land of his father's sojournings, in the land of Canaan.
²This is the history of the family of Jacob.

Joseph, being seventeen years old, was shepherding the flock with his brothers; he was a lad with the sons of Bilhah and Zilpah, his father's wives; and Joseph brought an ill report of them to their father. ³Now Israel loved Joseph more than any other of his children, because he was the son of his old age; and he made him a long robe with sleeves. ⁴But when his brothers saw that their father loved him more than all his brothers, they hated him, and could not speak peaceably to him.

⁵Now Joseph had a dream, and when he told it to his brothers they only hated him the more. ⁶He said to them, 'Hear this dream which I have dreamed: ⁷behold, we were binding sheaves in the field, and lo, my sheaf arose and stood upright; and behold, your sheaves gathered round it, and bowed down to my sheaf.' ⁸His brothers said to him, 'Are you indeed to reign over us? Or are you indeed to have dominion over us?' So they hated him yet more for his dreams and for his words. ⁹Then he dreamed another dream, and told it to his brothers, and said, 'Behold, I have dreamed another dream; and behold, the sun, the moon, and eleven stars were bowing down to me.' ¹⁰But when he told it to his father and to his brothers, his father rebuked him, and said to him, 'What is this dream that you have dreamed? Shall I and your mother and your brothers indeed come to bow ourselves to the ground before you?' ¹¹And his brothers were jealous of him, but his father kept the saying in mind.

¹²Now his brothers went to pasture their father's flock near Shechem. ¹³And Israel said to Joseph, 'Are not your brothers pasturing the flock at Shechem? Come, I will send you to them.' And he said to him, 'Here I am.' ¹⁴So he said to him, 'Go now, see if it is well with your brothers, and with the flock; and bring me word again.' So he sent him from the valley of Hebron, and he came to Shechem. ¹⁵And a man found him wandering in the fields; and the man asked him, 'What are you seeking?' ¹⁶'I am seeking my brothers,' he said, 'tell me, I pray you, where they are pasturing the flock.' ¹⁷And the man said, 'They have gone away, for I heard them say, "Let us go to Dothan."' So Joseph went after his brothers, and found them at

Dothan. ¹⁸*They saw him afar off, and before he came near to them they conspired against him to kill him.* ¹⁹*They said to one another, 'Here comes this dreamer.* ²⁰*Come now, let us kill him and throw him into one of the pits; then we shall say that a wild beast has devoured him, and we shall see what will become of his dreams.'* ²¹*But when Reuben heard it, he delivered him out of their hands, saying, 'Let us not take his life.'* ²²*And Reuben said to them, 'Shed no blood; cast him into this pit here in the wilderness, but lay no hand upon him'* — *that he might rescue him out of their hand, to restore him to his father.* ²³*So when Joseph came to his brothers, they stripped him of his robe, the long robe with sleeves that he wore;* ²⁴*and they took him and cast him into a pit. The pit was empty, there was no water in it.*

²⁵*Then they sat down to eat; and looking up they saw a caravan of Ishmaelites coming from Gilead, with their camels bearing gum, balm, and myrrh, on their way to carry it down to Egypt.* ²⁶*Then Judah said to his brothers, 'What profit is it if we slay our brother and conceal his blood?* ²⁷*Come, let us sell him to the Ishmaelites, and let not our hand be upon him, for he is our brother, our own flesh.' And his brothers heeded him.* ²⁸*Then Midianite traders passed by; and they drew Joseph up and lifted him out of the pit, and sold him to the Ishmaelites for twenty shekels of silver; and they took Joseph to Egypt.*

²⁹*When Reuben returned to the pit and saw that Joseph was not in the pit, he rent his clothes* ³⁰*and returned to his brothers and said, 'The lad is gone; and I, where shall I go?'* ³¹*Then they took Joseph's robe, and killed a goat, and dipped the robe in the blood;* ³²*and they sent the long robe with sleeves and brought it to their father, and said, 'This we have found; see now whether it is your son's robe or not.'* ³³*And he recognized it, and said, 'It is my son's robe; a wild beast has devoured him; Joseph is without doubt torn to pieces.'* ³⁴*Then Jacob rent his garments, and put sackcloth upon his loins, and mourned for his son many days.* ³⁵*All his sons and all his daughters rose up to comfort him; but he refused to be comforted, and said, 'No, I shall go down to Sheol to my son, mourning.' Thus his father wept for him.* ³⁶*Meanwhile the Midianites had sold him in Egypt to Potiphar, an officer of Pharaoh, the captain of the guard.*

It is remarkable how much of the Joseph narrative hinges on so ordinary a failing as a parent's favouritism. Jacob had seen the disasters wrought by parental favouritism in his own life and Esau's and yet, fool that he was, he openly made much of Joseph. Such a special relationship encourages tale-bearing, and Joseph was no better or wiser than other teenagers who note with dismay the unacceptable behaviour of older brothers. He reported it to his father (who had a right to know what was going on) and quite naturally incurred their hatred for putting them in their father's bad books. When, to add insult to injury, Jacob presented Joseph with a coat of many colours (AV), or a coat with long sleeves, which set him in a class apart and exempted him from the menial tasks of farming, the rest of the family were disgusted. It was an awkward situation in which Joseph became isolated and endangered by the hostility of his brothers, and yet it was not entirely of his making, and there was little he could do to put matters right. It is the kind of family background that can cause the youngster great pain and lead to a warped, inward-looking personality, full of fear and resentment. That it did not do so in Joseph's case is part of the charm of this story. His personality was remarkably resilient.

Now Joseph had a dream (5). This was no ordinary dream that could be dismissed as nonsense, but one that suggested that Joseph might even by favoured by providence, though our contemporaries would probably account for it by saying that it reflected self-centred ideas of greatness. Out in the harvest field Joseph's sheaf was central, while those of his brothers bowed down to it. When he dreamed that the sun, moon and eleven stars were bowing down to him, even his father resented the inference and rebuked him, though he *kept the saying in mind* (11), knowing that it could have been some divine pointer to the destiny of his son. So far as his brothers were concerned, however, the dreams only intensified their hatred and jealousy of him (verses 5, 8, 11).

The journey on which Joseph was sent by his father, in order to make sure that the news of his brothers and their flocks was good, endangered the life of Joseph. (Did Jacob suspect them of some underhand dealings?) From Hebron to Shechem was a journey of 50 miles (80 km), and to find his brothers in unfamiliar country would involve a wearying search in all directions. *Dothan* was another 15 miles (24 km) further on through hilly country. Incidentally, there is evidence that Dothan was a city in this period.[3] Thanks to the help he received from a stranger, Joseph found his brothers, and they ominously saw him coming. So far from home, the brothers think they can safely plan the dreamer's murder. The body could be disposed of easily in one of the cisterns used for collecting surface water during the winter rains (the subsequent pollution of

---

[3] 'Excavations at Tel Dothan have uncovered no evidence from MB I, but have revealed an urban centre of the MB II period', J. J. Bimson, *EOPN*, p. 79. He refers to J. P. Free, *BASOR* 152 (1958), pp. 14ff.

drinking-water was of no concern to them), and wild animals were always a danger (*cf.* 1 Sa. 17:36). An unexplained death could always be put down to their activity. The ultimate attraction was to thwart Joseph's dreams of supremacy and to remove this mischief-maker from their midst. Reuben, the eldest, who was ultimately responsible, intervened with a counter-suggestion. If they threw Joseph alive into the cistern they would not be guilty of shedding blood, and the end result would be the same, except that Reuben secretly planned Joseph's rescue. In this way Joseph was saved from an immediate death, and found himself in the dried-out cistern near the trade route that ran through the valley of Jezreel close to Dothan.

When some Ishmaelite traders came along, Judah, another of the older brothers, had a brilliant idea. Why kill their brother when they could sell him, and so avoid the extreme expedient of murdering their own kith and kin? Moreover Joseph's appeals for mercy had some effect (42:21), and within a short time he was being sold to the travelling merchants, now referred to as *Midianites*.[4] Joseph was being subjected to a terrifying experience, especially as he was being removed from the land where the Lord was working out his covenant, and from his father, on whom the promises had been conferred. Joseph's prospects were bleak indeed. The twenty pieces of silver, named as the price of a slave between the ages of five and twenty (Lv. 27:5), was evidently the currently accepted price for an adult male in the early second millennium.[5] Though he could not know it, Joseph was going through an experience which was to become a major theme of the Bible. The godly Servant was despised and rejected, only to become the rescuer of those who abused him (Is. 53:3–6); the Lord's shepherd was underrated (Zc. 11:12–13), was struck down and his sheep scattered, but the 'sheep' found they were the Lord's people (Zc. 13:7–9); the way of the cross involved for Jesus betrayal by a friend, as well as agony and death, but it was the way to life for all believers.

In the mean time Reuben, who may have been taking his turn to guard the flock and therefore had missed the latest episode, had

---

[4] Three names occur in this story: Ishmaelites, Midianites and (in the Hebrew text) Medanites (see RV mg., NIV mg.). All three groups derive from Abraham (Gn. 25:2, 12) and occupy the desert to the east and south of the Dead Sea, beyond that of Moab and Edom. The terms to some extent overlap (*cf.* Jdg. 8:24), though at the time of writing each no doubt had a distinctive feature.

[5] K. A. Kitchen, art. 'Slave, Slavery', *IBD*, 3, p. 1462. By the 15th century BC the price was to rise to 30 shekels, and in the first millennium went up to between 50 and 120 shekels.

returned to the well to lift out Joseph. With dismay he presumed him dead, and went grief-stricken and guilty to those responsible, who were using goat's blood to deceive their father into thinking that Joseph had been attacked by a beast and his distinctive robe stained with his blood. The ruse was successful, and Jacob once again was tricked as he himself had tricked his father many years before with goat meat (27:9). Nor was this cruel hoax soon forgotten. During a long period of mourning the sons and their wives (Jacob's 'daughters', 35) kept up a pretence of mourning with their father, as was expected of them. It would be unlikely to ring true so far as the sons were concerned, and their consciences must have troubled them. Little wonder that they tried to comfort their father and encourage him to forget Joseph, for whom he continued to mourn and weep, so unwittingly embarrassing them.

Mention of Joseph's arrival in Egypt and of his slave status in the house of a distinguished Egyptian sets the scene for a later episode, which will take up his story. But first something must be said of one of the other brothers, Judah.

Genesis 38:1–30

Judah's marriage and family

It happened at that time that Judah went down from his brothers, and turned in to a certain Adullamite, whose name was Hirah. ²There Judah saw the daughter of a certain Canaanite whose name was Shua; he married her and went in to her, ³and she conceived and bore a son, and he called his name Er. ⁴Again she conceived and bore a son, and she called his name Onan. ⁵Yet again she bore a son, and she called his name Shelah. She was in Chezib when she bore him. ⁶And Judah took a wife for Er his first-born, and her name was Tamar. ⁷But Er, Judah's first-born, was wicked in the sight of the Lord; and the Lord slew him. ⁸Then Judah said to Onan, 'Go in to your brother's wife, and preform the duty of a brother-in-law to her, and raise up offspring for your brother.' ⁹But Onan knew that the offspring would not be his; so when he went in to his brother's wife he spilled the semen on the ground, lest he should give offspring to his brother. ¹⁰And what he did was displeasing in the sight of the Lord, and he slew him also. ¹¹Then Judah said to Tamar his daughter-in-law, 'Remain a widow in your father's house, till Shelah my son grows up' — for he feared that he would die, like his brothers. So Tamar went and dwelt in her father's house. ¹²In course of time the wife of Judah, Shua's daughter, died; and when

Judah was comforted, he went up to Timnah to his sheepshearers, he and his friend Hirah the Adullamite. ¹³*And when Tamar was told, 'Your father-in-law is going up to Timnah to shear his sheep,'* ¹⁴*she put off her widow's garments, and put on a veil, wrapping herself up, and sat at the entrance to Enaim, which is on the road to Timnah; for she saw that Shelah was grown up, and she had not been given to him in marriage.* ¹⁵*When Judah saw her, he thought her to be a harlot, for she had covered her face.* ¹⁶*He went over to her at the road side, and said, 'Come, let me come in to you,' for he did not know that she was his daughter-in-law. She said, 'What will you give me, that you may come in to me?'* ¹⁷*He answered, 'I will send you a kid from the flock.' And she said, 'Will you give me a pledge, till you send it?'* ¹⁸*He said, 'What pledge shall I give you?' She replied, 'Your signet and your cord, and your staff that is in your hand.' So he gave them to her, and went in to her, and she conceived by him.* ¹⁹*Then she arose and went away, and taking off her veil she put on the garments of her widowhood.*

²⁰*When Judah sent the kid by his friend the Adullamite, to receive the pledge from the woman's hand, he could not find her.* ²¹*And he asked the men of the place, 'Where is the harlot who was at Enaim by the wayside?' And they said, 'No harlot has been here.'* ²²*So he returned to Judah, and said, 'I have not found her; and also the men of the place said, "No harlot has been here."'* ²³*And Judah replied, 'Let her keep the things as her own, lest we be laughed at; you see, I sent this kid, and you could not find her.'*

²⁴*About three months later Judah was told, 'Tamar your daughter-in-law has played the harlot; and moreover she is with child by harlotry.' And Judah said, 'Bring her out, and let her be burned.'* ²⁵*As she was being brought out, she sent word to her father-in-law, 'By the man to whom these belong, I am with child.' And she said, 'Mark, I pray you, whose these are, the signet and the cord and the staff.'* ²⁶*Then Judah acknowledged them and said, 'She is more righteous than I, inasmuch as I did not give her to my son Shelah.' And he did not lie with her again.*

²⁷*When the time of her delivery came, there were twins in her womb.* ²⁸*And when she was in labour, one put out a hand; and the midwife took and bound on his hand a scarlet thread, saying, 'This came out first.'* ²⁹*But as he drew back his hand, behold, his brother came out; and she said, 'What a breach you have made for yourself!' Therefore his name was called Perez.* ³⁰*Afterward his brother came out with the scarlet thread upon his hand; and his name was called Zerah.*

The intrusion of this story into the Joseph narrative gives the incident particular prominence. While the reader is in suspense to know how Joseph fared in Egypt, he is forced to attend to this review of Judah's private life, a review which was destined to become public property for centuries to come. Judah is, of course, to reappear in the Joseph narrative, where he has a sensitivity and self-forgetfulness, the very opposite of which dominate in this story. It may be that his public humiliation following the Tamar scandal genuinely humbled him and transformed him into the kindly man who was concerned for his aged father and young brother. 'The principle of divine election makes few concessions to greatness or even merit (*cf.* Deut. 7:6ff.). ... Nevertheless the motif of the readiness of God to forgive and continue with his people is thus introduced.'[6] This truth should give new heart to every defeated Christian.

Though Judah was the fourth son of Jacob, he began to take precedence after his older brothers had disqualified themselves for leadership. Reuben had taken his father's concubine (35:22), and Simeon and Levi had attacked the Shechemites (chapter 34). Judah therefore began to come to the fore and his lineage assumed a special interest, but, like Abraham and Isaac before him, he was in danger of having no son to succeed him.

It all began when Judah broke away from his brothers in order to reside with a Canaanite family, that of Hirah of Adullam, best known for the cave in which at a later period David was to take refuge (1 Sa. 22:1–2). It was south-west of Jerusalem in the Judean foothills. There Judah married a Canaanite wife, whose name is never given, but who bore him three sons, Er, Onan and Shelah. The note that *she was in Chezib* (or Achzib, a nearby village) *when she bore him* [Shelah] (5) is apparently inconsequential, but the name is related to the Hebrew verb meaning 'to tell a lie', and so, when Jacob proved to be deceitful regarding his son (14), did the wiseacres recall that he was born at Chezib? What could you expect?

Disaster began to strike when Judah chose, as a wife for Er, Tamar, whose name, meaning 'date-palm', suggested that she had a lovely figure (*cf.* Song 7:7). Her husband's early death was accounted for by his wicked ways and attributed to divine judgment. Tamar, left childless, was not devoid of all hope for the future, even so. A widespread custom, known as levirate marriage, operated on the assumption that the family as a whole was responsible to ensure the continuity of the line of the dead relative. If he had a brother it

[6] J.G. McConville, *Chronicles* in *The Daily Study Bible* (St. Andrew Press, 1984), pp. 9–10, in a comment on the genealogy of Judah (1 Ch. 2:3 – 4:23).

would fall to him to take the bereaved wife, and any children of the union would become the heirs of the dead man. In the book of Ruth the same principle of family responsibility is seen operating when the young widow, Ruth, is sent to a near relative of her late husband to ask for marriage.[7] In Tamar's case her father-in-law, Judah, ordered his second son, Onan, to perform his duty as a brother-in-law. It is not clear whether Onan was already married, but he was determined not to perpetuate his brother's family. Such animosity against the dead man, and such lack of concern for his posterity, was considered inexcusable, so when he died within a short time there was no doubt in the mind of the writer that the Lord *slew him also* (10).

Judah, however, took a superstitious view of events, and contrived to rid himself of this ill-omened woman, to whom he attributed the death of his sons. Though he implied that he would give her to his third son, Shelah, when he was old enough, the fact that he sent her back to her father's house indicated his true intention. He feared for the safety of Shelah, and found him another wife (14).

Tamar's daring escapade

Time passed, during which Judah's wife died, and Tamar, virtually forgotten in her parental home, determined to take matters into her own hands. Sheep-shearing was a traditional excuse for merry-making (*cf.* 1 Sa. 25:4 and the appeal of David for a small share of the abundant supply of food). News reached her that Judah, with his friend Hirah of Adullam, was going to the sheep-shearing festivities at Timnah, so she resolved to get there first.

Such was Judah's reputation that Tamar was confident that she could get the better of him by posing as a prostitute.[8] It was

Ru. 3:9. Boaz is not free to assume responsibility for Ruth until the nearest relative has declined to do so. Community law laid down the rights and obligations involved in levirate marriage, a term coined from the Latin *levir*, meaning 'brother-in-law'.

[8] Two Hebrew words are used in this passage. Judah took the woman at the road side to be a common prostitute, *zōnā*, whereas Hiram and the men of Timnah talked about a cult prostitute, *q'dēšâ*. The latter would be attached to a shrine associated with the local religion, which was considered to be essential to the fertility of the fields and livestock. Men and women served at these shrines, giving their bodies for ritual purposes to worshippers, in order to encourage the gods and goddesses to sexual activity, which was supposed to ensure fertility and growth in the homes and farms of humans. The pernicious influence of this cult was a constant threat to Israel's life and witness, hence its frequent condemnation by the prophets (*e.g.* Je. 2:20ff.; 3:1ff.; Ezk. 23:37–45; Ho. 2:2–5).

evidently the custom for prostitutes to wrap themselves in a large shawl, and in the process to cover their faces. This loss of identity suited Tamar well, as she sat at the entrance to the village of Enaim, which was on Judah's route. She had judged right that he would approach her. As her side of the bargain Tamar arranged that she should receive a kid, and as a pledge that this would be forthcoming she contrived to take Judah's personal seal, worn on a cord round his neck, and his staff, which would be equally distinctive. When Hiram returned with Judah's kid to fulfil his obligation, no prostitute was known in the place. The indication is that Canaanite cult-prostitution was not common in all the villages, and that Tamar had not long been there when Judah arrived. Rather than make himself a laughing-stock Judah let the matter drop.

When news reached Judah that Tamar was pregnant as a result of prostitution he reacted with righteous indignation. Since she was still under his jurisdiction he ordered her to be brought out and burnt. Thereupon she brought out her trump card: Judah was obliged to acknowledge as his the tokens she sent him, and he admitted that he had deceived her over his son Shelah. The guilt was first and foremost his own. It was a costly and humiliating confession, and an implicit warning against casual liaisons that bring disgrace (Pr. 6:33). Though all this happened before the law of Moses was given, the world of the patriarchs was permeated by standards of right and wrong, recognizably the same as those which the law was to encapsulate. By consorting with Canaanites Judah had opted for a less demanding way of life than that of his fathers, but his conscience, dulled though it may have been, still condemned his wayward self-seeking.

Judah, like his grandfather Isaac, became the father of twins. History repeated itself also in that there was some uncertainty over which of the two was the elder. The hand that first appeared and was marked by the scarlet thread did not belong to the child that was first-born; he was considered to have broken through 'out of turn', hence his name *Perez*, meaning 'breach'.[9] It was he who was to appear in the key genealogies that led to David and so to the Christ (Ru. 4:18; Mt. 1:3; Lk. 3:33). In the providence of God the lineage

---

[9] 'There is in Genesis ... an account of the birth of locked twins with in one case a transverse presentation. Tamar, the mother, was fortunate to have survived. The midwife must have been a woman of skill and resource to diagnose correctly such a rare and difficult condition, and to bring her patient through successfully.' A. Rendle Short, *The Bible and Modern Medicine* (Paternoster Press, 1955), p. 35.

of Judah fulfilled God's purpose, which had of necessity to bear with human sinfulness in order to redeem it. That God saves by grace and not by merit needs to be writ large so that all may read and understand.

Genesis 39:1–23

Joseph, blessed of the Lord

Now Joseph was taken down to Egypt, and Potiphar, an officer of Pharaoh, the captain of the guard, an Egyptian, bought him from the Ishmaelites who had brought him down there. [2]The Lord was with Joseph, and he became a successful man; and he was in the house of his master the Egyptian, [3]and his master saw that the Lord was with him, and that the Lord caused all that he did to prosper in his hands. [4]So Joseph found favour in his sight and attended him, and he made him overseer of his house and put him in charge of all that he had. [5]From the time that he made him overseer in his house and over all that he had the Lord blessed the Egyptian's house for Joseph's sake; the blessing of the Lord was upon all that he had, in house and field. [6]So he left all that he had in Joseph's charge; and having him he had no concern for anything but the food which he ate.

Now Joseph was handsome and good-looking. [7]And after a time his master's wife cast her eyes upon Joseph, and said, 'Lie with me.' [8]But he refused and said to his master's wife, 'Lo, having me my master has no concern about anything in the house, and he has put everything that he has in my hand; [9]he is not greater in this house than I am; nor has he kept back anything from me except yourself, because you are his wife; how then can I do this great wickedness, and sin against God?' [10]And although she spoke to Joseph day after day, he would not listen to her, to lie with her or to be with her. [11]But one day, when he went into the house to do his work and none of the men of the house was there in the house, [12]she caught him by his garment, saying, 'Lie with me.' But he left his garment in her hand, and fled and got out of the house. [13]And when she saw that he had left his garment in her hand, and had fled out of the house, [14]she called to the men of her household and said to them, 'See, he has brought among us a Hebrew to insult us; he came in to me to lie with me, and I cried out with a loud voice; [15]and when he heard that I lifted up my voice and cried, he left his garment with me, and fled and got out of the house.' [16]Then she laid up his garment by her until his master came home, [17]and she told him the same story, saying, 'The Hebrew servant, whom you have brought among us, came in to me to insult me; [18]but as soon as I lifted up my voice and cried, he left his garment with

me, and fled out of the house.'
 ¹⁹*When his master heard the words which his wife spoke to him, 'This is the way your servant treated me,' his anger was kindled.* ²⁰*And Joseph's master took him and put him into the prison, the place where the king's prisoners were confined, and he was there in prison.* ²¹*But the Lord was with Joseph and showed him steadfast love, and gave him favour in the sight of the keeper of the prison.* ²²*And the keeper of the prison committed to Joseph's care all the prisoners who were in the prison; and whatever was done there, he was the doer of it;* ²³*the keeper of the prison paid no heed to anything that was in Joseph's care, because the Lord was with him; and whatever he did, the Lord made it prosper.*

'The Lord bless you and keep you' (Nu. 6:24) is a pronouncement often used in our Sunday worship. This chapter gives substance to the verb 'bless' by showing how God's blessing worked out in the life of Joseph. After the interlude in which Judah's way of life was sampled (chapter 38), the contrast in Joseph's conduct is all the more striking. *The Lord was with Joseph* becomes almost a refrain (verses 2, 3, 21, 23), together with the words 'successful' and 'prosper', which translate the same Hebrew word. Nevertheless the blessing did not enable him to avoid trouble and testing. Yet the injustice he suffered played its part in preparing him for the position of leadership he was to fill later in life.

To begin with all went well. Joseph's work in Potiphar's house was appreciated by his master, and he was given more and more responsibility. God's blessing upon Joseph brought blessing in terms of material prosperity to those with whom he served, as well as favour upon himself. Not surprisingly Joseph was made estate manager, and Potiphar left all the business to him. The fact is reiterated that *the Lord blessed the Egyptian's house for Joseph's sake* (5), so illustrating the way in which blessing overflows to others, and makes them 'rich' (Pr. 10:22), in this case literally.

Subsequent events which resulted in Joseph's imprisonment are not so easily seen in terms of blessing. Despite Joseph's refusal to co-operate with the adulterous intentions of Potiphar's wife, and his deliberate policy of keeping out of her way to avoid *this great wickedness* and sinning *against God* (9), he nevertheless became implicated. The injustice of her accusation, made to clear herself at Joseph's expense, was something a slave simply had to accept. It would be surprising if no-one else suspected the true situation (perhaps that is why he did not receive the death penalty), but

Joseph had no rights and no court of appeal. Even if Potiphar had misgivings in punishing Joseph and so depriving himself of a dependable steward, he could hardly risk disregarding his wife's accusation. Understandably he was angry. Joseph therefore was summarily dismissed and sent to prison. Not, however, to the common prison, but to the place where the king's prisoners were held. He was, therefore, in a special category, and it was by contact with servants of the Pharaoh that Joseph was eventually to come to the notice of the king. But at the time there was little cause for hope; only isolation and loneliness.

Despite the injustice of his imprisonment Joseph evidently did not sulk or complain, but did his best to be helpful. *The Lord was with Joseph* in the prison as he had been in Potiphar's house, showing him *steadfast love* and giving him *favour in the sight of the keeper of the prison* (21). For the second time Joseph became the victim of other people's spite, but he was learning to submit without resentment and to rejoice in the Lord's faithfulness to his word to his great-grandfather Abraham, when he specifically pronounced the promise of the birth of a son (17:19). Though Joseph had displeased his human master, the Lord God was well pleased with him and caused him to prosper. He was not, after all, alone.

Genesis 40:1–23

Two significant dreams

Some time after this, the butler of the king of Egypt and his baker offended their lord the king of Egypt. ²And Pharaoh was angry with his two officers, the chief butler and the chief baker, ³and he put them in custody in the house of the captain of the guard, in the prison where Joseph was confined. ⁴The captain of the guard charged Joseph with them, and he waited on them; and they continued for some time in custody. ⁵And one night they both dreamed — the butler and the baker of the king of Egypt, who were confined in the prison — each his own dream, and each dream with its own meaning. ⁶When Joseph came to them in the morning and saw them, they were troubled. ⁷So he asked Pharaoh's officers who were with him in custody in his master's house, 'Why are your faces downcast today?' ⁸They said to him, 'We have had dreams, and there is no one to interpret them.' And Joseph said to them, 'Do not interpretations belong to God? Tell them to me, I pray you.'

⁹So the chief butler told his dream to Joseph, and said to him, 'In my dream there was a vine before me, ¹⁰and on the vine there were three branches: as soon as it budded, its blossoms shot forth, and the clusters ripened into grapes. ¹¹Pharaoh's cup was in my hand; and I took the grapes and pressed them into Pharaoh's cup, and placed the cup in Pharaoh's hand.' ¹²Then Joseph said to him, 'This is its interpretation: the three branches are three days; ¹³within three days Pharaoh will lift up your head and restore you to your office; and you shall place Pharaoh's cup in his hand as formerly, when you were his butler. ¹⁴But remember me, when it is well with you, and do me the kindness, I pray you, to make mention of me to Pharaoh, and so get me out of this house. ¹⁵For I was indeed stolen out of the land of the Hebrews; and here also I have done nothing that they should put me into the dungeon.'

¹⁶When the chief baker saw that the interpretation was favourable, he said to Joseph, 'I also had a dream: there were three cake baskets on my head, ¹⁷and in the uppermost basket there were all sorts of baked food for Pharaoh, but the birds were eating it out of the basket on my head.' ¹⁸And Joseph answered, 'This is its interpretation: the three baskets are three days; ¹⁹within three days Pharaoh will lift up your head — from you! — and hang you on a tree; and the birds will eat the flesh from you.'

²⁰On the third day, which was Pharaoh's birthday, he made a feast for all his servants, and lifted up the head of the chief butler and the head of the chief baker among his servants. ²¹He restored the chief butler to his butlership, and he placed the cup in Pharaoh's hand; ²²but he hanged the chief baker, as Joseph had interpreted to them. ²³Yet the chief butler did not remember Joseph, but forgot him.

Other slaves besides Joseph experienced summary imprisonment without trial. While Joseph was assisting the prison governor with custody of other prisoners, two responsible men from the royal household were admitted: the butler, who served the king's wine, and the baker, who made his bread. If the king was unwell, either could have been accused of attempting to poison him, and since no sentence decreed how long their imprisonment was to last they had to await the king's pleasure, and hope that he would not forget them altogether.

One morning when they both awoke from vivid dreams, they were afraid that these were portents of their future destiny, *each dream with its own meaning* (5). But in prison they had no possibility of consulting the expert interpreters of dreams, who were part of Egyptian culture as they were of other cultures of the ancient Near East. Where there is no knowledge of God great importance becomes attached to portents of all kinds, and so, when God had

169

some message to disclose, he sometimes spoke by dreams, both to his covenant people and to others: Abimelech (Gn. 20:6–7), the Pharaoh (Gn. 41:1–8) and Nebuchadrezzar (Dn. 2:1ff.) on the one hand, Joseph (Gn. 37:5–11), Solomon (1 Ki. 3:5–9) and Joseph, husband of Mary (Mt. 1:20; 2:19), among his own people on the other hand. One of the ways in which God spoke to the prophets was by dreams (Dt. 13:1), and Joseph was already assured that dreams and their interpretation were from God, perhaps on the basis of his own experience, but more probably on the basis of his understanding of God. He attributed to God all authority and might: *Do not interpretations belong to God?* (8). This he believed to be the case even when those who had dreamed were Egyptians, who worshipped other gods. These gods could be disregarded for all practical purposes!

Christians brought up in the materialistic atmosphere of western society have long tended to be sceptical about messages through dreams, which they have been taught to regard as glimpses of their own subconscious minds. Fellow Christians in Asia and Africa, whose education and upbringing have been in a different mould, more often testify to having received warning and guidance through dreams. Recently there have been groups of Christians in western Christendom also who set great store by dreams, and the Old Testament generally accepts that a dream may become the means by which God speaks to men and women. The prophet sometimes received his revelation through a dream, but it was possible for impostors to make the claim that they had a word from the Lord through a dream, so their claims needed to be tested: first, against the broad truths taught in Scripture (Dt. 13:1–5), and secondly by the moral influence they brought to bear (Je. 23:16–17). Proverbial wisdom warned against the person who was always having 'dreams': 'For in a multitude of dreams there is futility' (Ec. 5:7, RSV mg.). It is a test which, like the other two, is applicable today.

The butler's dream, obviously appropriate, was of a prosperous vine with three branches shooting forth buds and simultaneously producing grapes, which the butler squeezed into Pharaoh's cup. The message was reassuring. Within three days the butler would be back at court serving the Pharaoh, with the opportunity to do Joseph a good turn by mentioning him to the Pharaoh, and pleading his just cause. Joseph blames no-one, but declares he has been *stolen out of the land of the Hebrews* (15) and is innocent of any crime.[10] No doubt Joseph thought that his own prayers for his release were about to be answered through this opportunity of interpreting a dream. Ultimately he was right, but he had to wait a little longer yet before God's time came for the redress of his twofold wrongs, to which the butler added a third. He forgot him.

The chief baker, by contrast, dreamed of birds eating the cakes from the three baskets on his head, and the sinister meaning was that within three days he would be hanged and his body left to become food for the birds of prey. The fact that the birthday decrees of the king coincided with the interpretation of Joseph confirmed his confidence in God as the interpreter of dreams, but his strangely long wait for the answer to his prayers was a severe test of patience and faith. It was as if he alone had been abandoned by God. But experiences like this were often part of the training of those whom God was going to use in outstanding roles. Abraham and Sarah had to wait until old age for the birth of Isaac; Moses was exiled for much of his life in an inhospitable desert; David lived under threat of death at the hand of Saul, and was on the run for months, if not years. Yet in every case the purpose of God was being worked out and in due course came to fruition. Indeed it has been said that only those with faith in God experience his testing, which after all is self-evident, for it is designed to put steel into faith so that it becomes steadfast and mature (Jas 1:2–4), and can testify to the tender love of the Lord in designing the suffering. This was to be outstandingly true of Joseph, who was fully aware of his brothers' hatred but who saw that God had meant it for good (50: 20). That is the kind of conviction that results from patient, enduring trust in the loving intentions of God, when outward circumstances seem to belie that love.

Genesis 41:1–57

The king's dream

After two whole years, Pharaoh dreamed that he was standing by the Nile, [2]and behold, there came up out of the Nile seven cows sleek and fat, and they fed in the reed grass. [3]And behold, seven other cows, gaunt and thin, came

[10]*The land of the Hebrews* is an unusual way of referring to Canaan. The word 'Hebrew' has a derogatory overtone in 39:14, 17; the word has sometimes been equated with *Habiru*, landless peasants who are mentioned in numerous texts of the second millennium BC, but this expression would give the lie to that identification. What can be said is that in the early Old Testament period the word *Hebrew* is used in contacts with non-Israelites, and seems to have a wider connotation than the family of Abraham.

up out of the Nile after them, and stood by the other cows on the bank of the Nile. ⁴And the gaunt and thin cows ate up the seven sleek and fat cows. And Pharaoh awoke. ⁵And he fell asleep and dreamed a second time; and behold, seven ears of grain, plump and good, were growing on one stalk. ⁶And behold, after them sprouted seven ears, thin and blighted by the east wind. ⁷And the thin ears swallowed up the seven plump and full ears. And Pharaoh awoke, and behold, it was a dream. ⁸So in the morning his spirit was troubled; and he sent and called for all the magicians of Egypt and all its wise men; and Pharaoh told them his dream, but there was none who could interpret it to Pharaoh.

⁹Then the chief butler said to Pharaoh, 'I remember my faults today. ¹⁰When Pharaoh was angry with his servants, and put me and the chief baker in custody in the house of the captain of the guard, ¹¹we dreamed on the same night, he and I, each having a dream with its own meaning. ¹²A young Hebrew was there with us, a servant of the captain of the guard; and when we told him, he interpreted our dreams to us, giving an interpretation to each man according to his dream. ¹³And as he interpretated to us, so it came to pass; I was restored to my office, and the baker was hanged.'

¹⁴Then Pharaoh sent and called Joseph, and they brought him hastily out of the dungeon; and when he had shaved himself and changed his clothes, he came in before Pharaoh. ¹⁵And Pharaoh said to Joseph, 'I have had a dream, and there is no one who can interpret it; and I have heard it said of you that when you hear a dream you can interpret it.' ¹⁶Joseph answered Pharaoh, 'It is not in me; God will give Pharaoh a favourable answer.' ¹⁷Then Pharaoh said to Joseph, 'Behold, in my dream I was standing on the banks of the Nile; ¹⁸and seven cows, fat and sleek, came up out of the Nile and fed in the reed grass; ¹⁹and seven other cows came up after them, poor and very gaunt and thin, such as I had never seen in all the land of Egypt. ²⁰And the thin and gaunt cows ate up the first seven fat cows, ²¹but when they had eaten them no one would have known that they had eaten them, for they were still as gaunt as at the beginning. Then I awoke. ²²I also saw in my dream seven ears growing on one stalk, full and good; ²³and seven ears, withered, thin, and blighted by the east wind, sprouted after them, ²⁴and the thin ears swallowed up the seven good ears. And I told it to the magicians, but there was no one who could explain it to me.'

²⁵Then Joseph said to Pharaoh, 'The dream of Pharaoh is one; God has revealed to Pharaoh what he is about to do. ²⁶The seven good cows are seven years, and the seven good ears are seven years; the dream is one. ²⁷The seven lean and gaunt cows that came up after them are seven years, and the seven empty ears blighted by the east wind are also seven years of famine. ²⁸It is as I told Pharaoh, God has shown to Pharaoh what he is about to do. ²⁹There

will come seven years of great plenty throughout all the land of Egypt, [30]but after them there will arise seven years of famine, and all the plenty will be forgotten in the land of Egypt; the famine will consume the land, [31]and the plenty will be unknown in the land by reason of that famine which will follow, for it will be very grievous. [32]And the doubling of Pharaoh's dream means that the thing is fixed by God, and God will shortly bring it to pass. [33]Now therefore let Pharaoh select a man discreet and wise, and set him over the land of Egypt. [34]Let Pharaoh proceed to appoint overseers over the land, and take the fifth part of the produce of the land of Egypt during the seven plenteous years. [35]And let them gather all the food of these good years that are coming, and lay up grain under the authority of Pharaoh for food in the cities, and let them keep it. [36]That food shall be a reserve for the land against the seven years of famine which are to befall the land of Egypt, so that the land may not perish through the famine.'

[37]This proposal seemed good to Pharaoh and to all his servants. [38]And Pharaoh said to his servants, 'Can we find such a man as this, in whom is the Spirit of God?' [39]So Pharaoh said to Joseph, 'Since God has shown you all this, there is none so discreet and wise as you are; [40]you shall be over my house, and all my people shall order themselves as you command; only as regards the throne will I be greater than you.' [41]And Pharaoh said to Joseph, 'Behold, I have set you over all the land of Egypt.' [42]Then Pharaoh took his signet ring from his hand and put it on Joseph's hand, and arrayed him in garments of fine linen, and put a gold chain about his neck; [43]and he made him to ride in his second chariot; and they cried before him, 'Bow the knee!' Thus he set him over all the land of Egypt. [44]Moreover Pharaoh said to Joseph, 'I am Pharaoh, and without your consent no man shall lift up hand or foot in all the land of Egypt.' [45]And Pharaoh called Joseph's name Zaphenath-paneah; and he gave him in marriage Asenath, the daughter of Potiphera priest of On. So Joseph went out over the land of Egypt.

[46]Joseph was thirty years old when he entered the service of Pharaoh king of Egypt. And Joseph went out from the presence of Pharaoh, and went through all the land of Egypt. [47]During the seven plenteous years the earth brought forth abundantly, [48]and he gathered up all the food of the seven years when there was plenty in the land of Egypt, and stored up food in the cities; he stored up in every city the food from the fields around it. [49]And Joseph stored up grain in great abundance, like the sand of the sea, until he ceased to measure it, for it could not be measured.

[50]Before the year of famine came, Joseph had two sons, whom Asenath, the daughter of Potiphera priest of On, bore to him. [51]Joseph called the name of the first-born Manasseh, 'For,' he said, 'God has made me forget all my hardship and all my father's house.' [52]The name of the second he called

Ephraim, 'For God has made me fruitful in the land of my affliction.'

⁵³The seven years of plenty that prevailed in the land of Egypt came to an end; ⁵⁴and the seven years of famine began to come, as Joseph had said. There was famine in all lands; but in all the land of Egypt there was bread. ⁵⁵When all the land of Egypt was famished, the people cried to Pharaoh for bread; and Pharaoh said to all the Egyptians, 'Go to Joseph; what he says to you, do.' ⁵⁶So when the famine had spread over all the land, Joseph opened all the storehouses, and sold to the Egyptians, for the famine was severe in the land of Egypt. ⁵⁷Moreover, all the earth came to Egypt to Joseph to buy grain, because the famine was severe over all the earth.

All unbeknown to Joseph, the time for his release from prison had come. The king had two dreams in the same night which had much in common and which appeared to belong together, the repetition reinforcing the importance of their meaning. When he put the dreams to the wise men of Egypt they could not give their interpretation, because these were not usual dreams that arise out of the human subconscious, and therefore they did not have any mention in the dream manuals. When the Lord spoke by dreams neither Egypt nor Babylon had any precedent (Dn. 2:10; 4:7); only the man of God, a Joseph or a Daniel, could give the meaning.

The king's need of an interpreter of dreams suddenly reminded the chief butler of Joseph, who had accurately explained the dreams of the baker and himself in prison. The Pharaoh was sure this was the man he needed, and he lost no time in sending for him. Joseph's rapid transformation from prisoner to king's adviser required not only a change of clothes but also a shave, because the Egyptians were clean-shaven, and the beard was therefore foreign and unwelcome.[11] Once in the presence of the king Joseph was quick to insist that, whereas he had no special powers of interpretation, God would *give Pharaoh a favourable answer.* Thus he nailed his colours to the mast from the beginning and staked everything on God's ability to give him the message he needed. Whatever the outcome, he had made his position clear and would not be in danger of compromise.

The Pharaoh had dreamed he was beside the Nile and saw seven fat cows leave the water for *the reed grass* or papyrus, which once grew in Egypt but is now prolific only in the upper reaches of the river.

[11] 'In Egypt, white linen dress and clean-shaven face are customary in the tomb- and temple-scenes and are presupposed in Genesis 41:14, 42; while in Western Asia the Semitic and other peoples appreciated fine beards and often multi-coloured garments.' K.A. Kitchen, *AOOT*, p. 167.

Seven starved cows followed and ate the fat ones, but put on no weight. This last detail had not been mentioned in verse 4, but the variation sustains interest. The second dream also featured the number seven. Seven full ears of corn on one stem were followed by seven poor ears, *blighted by the east wind*, that is, the desert wind known in north Africa as the *ḥamsin*; the thin ears then devoured the fat ears.

Once Joseph's interpretation is known it seems incredible that the Pharaoh did not see it for himself, so clear and fitting is the meaning. The word of God, however it is given, is meant to be understood and acted upon. God never speaks without authenticating his word, or giving someone to explain it. Once the Pharaoh heard Joseph's explanation, he accepted it without question: *God has revealed to Pharaoh what he is about to do* (25). Seven years of plentiful harvests will be followed by seven years when extreme famine conditions will prevail. This is not presented as a judgment for wrongdoing, but rather as 'an act of God', predetermined (32) and now announced in advance so that the kingdom of Egypt can take necessary steps to provide for the famine years. An organizer should be appointed to be responsible to the king; overseers should enforce a 20% tax during the good years, this grain to be stored and protected until it was needed. It was a simple but effective plan, if it could be carried out conscientiously in every district of the land, and if distribution was on an equal basis, free from the distortions caused by bribery and élitism. Once there is a shortage the temptation to favour the influential becomes powerful; hence Joseph's advice that *a man discreet and wise* be selected. Under such a leader Egypt will survive the famine.

Joseph's advice commended itself for its sheer good sense, and the king decided on the spot that he would never find anyone better to take the new appointment than the one who had proposed it, *in whom is the Spirit of God* (38). The king takes up the confession of Joseph that God would speak through him, and accepts it as the truth. As for Joseph, his faith in God has been publicly vindicated. The Egyptian court acknowledges the supremacy of God (*Elohim*) and his direction of the course of history, implicit in the advance announcement of the coming famine. God's man must direct conservation of crops, and since, in order to fulfil this task, he needs authority, the Pharaoh sets Joseph over the royal estate (the word translated *house* (40) should have this meaning) and *over all the land of Egypt* (41). He is second only to the king, and he wears the king's

175

signet ring, with which to 'sign' documents, and over his linen robes a gold chain of office. In his proclamation procession he was in the chariot behind the Pharaoh; the very use of chariots would have had prestige value at that early date,[12] and the population of the capital was made to acknowledge his rank. The meaning of the word *Abrek* (RSV mg.), translated *Bow the knee!* (43), has been a problem since antiquity, but an old suggestion that it means 'grand vizier' has recently been argued afresh.[13] By royal decree Joseph had executive authority throughout the land. His Egyptian name *Zaphenath-paneah* was necessary to give him acceptance as an Egyptian, and his marriage to the daughter of *Potiphera, priest of On* (later called Heliopolis, the city at the southern tip of the Nile delta), would give him added support in the hierarchy at court.

Soon Joseph's responsibilities took him the length and breadth of the land (45–46). At thirty years of age he was old enough to win respect, and adaptable enough to adjust to high office, with all its demands, conflicts and temptations. Having been in custody for years he would have extra zest for a demanding and worth-while job, commensurate with his gifts, and, more reassuring still, he had the consciousness that the Lord was in these extraordinary developments, though what they were to lead to he could not yet have known. His policy of storing grain from the fields in the nearest city ensured fair distribution and access to food for the whole population from the overflowing granaries.

The birth of Joseph's two sons during the prosperous years (50–52) helped to establish his identity as an Egyptian citizen. Though his father-in-law was a priest of the sun god Ra (this at least is suggested by the last syllable of his name), Joseph made no concessions when he named his first-born son with a Hebrew name, *Manasseh*, 'made to forget'; the name summed up Joseph's attitude to all the hurt he had had to suffer in the recent past. *'God has made me forget all my hardship and all my father's house'* showed a healthy refusal to allow memories of injustice to fester; any temptation to do so was countered by deliberate gratitude for God's deliverance. Now that he had a wife and baby son home would be in Egypt, and he would cease to hanker after those he had left behind in Canaan. It

---

[12] 'The true chariot ... did not appear until the 2nd millennium. It is probable that the horse was introduced by the peoples of the S Russian steppe. ... Perhaps ... the northerners developed the light horse-drawn war-chariot' and took it with them when they entered Egypt. T.C. Mitchell, art. 'Chariot', *IBD*, I, p. 259.

[13] W. W. Hallo, *BA* 46.1 (Winter 1983). He says it is the Assyrian *abarakku*, 'vizier'; *cf.* BDB, p. 8.

was in this sense that he 'forgot' them all. By an act of will he left the past behind and lived in the present. It is by a similar act of will that the Christian is to 'hate' his own life, and 'hate' his father and mother, in the sense of relegating all to a subsidiary place so that the disciple can give total allegiance to Jesus Christ (Lk. 14:26). That Joseph did not forget his family in any absolute sense is proved by his reactions when unexpectedly his brothers presented themselves before him.

The name of the second son, *Ephraim*, reflected the joy his birth had given: *God has made me fruitful.* After the loneliness and fear of the kidnapping and all that led up to imprisonment, to have a wife and family called for celebration in the naming of this second son. Paul, too, advocated forgetting the past and pressing forward into God's plan (Phil. 3:13).

The famine which Joseph had predicted was not confined to Egypt, but engulfed all the countries around. Thanks to the careful organization and execution of Joseph's policy, there was famine relief available, though it is noteworthy that the grain was sold and not given away. News spread that food was available in Egypt, so foreigners travelled there to buy grain. Joseph was proving to be a blessing to the Pharaoh, to Egypt as a whole, and further afield. Ironically, when Joseph had overcome his homesickness and had resolved to 'forget' all his father's house (51), his father was planning to send his brothers to Egypt. The unexpected developments of God's plan were only just beginning to unfold, even though so much had happened already.

Genesis 42:1–38

Joseph's brothers come to buy grain

When Jacob learned that there was grain in Egypt, he said to his sons, 'Why do you look at one another?' ²And he said, 'Behold, I have heard that there is grain in Egypt; go down and buy grain for us there, that we may live, and not die.' ³So ten of Joseph's brothers went down to buy grain in Egypt. ⁴But Jacob did not send Benjamin, Joseph's brother, with his brothers, for he feared that harm might befall him. ⁵Thus the sons of Israel came to buy among the others who came, for the famine was in the land of Canaan.

⁶Now Joseph was governor over the land; he it was who sold to all the people of the land. And Joseph's brothers came, and bowed themselves before him with their faces to the ground. ⁷Joseph saw his brothers, and knew them, but he treated them like strangers and spoke roughly to them. 'Where do you come from?' he said. They said, 'From the land of Canaan, to buy food.' ⁸Thus Joseph knew his brothers, but they did not know him. ⁹And Joseph remembered the dreams which he had dreamed of them; and he said to them, 'You are spies, you have come to see the weakness of the land.' ¹⁰They said to him, 'No, my lord, but to buy food have your servants come. ¹¹We are all sons of one man, we are honest men, your servants are not spies.' ¹²He said to them, 'No, it is the weakness of the land that you have come to see.' ¹³And they said, 'We, your servants, are twelve brothers, the sons of one man in the land of Canaan; and behold, the youngest is this day with our father, and one is no more.' ¹⁴But Joseph said to them, 'It is as I said to you, you are spies. ¹⁵By this you shall be tested: by the life of Pharaoh, you shall not go from this place unless your youngest brother comes here. ¹⁶Send one of you, and let him bring your brother, while you remain in prison, that your words may be tested, whether there is truth in you; or else, by the life of Pharaoh, surely you are spies.' ¹⁷And he put them all together in prison for three days.

¹⁸On the third day Joseph said to them, 'Do this and you will live, for I fear God: ¹⁹if you are honest men, let one of your brothers remain confined in your prison, and let the rest go and carry grain for the famine of your households, ²⁰and bring your youngest brother to me; so your words will be verified, and you shall not die.' And they did so. ²¹Then they said to one another, 'In truth we are guilty concerning our brother, in that we saw the distress of his soul, when he besought us and we would not listen; therefore is this distress come upon us.' ²²And Reuben answered them, 'Did I not tell you not to sin against the lad? But you would not listen. So now there comes a reckoning for his blood.' ²³They did not know that Joseph understood them, for there was an interpreter between them. ²⁴Then he turned away from them and wept; and he returned to them and spoke to them. And he took Simeon from them and bound him before their eyes. ²⁵And Joseph gave orders to fill their bags with grain, and to replace every man's money in his sack, and to give them provisions for the journey. This was done for them.

²⁶Then they loaded their asses with their grain, and departed. ²⁷And as one of them opened his sack to give his ass provender at the lodging place, he saw his money in the mouth of his sack; ²⁸and he said to his brothers, 'My money has been put back; here it is in the mouth of my sack!' At this their hearts failed them, and they turned trembling to one another, saying, 'What is this that God has done to us?'

²⁹When they came to Jacob their father in the land of Canaan, they told him all that had befallen them, saying, ³⁰'The man, the lord of the land,

spoke roughly to us, and took us to be spies of the land. ³¹*But we said to him, "We are honest men, we are not spies;* ³²*we are twelve brothers, sons of our father; one is no more, and the youngest is this day with our father in the land of Canaan."* ³³*Then the man, the lord of the land, said to us, "By this I shall know that you are honest men: leave one of your brothers with me, and take grain for the famine of your households, and go your way.* ³⁴*Bring your youngest brother to me; then I shall know that you are not spies but honest men, and I will deliver to you your brother, and you shall trade in the land."'*

³⁵*As they emptied their sacks, behold, every man's bundle of money was in his sack; and when they and their father saw their bundles of money, they were dismayed.* ³⁶*And Jacob their father said to them. 'You have bereaved me of my children: Joseph is no more, and Simeon is no more, and now you would take Benjamin; all this has come upon me.'* ³⁷*Then Reuben said to his father, 'Slay my two sons if I do not bring him back to you; put him in my hands, and I will being him back to you.'* ³⁸*But he said, 'My son shall not go down with you, for his brother is dead, and he only is left. If harm should befall him on the journey that you are to make, you would bring down my grey hairs with sorrow to Sheol.'*

Back in Canaan the famine was putting a severe strain on food supplies, and it caused Jacob and his sons to hold a consultation. Whereas in the past Jacob had had difficulty in bearing with his headstrong family (34:25–31; 35:22), now it is the old man who shows initiative and gives his clear directive to his resourceless sons; *'I have heard that there is grain in Egypt; go down and buy grain for us there, that we may live, and not die.'* Thought of the long return journey, transporting sacks of grain, was enough to make anyone reluctant, but ten asses would be able to carry about half a ton of food, which would make a significant difference. Benjamin, Rachel's son, and the youngest of the family, did not go. Jacob was cautious enough to keep him at home, having lost his brother, Joseph.

Though there was grain to be bought in every part of Egypt, and Joseph could not have superintended every sale, it so happened that these foreigners arrived at the main supply base, where Joseph was in charge. He may, of course, have asked to be kept informed if anyone from his part of Canaan arrived to buy grain. All who travelled from Canaan came first to the delta region, where it seems likely that Joseph lived. In the early second millennium the capital was Memphis, only 20 miles or so up the Nile from the apex of the

179

delta. To his astonishment Joseph recognized his brothers among the foreigners buying grain, and he watched them bow to the ground before him, so unwittingly fulfilling his first dream (37:5–8). Understandably he took the opportunity both to find out some news and to give himself time to decide on a course of action, which would bring the whole family to bow before him, and so fulfil his second dream (37:9–10).

By his gruff manner and unwarranted accusations Joseph put his brothers on the spot and at the same time elicited the essential facts. His father was still alive, and so was the missing brother, Benjamin. *'We ... are twelve brothers, the sons of one man ...; and behold, the youngest is this day with our father.'* (Who ever heard of a spy ring consisting of ten brothers?) But it was impossible to prove their relationship, and the accusation was repeated; *'it is the weakness of the land that you have come to see.'* The inference was that they were spies reconnoitring for military purposes. In the light of subsequent history the suggestion was not without plausibility, for Asiatics infiltrated Egypt, and in the eighteenth century BC were to effect a take-over and set up a foreign dynasty. These Asiatic Pharaohs were known as *Hyksos*, which means 'foreign chiefs'.[14] The Pharaohs of the Middle Kingdom (21st – 18th centuries BC) called by the name *Hyksos* the princes of Palestine and south Syria, over which Egypt nominally ruled, and the people of these countries seem to have adopted the name. The accusation made by Joseph seemed expedient, therefore, as did the summary imprisonment, though the brothers insisted on their innocence. The only way to prove it was to agree to send for Benjamin, but they knew what it would cost their old father to part with him. It was a clever ploy on the part of Joseph thus to put his brothers under pressure, and at the same time to contrive to bring Benjamin to Egypt.

Since nine of the brothers had expected to have to remain in the prison, the new stipulation that instead one should remain hostage (19) came as good news. Nine were permitted to return home with grain, on the understanding that they would bring back their youngest brother with them. Despite the relaxed sentence, the brothers were deeply uneasy, and revealed in their conversation between themselves, which they assumed the Egyptian overlord

[14]Pharaoh Amenemhet I (1991–1962) built a chain of forts, known as 'the Prince's Wall', across the Isthmus of Suez to guard the land from the incursions of Semitic bands. This is sufficient proof that at that time the threat to Egypt came from the direction of Canaan. *Cf.* John Bright, *A History of Israel*[2] (SCM Press, 1972), p. 52; S. Herrmann, *Israel in Egypt* (SCM Press, 1973), p. 8.

could not understand, that they still had their cruelty to Joseph heavy on their consciences. What worried them in particular was their callous refusal to respond when Joseph had shouted for mercy: *we saw the distress of his soul ... and we would not listen'* (21). This revelation was too much for Joseph, who wept with emotion, so deeply did he want to be reunited with his own family, now repentant. But the time for disclosure had not yet come and he steeled himself to make Simeon, the second eldest, his prisoner. Reuben, who had tried to rescue him, he spared. Still longing, however, to do all he could for them, Joseph gave them more than they asked (25) and even returned to their sacks the money they had brought. It was a loving gesture, misunderstood by the brothers, who regarded with suspicion this unexpected generosity. To their minds it could only be mysterious and ominous, an act of God, of whom they were afraid (28). Sheer grace they found frankly perplexing.

Even Jacob reacted as they had done when he heard their story and saw the money returned in each of the sacks. The suggestion that he should permit Benjamin to go to Egypt, even though Reuben was prepared to go surety for him, was out of the question. *'My son shall not go down with you'* (38). The risk was too great, for he loved Benjamin too much to be able to endure his death, and doubted whether he could survive without him. The desperate life and death situation was bringing out in various members of the family the depth of the bond between them, and the lengths to which each one would go to reassure his father. If it had not been for this famine they would not have known how much they loved him.

Genesis 43:1 – 44:34

The brothers' second visit

Now the famine was severe in the land. ²And when they had eaten the grain which they had brought from Egypt, their father said to them, 'Go again, buy us a little food.' ³But Judah said to him, 'The man solemnly warned us, saying, "You shall not see my face, unless your brother is with you." ⁴If you will send our brother with us, we will go down and buy you food; ⁵but if you will not send him, we will not go down, for the man said to us, "You shall not see my face, unless your brother is with you."' ⁶Israel said, 'Why did you treat me so ill as to tell the man that you had another brother?' ⁷They replied, 'The man questioned us carefully about ourselves and our

181

kindred, saying, "Is your father still alive? Have you another brother?" What we told him was in answer to these questions; could we in any way know that he would say, "Bring your brother down"?' [8]And Judah said to Israel his father, 'Send the lad with me, and we will arise and go, that we may live and not die, both we and you and also our little ones. [9]I will be surety for him; of my hand you shall require him. If I do not bring him back to you and set him before you, then let me bear the blame for ever; [10]for if we had not delayed, we would now have returned twice.'

[11]Then their father Israel said to them, 'If it must be so, then do this: take some of the choice fruits of the land in your bags, and carry down to the man a present, a little balm and a little honey, gum, myrrh, pistachio nuts, and almonds. [12]Take double the money with you; carry back with you the money that was returned in the mouth of your sacks; perhaps it was an oversight. [13]Take also your brother, and arise, go again to the man; [14]may God Almighty grant you mercy before the man, that he may send back your other brother and Benjamin. If I am bereaved of my children, I am bereaved.' [15]So the men took the present, and they took double the money with them, and Benjamin; and they arose and went down to Egypt, and stood before Joseph.

[16]When Joseph saw Benjamin with them, he said to the steward of his house, 'Bring the men into the house, and slaughter an animal and make ready, for the men are to dine with me at noon.' [17]The man did as Joseph bade him, and brought the men to Joseph's house. [18]And the men were afraid because they were brought to Joseph's house, and they said, 'It is because of the money, which was replaced in our sacks the first time, that we are brought in, so that he may seek occasion against us and fall upon us, to make slaves of us and seize our asses.' [19]So they went up to the steward of Joseph's house, and spoke with him at the door of the house, [20]and said, 'Oh, my lord, we came down the first time to buy food; [21]and when we came to the lodging place we opened our sacks, and there was every man's money in the mouth of his sack, our money in full weight; so we have brought it again with us, [22]and we have brought other money down in our hand to buy food. We do not know who put our money in our sacks.' [23]He replied, 'Rest assured, do not be afraid; your God and the God of your father must have put treasure in your sacks for you; I received your money.' Then he brought Simeon out to them. [24]And when the man had brought the men into Joseph's house, and given them water, and they had washed their feet, and when he had given their asses provender, [25]they made ready the present for Joseph's coming at noon, for they heard that they should eat bread there.

[26]When Joseph came home, they brought into the house to him the present which they had with them, and bowed down to him to the ground. [27]And he

inquired about their welfare, and said, 'Is your father well, the old man of whom you spoke? Is he still alive?' ²⁸*They said, 'Your servant our father is well, he is still alive.' And they bowed their heads and made obeisance.* ²⁹*And he lifted up his eyes, and saw his brother Benjamin, his mother's son, and said, 'Is this your youngest brother, of whom you spoke to me? God be gracious to you, my son!'* ³⁰*Then Joseph made haste, for his heart yearned for his brother, and he sought a place to weep. And he entered his chamber and wept there.*³¹ *Then he washed his face and came out; and controlling himself he said, 'Let food be served.'* ³²*They served him by himself, and them by themselves, and the Egyptians who ate with him by themselves, because the Egyptians might not eat bread with the Hebrews, for that is an abomination to the Egyptians.* ³³*And they sat before him, the first-born according to his birthright and the youngest according to his youth; and the men looked at one another in amazement.* ³⁴*Portions were taken to them from Joseph's table, but Benjamin's portion was five times as much as any of theirs. So they drank and were merry with him.*

^{44:1}*Then he commanded the steward of his house, 'Fill the men's sacks with food, as much as they can carry, and put each man's money in the mouth of his sack,* ²*and put my cup, the silver cup, in the mouth of the sack of the youngest, with his money for the grain.' And he did as Joseph told him.* ³*As soon as the morning was light, the men were sent away with their asses.* ⁴*When they had gone but a short distance from the city, Joseph said to his steward, 'Up, follow after the men; and when you overtake them, say to them, "Why have you returned evil for good? Why have you stolen my silver cup?* ⁵*Is it not from this that my lord drinks, and by this that he divines? You have done wrong in so doing."'*

⁶*When he overtook them, he spoke to them these words.* ⁷*They said to him, 'Why does my lord speak such words as these? Far be it from your servants that they should do such a thing!* ⁸*Behold, the money which we found in the mouth of our sacks, we brought back to you from the land of Canaan; how then should we steal silver or gold from your lord's house?* ⁹*With whomever of your servants it be found, let him die, and we also will be my lord's slaves.'* ¹⁰*He said, 'Let it be as you say: he with whom it is found shall be my slave, and the rest of you shall be blameless.'* ¹¹*Then every man quickly lowered his sack to the ground, and every man opened his sack.* ¹²*And he searched, beginning with the eldest and ending with the youngest; and the cup was found in Benjamin's sack.* ¹³*Then they rent their clothes, and every man loaded his ass, and they returned to the city.*

¹⁴*When Judah and his brothers came to Joseph's house, he was still there; and they fell before him to the ground.* ¹⁵*Joseph said to them, 'What deed is this that you have done? Do you not know that such a man as I can indeed*

divine?' [16]And Judah said, 'What shall we say to my lord? What shall we speak? Or how can we clear ourselves? God has found out the guilt of your servants; behold, we are my lord's slaves, both we and he also in whose hand the cup has been found.' [17]But he said, 'Far be it from me that I should do so! Only the man in whose hand the cup was found shall be my slave; but as for you, go up in peace to your father.'

[18]Then Judah went up to him and said, 'O my lord, let your servant, I pray you, speak a word in my lord's ears, and let not your anger burn against your servant; for you are like Pharaoh himself. [19]My lord asked his servants, saying, "Have you a father or a brother?" [20]And we said to my lord, "We have a father, an old man, and a young brother, the child of his old age; and his brother is dead, and he alone is left of his mother's children; and his father loves him." [21]Then you said to your servants, "Bring him down to me, that I may set my eyes upon him." [22]We said to my lord, "The lad cannot leave his father, for if he should leave his father, his father would die." [23]Then you said to your servants, "Unless your youngest brother comes down with you, you shall see my face no more." [24]When we went back to your servant my father we told him the words of my lord. [25]And when our father said, "Go again, buy us a little food," [26]we said, "We cannot go down. If our youngest brother goes with us, then we will go down; for we cannot see the man's face unless our youngest brother is with us." [27]Then your servant my father said to us, "You know that my wife bore me two sons; [28]one left me, and I said, Surely he has been torn to pieces; and I have never seen him since. [29]If you take this one also from me, and harm befalls him, you will bring down my grey hairs in sorrow to Sheol." [30]Now therefore, when I come to your servant my father, and the lad is not with us, then, as his life is bound up in the lad's life, [31]when he sees that the lad is not with us, he will die; and your servants will bring down the grey hairs of your servant our father with sorrow to Sheol. [32]For your servant became surety for the lad to my father, saying, "If I do not bring him back to you, then I shall bear the blame in the sight of my father all my life." [33]Now therefore, let your servant, I pray you, remain instead of the lad as a slave to my lord; and let the lad go back with his brothers. [34]For how can I go back to my father if the lad is not with me? I fear to see the evil that would come upon my father.'

Jacob in his old age bears all the characteristics we are accustomed to associate with the very elderly. He dominates the family, sees issues in stark terms of black and white and makes assertions which express his own passionate feelings; but everyone knows that he will have to go back on what he has so categorically stated. He could afford to refuse Reuben's offer because it was made at a time when there was food in store, but continuing shortage of rain forced the family to live on its stocks, until the situation was again becoming desperate. '*Go again, buy us a little food*,' said Jacob at last (43:2). The brothers did not need coaxing, but first their father had to be cajoled into facing the facts. It was useless to return without Benjamin, as Judah, acting this time as spokesman, pointed out. How 'the man' knew that there was one more brother was by this time irrelevant, but the argument enabled Jacob to project on to someone else his intense disquiet. His own world was in jeopardy and he was trying desperately to salvage it. As Judah reminded him, life was at stake, and there were 'little ones', grandchildren of Jacob, to consider, as well as Benjamin. '*If we had not delayed*,' the reason for the delay being tactfully omitted, '*we would now have returned twice* (10).

At last the matter was settled. Benjamin could go, his safe return assured by Judah. There were still fruit, honey and nuts to be had, and luxury items such as balm and myrrh from surviving shrubs; from all these a suitable present could be put together to take for the man in charge. Jacob ordered them to take double the silver they expected to need so that they could pay for the first load as well as the second, and prayed that *God Almighty*, who disclosed himself to Abraham by that name when the covenant sign of circumcision was given (17:1), would grant mercy to his sons, so that the family could be reunited once more. But Jacob was not very hopeful of a happy outcome. Bereavement seemed to be his lot.

The story continues from the point of view of Joseph, who treated his brothers with the very special favour reserved for the few. They were invited to a feast at his residence; but again they misinterpreted Joseph's intention, because they did not realize why they had been singled out from all the other famine victims buying food. They suspected a trap and imagined that it could be connected with their failure to pay for the grain, because their money had been returned. They were no less mystified when the steward in charge said he had received their money, and suggested that their money had been put in their sacks by their God. It was astonishing to find an Egyptian implying that they worshipped a living God who intervened in human life to the extent of supplying silver in sacks of grain! What could he know about the God they worshipped? It was reassuring to have Simeon back with them, and they gladly got ready for the special meal arranged by their host.

It was at this point that they handed over their present, and for the second time bowed down to the ground before Joseph (26; cf. 42:6). The great man made conversation by enquiring about their father, and correctly surmised which of the eleven men before him was the youngest, whom they had brought for the first time; the man had an uncanny memory! His prayer, 'God be gracious to you, my son!', was as unexpected as the steward's comment about their God (Elohim). For Joseph, mention of his God and the sight of his own mother's son overwhelmed him with emotion. Prayer was being answered beyond all his expectations.

When the brothers were ushered into the dining-room they found that they had been placed in order of age, another unaccountable and disturbing factor, at a table by themselves, while the grand vizier ate in lonely splendour before them. They would not be surprised that the Egyptian ate separately, because there was a taboo against their sharing meals with foreigners, who were regarded as defiling the food. The brothers, however, shared the specialities from the high table, Benjamin being specially honoured with an extra large portion. Well fed and fully satisfied after their journey, the brothers relaxed and enjoyed themselves with their host.

The brusque treatment they received in the morning was out of keeping with the entertainment of the night before, but Joseph could not let them leave now in case he did not see them again. Accordingly he devised a means of enforcing their return, and at the same time put them in the wrong though they were innocent. He wanted to have a reason for arresting Benjamin, hence the choice of his sack in which to bury the divining-cup. Someone would be put on the spot and would reveal what lay beneath the polite exterior. Though he loved his brothers so much, he dare not assume that they would not still plot his murder if they had the chance, and to gloss over the wrong they had done him, without ensuring that they had truly repented, would not bring about an effective reconciliation. For this reason Joseph moved forward step by step, in an endeavour to evoke their reactions under stress, especially where their father was involved.

As the brothers were making the most of an early start on their return journey, it was disconcerting to be overtaken by the steward, who had so courteously received them the day before, and to be accused of stealing his master's silver cup. But the accusation was so wild as to be easily refuted, and all agreed that if the cup was found in their possession, the guilty one should die and the rest would become slaves; but the steward decreed that only the guilty one should be punished, and that by being made his slave. To the dismay of all the brothers Benjamin had the cup.

Having retraced their steps they prostrated themselves for the third time before Joseph, who accused them of stupidity in thinking that they could get away with stealing from someone who could solve mysteries by divination. (Whether he could or not is beside the point; it was all part of Joseph's put-up job.) Now they had been found out there was nothing they could say in explanation. God, not divination, had exposed their guilt, of which they were only too aware, and now they must pay the penalty. All of them, not just Benjamin, would become slaves to the grand vizier. But Joseph desired to keep only Benjamin, and the rest could return to their father. It was this offer of freedom that prompted Judah's revealing response, for he depicted the scene back in Canaan, and their father's reluctance to part with Benjamin, that explained the delay in their return. Incidentally Joseph learnt how sorely his father had missed him (28). Fearing lest their father would die if Benjamin was not with them when they returned, Judah begged to be allowed to become a substitute for Benjamin. He could not have proved more effectively the genuineness of his love for his father and of his repentance for the blame he had incurred in selling Joseph (37:26). It is a vivid example of the change that God can bring about in a person, even someone as 'earthy' as Judah. The Lord had been at work to make his people what he wanted them to become.

Genesis 45:1–28

Joseph's disclosure of his identity

Then Joseph could not control himself before all those who stood by him; and he cried, 'Make every one go out from me.' So no one stayed with him when Joseph made himself known to his brothers. ²And he wept aloud, so that the Egyptians heard it, and the household of Pharaoh heard it. ³And Joseph said to his brothers, 'I am Joseph; is my father still alive?' But his brothers could not answer him, for they were dismayed at his presence.

⁴So Joseph said to his brothers, 'Come near to me, I pray you.' And they came near. And he said, 'I am your brother, Joseph, whom you sold into Egypt. ⁵And now do not be distressed, or angry with yourselves, because you sold me here; for God sent me before you to preserve life. ⁶For the famine has been in the land these two years; and there are yet five years in which there will be neither ploughing nor harvest. ⁷And God sent me before you to

187

preserve for you a remnant on earth, and to keep alive for you many survivors. [8]So it was not you who sent me here, but God; and he has made me a father to Pharaoh, and lord of all his house and ruler over all the land of Egypt. [9]Make haste and go up to my father and say to him, 'Thus says your son Joseph, God has made me lord of all Egypt; come down to me, do not tarry; [10]you shall dwell in the land of Goshen, and you shall be near me, you and your children and your children's children, and your flocks, your herds, and all that you have; [11]and there I will provide for you, for there are yet five years of famine to come; lest you and your household, and all that you have, come to poverty.' [12]And now your eyes see, and the eyes of my brother Benjamin see, that it is my mouth that speaks to you. [13]You must tell my father of all my splendour in Egypt, and of all that you have seen. Make haste and bring my father down here.' [14]Then he fell upon his brother Benjamin's neck and wept; and Benjamin wept upon his neck. [15]And he kissed all his brothers and wept upon them; and after that his brothers talked with him.

[16]When the report was heard in Pharaoh's house, 'Joseph's brothers have come,' it pleased Pharaoh and his servants well. [17]And Pharaoh said to Joseph, 'Say to your brothers, "Do this: load your beasts and go back to the land of Canaan; [18]and take your father and your households, and come to me, and I will give you the best of the land of Egypt, and you shall eat the fat of the land." [19]Command them also, "Do this; take wagons from the land of Egypt for your little ones and for your wives, and bring your father, and come. [20]Give no thought to your goods, for the best of all the land of Egypt is yours."'

[21]The sons of Israel did so; and Joseph gave them wagons, according to the command of Pharaoh, and gave them provisions for the journey. [22]To each and all of them he gave festal garments, but to Benjamin he gave three hundred shekels of silver and five festal garments. [23]To his father he sent as follows: ten asses loaded with the good things of Egypt, and ten she-asses loaded with grain, bread, and provision for his father on the journey. [24]Then he sent his brothers away, and as they departed, he said to them, 'Do not quarrel on the way.' [25]So they went up out of Egypt, and came to the land of Canaan to their father Jacob. [26]And they told him, 'Joseph is still alive, and he is ruler over all the land of Egypt.' And his heart fainted, for he did not believe them. [27]But when they told him all the words of Joseph, which he had said to them, and when he saw the wagons which Joseph had sent to carry him, the spirit of their father Jacob revived; [28]and Israel said, 'It is enough; Joseph my son is still alive; I will go and see him before I die."

The spacious dignity of an audience chamber, flanked by retainers, was no setting for a family reunion and the complex emotions it was to evoke. Even when the observers had left, Joseph was still the man of power, with all the might of Egypt behind him. No wonder the brothers kept their distance when he said amid tears, '*I am Joseph; is my father still alive?*' (and well, understood). Despite the many coincidences that might have pointed to 'the man' being their own brother, such a possibility had never crossed their minds, and now the shock was demoralizing. The last thing they felt like doing was to *come near*, as Joseph requested.

He had much that he wanted to say to them, not least that he had no desire to take revenge, despite the fact that they had sold him into slavery. Joseph had been able to come to terms with the situation because he had been able to trace the hand of God in all that had happened to him. Three times over he says '*God sent me*', and the purpose was also plain: it was to save life. It was obvious from the crowds flocking from many countries around that this applied not merely to Egypt, nor only to Jacob's family, but to human beings in general. Through Joseph God had made survival possible during this long period of famine. The unmistakably evil plans of Joseph's brothers, when they sold him at Dothan, had been incorporated into God's greater and altogether good purpose of saving life. Indeed, though many benefited, at the centre of God's concern were the very people who had so blatantly planned to murder their brother, namely the covenant family: '*God sent me before you to preserve for you a remnant on earth, and to keep alive many survivors*' (7), in accordance with the promise of descendants as numerous as the stars or the grains of sand on the seashore. A severe threat to the covenant family had been averted, and all twelve brothers survived to become the progenitors of Israel's tribes, thanks to the providential care of their covenant God.

The life of Joseph so perfectly illustrates the overruling providence of God that it is important to consider its relevance for ourselves and the troubles we encounter in our lives. First, Joseph was undoubtedly the victim of jealousy; the youngster had been provocative, with his self-centred dreams, but he had not deserved the treatment he got at the hand of his brothers. They hated him and intended to murder him (37:20). Secondly, during the course of his adventures Joseph might frequently have asked why God had allowed him to be isolated from his family, sold, tossed from pillar to post and imprisoned when he had done nothing to deserve it. We complain bitterly over much less. Thirdly, whether he complained or not, Joseph in the end saw clearly that he had not by any means been abandoned by his God. In a mysterious way God had made use of the ill will of his brothers to achieve their rescue in time of famine. This enabled Joseph to say, '*so it was not you who sent me here, but God*' (8); God not only thwarted the intentions of the brothers, but worked for their good.

The things that happened to Joseph, and to other people in the Bible, could have been confined to them as members of the covenant family, the survival of which was ensured because it was essential to the fulfilment of God's saving purpose. The question has to be asked, whether God's providential keeping extends to our own generation and to ourselves. On the surface the world does not look as if God were directing it; at best the evidence is ambiguous. But then it did not look to Joseph as if God were directing *his* steps. It is at certain moments that God lets his presence be seen, in blessing and in judgment, but Scripture insists that the God who created all things takes a personal interest in so insignificant a creature as the common sparrow, and Jesus assured his disciples that they were 'of more value than many sparrows' (Mt. 10:29–31). Of course it is not always given to us to know exactly what God is doing with us, when troubles overwhelm us and cause us to cry out for mercy; the secret is to cling to what God has shown us of himself in his word, and to believe that he intends it for good. Then we shall be able to 'count it all joy' when trials come (Jas. 1:2).

But the famine was not yet over, and five more years of drought were still to come. For this reason some long-term solution to the food problem was essential, and Joseph determined that the whole family should move to be near him. In his status as 'father to Pharaoh' and ruler over the land of Egypt Joseph was well placed to provide a home for his father and brothers, together with their families, their possessions and their farm stock. They required an undeveloped area of land where they could pursue their own way of life, and this Joseph had in mind in the land of *Goshen*, called in 47:11 the land of Rameses, and designated 'the best of the land'. It sounds as if it was part of the royal estates, unpopulated for that reason, and yet available to Joseph because of his privileged position at court. The name 'Goshen' is not attested outside the Bible.

Joseph commissioned his brothers to hurry back to Canaan with the message, '*God has made me lord of all Egypt*', and with his invitation to take up residence there and enjoy the plenty he could provide. But first he gave Benjamin a passionate embrace, and affectionately greeted all the others, who by this time were sufficiently reassured to talk to him. A further honour came their way when the Pharaoh not only endorsed all that Joseph had said, but also added that *he* would give Joseph's father and brothers the best of the land of Egypt. His provision of transport was especially thoughtful in the light of Jacob's years; though the ox-drawn cart would hardly have been the height of comfort, not everyone was so honoured as to travel in one of the Pharaoh's 'coaches', and to be offered by the king himself all the best that Egypt could provide.

Finally Joseph produced lavish presents for them all, and provisions sufficient for the double journey, not only for themselves but also for all who would be accompanying them on their return to Egypt. Benjamin was selected for specially generous gifts, but bountiful supplies of presents were taken to Jacob by ten pairs of asses. In the light of the confessions that were going to be called for when they came to their father, Joseph was realistic in dismissing his brothers with the warning, *'Do not quarrel on the way'*.

The incredible story was almost too much for Jacob, who could not take in the news and did not believe his sons. Nevertheless he could not otherwise account for all the things that Joseph had sent, along with his special message, and having once accepted that Joseph was alive, he had a new incentive for living. *'I will go and see him before I die.'*

Genesis 46:1 – 47:26

Jacob's descent into Egypt

So Israel took his journey with all that he had, and came to Beer-sheba, and offered sacrifices to the God of his father Isaac. ²And God spoke to Israel in visions of the night, and said, 'Jacob, Jacob.' And he said, 'Here am I.' ³Then he said, 'I am God, the God of your father; do not be afraid to go down to Egypt; for I will there make of you a great nation. ⁴I will go down with you to Egypt, and I will also bring you up again; and Joseph's hand shall close your eyes.' ⁵Then Jacob set out from Beer-sheba; and the sons of Israel carried Jacob their father, their little ones, and their wives, in the wagons which Pharaoh had sent to carry him. ⁶They also took their cattle and their goods, which they had gained in the land of Canaan, and came into Egypt, Jacob and all his offspring with him, ⁷his sons, and his sons' sons with him, his daughters, and his sons' daughters; all his offspring he brought with him into Egypt. ...

²⁸*He sent Judah before him to Joseph, to appear before him in Goshen; and they came into the land of Goshen.* ²⁹*Then Joseph made ready his chariot and went up to meet Israel his father in Goshen; and he presented himself to him, and fell on his neck, and wept on his neck a good while.* ³⁰*Israel said to Joseph, 'Now let me die, since I have seen your face and know that you are still alive.'* ³¹*Joseph said to his brothers and to his father's household, 'I will go up and tell Pharaoh, and will say to him, "My brothers and my father's household, who were in the land of Canaan, have come to me;* ³²*and the men are shepherds, for they have been keepers of cattle; and they have brought their flocks, and their herds, and all that they have."* ³³*When Pharaoh calls you, and says, "What is your occupation?"* ³⁴*you shall say, "Your servants have been keepers of cattle from our youth even until now, both we and our fathers," in order that you may dwell in the land of Goshen; for every shepherd is an abomination to the Egyptians.'*

⁴⁷:¹*So Joseph went in and told Pharaoh, 'My father and my brothers, with their flocks and herds and all that they possess, have come from the land of Canaan; they are now in the land of Goshen.'* ²*And from among his brothers he took five men and presented them to Pharaoh.* ³*Pharaoh said to his brothers, 'What is your occupation?' And they said to Pharaoh, 'Your servants are shepherds, as our fathers were.'* ⁴*They said to Pharaoh, 'We have come to sojourn in the land; for there is no pasture for your servants' flocks, for the famine is severe in the land of Canaan; and now, we pray you, let your servants dwell in the land of Goshen.'* ⁵*Then Pharaoh said to Joseph, 'Your father and your brothers have come to you,* ⁶*The land of Egypt is before you; settle your father and your brothers in the best of the land; let them dwell in the land of Goshen; and if you know any able men among them, put them in charge of my cattle.'*

⁷*Then Joseph brought in Jacob his father, and set him before Pharaoh, and Jacob blessed Pharaoh.* ⁸*And Pharaoh said to Jacob, 'How many are the days of the years of your life?'* ⁹*And Jacob said to Pharaoh, 'The days of the years of my sojourning are a hundred and thirty years; few and evil have been the days of the years of my life, and they have not attained to the days of the years of the life of my fathers in the days of their sojourning.'* ¹⁰*And Jacob blessed Pharaoh, and went out from the presence of Pharaoh.* ¹¹*Then Joseph settled his father and his brothers, and gave them a possession in the land of Egypt, in the best of the land, in the land of Rameses, as Pharaoh had commanded.* ¹²*And Joseph provided his father, his brothers, and all his father's household with food, according to the number of their dependants.*

¹³*Now there was no food in all the land; for the famine was very severe, so that the land of Egypt and the land of Canaan languished by reason of the famine.* ¹⁴*And Joseph gathered up all the money that was found in the*

*land of Egypt and in the land of Canaan, for the grain which they bought;
and Joseph brought the money into Pharaoh's house.* ¹⁵*And when the money
was all spent in the land of Egypt and in the land of Canaan, all the
Egyptians came to Joseph, and said, 'Give us food; why should we die before
your eyes? For our money is gone.'* ¹⁶*And Joseph answered, 'Give your
cattle, and I will give you food in exchange for your cattle, if your money is
gone.'* ¹⁷*So they brought their cattle to Joseph; and Joseph gave them food in
exchange for the horses, the flocks, the herds, and the asses: and he supplied
them with food in exchange for all their cattle that year.* ¹⁸*And when that
year was ended, they came to him the following year, and said to him, 'We
will not hide from my lord that our money is all spent; and the herds of cattle
are my lord's; there is nothing left in the sight of my lord but our bodies and
our lands.* ¹⁹*Why should we die before your eyes, both we and our land?
Buy us and our land for food, and we with our land will be slaves to
Pharaoh; and give us seed, that we may live, and not die, and that the land
may not be desolate.'*

²⁰*So Joseph bought all the land of Egypt for Pharaoh; for all the
Egyptians sold their fields, because the famine was severe upon them. The
land became Pharaoh's;* ²¹*and as for the people, he made slaves of them from
one end of Egypt to the other.* ²²*Only the land of the priests he did not buy;
for the priests had a fixed allowance from Pharaoh, and lived on the
allowance which Pharaoh gave them; therefore they did not sell their land.*
²³*Then Joseph said to the people, 'Behold, I have this day bought you and
your land for Pharaoh. Now here is seed for you, and you shall sow the
land.* ²⁴*And at the harvests you shall give a fifth to Pharaoh, and four
fifths shall be your own, as seed for the field and as food for yourselves and
your households, and as food for your little ones.'* ²⁵*And they said, 'You
have saved our lives; may it please my lord, we will be slaves to Pharaoh.'*
²⁶*So Joseph made it a statute concerning the land of Egypt, and it stands to
this day, that Pharaoh should have the fifth; the land of the priests alone
did not become Pharaoh's.*

Whereas in a time of famine Abraham had migrated to Egypt for the
duration of the food-shortage and had been summarily expelled,
Jacob had carefully avoided even travelling to Egypt, though he had
sent his sons there to buy food. His father Isaac had been expressly
forbidden by the Lord to go to Egypt in search of grain (26:2) and
was careful to remain within the territory promised to his family by
going to Gerar, which was in Philistine hands. Joseph had had no
option, but had been sent to Egypt and had married into an
Egyptian, priestly family. It is an interesting example of the

differing guidance God may give to his people in differing circumstances; what was not God's will for Isaac seemed to be the way God had specially prepared for Jacob. He had assumed that Joseph's invitation, with the wonderful prospect of reunion with his long-lost son, must be part of the Lord's providential ordering of his life. But was it so? The family travelled south, through areas evocative of the Lord's dealings with Abraham and Isaac. Beersheba was associated with both of them, but particularly with his father Isaac, to whose God Jacob offered sacrifices, and from whom he implicitly sought reassurance.

And God spoke to Israel in visions of the night (46:2). 'Ask, and it will be given you,' said Jesus (Mt. 7:7), so assuring all believers that God responds when we call. For Jacob the permission he sought to continue his journey was given in *visions of the night*. The command which Isaac had had to obey was not applicable in Jacob's new situation. Jacob was to be the one to take the family into 'a land that is not theirs' (Gn. 15:13), where they would become a great nation bearing his God-given name, Israel. Whatever the perils involved in this adventure, Jacob knew that the God of his fathers was with him in it, that he would die in Egypt in the presence of Joseph, and that God would take care of the family, bringing them back to the land of his promise (3–4). Reassured, the large company of people, flocks and herds, set off again across the desert to the south and west towards Egypt. Genesis insists that all the family left Canaan, including daughters and granddaughters, who might have stayed, intermarried into other families, and have remembered their forefathers, handing on the traditions so that at the time of the conquest there would have been related people to welcome the invaders. Historians have conjectured that even some of the brothers remained in Canaan, but the account here totally denies that this was the case.[15]

The names of Jacob's sons and grandsons (8–27) read like entries into a family record. All the sons born are recorded, even though some, like Er and Onan (12), died in Canaan. They are grouped, not in order of age, but according to their mothers, the children of Leah and Zilpah first, followed by the children of Rachel and her handmaid, Bilhah. The total including Jacob, and Joseph with his two sons who were already in Egypt, numbered seventy, not counting daughters-in-law.

[15]*E.g.* Martin Noth, *The History of Israel* (A. & C. Black, 1958), Ch. 2, especially pp. 116–118; J.H. Hayes and J.M. Miller, *Israelite and Judean History* (SCM Press, 1977), p. 242.

Once in Egyptian territory, *Jacob sent Judah ahead of him to Joseph to get directions to Goshen* (28, NIV). Thus Joseph was alerted to the fact that his father had arrived, and Joseph sped to meet him in Goshen. The inference is that Goshen lay somewhere between Egypt's eastern border and the residence of Joseph, possibly in the ancient capital, Memphis. An area in the delta region may well be right; well watered, fertile and yet away from Egypt's centres of activity. Above all, it was on the convenient side of the country for eventual escape. Joseph thought out every move with an eye to God's purposes, for this much he knew, that his family would eventually have to return to the land of promise.

Emotion welled up as father and son were reunited. For Jacob it was the crowning moment of his life, one of God's marvellous surprises that enabled past sorrows to be forgotten and evil deeds forgiven. In the light of all that God had done the selling of Joseph looked particularly mean and despicable. But bitter hatred had been rewarded with kindness and generosity. No wonder the tears flowed at the experience of such a gracious reception.

Pharaoh still had to meet Joseph's family and approve their plans to settle in Goshen; though he had promised the best of the land, he had not specified in advance where it was to be. Joseph had his idea, but this still had to be verified by the Pharaoh, hence Joseph's instructions to his family. Did they look somewhat grotesque at court, with their unshaved faces and bright clothes? Their foreign appearance would tend to emphasize the fact that Joseph himself was not an Egyptian, though there is no suggestion that at the time this was in any way detrimental to his reputation. Egypt was too dependent on him for that to be the case, and in the event the audience of five of the brothers (47:2–6) with the Pharaoh resulted in exactly the outcome that Joseph had planned. Goshen was to become their home while they lived in Egypt, and the Pharaoh would gladly employ their best men to look after his own cattle. This was not the kind of work that appealed to the Egyptians (46:34), and it brought the settlers into the community without alienating the host nation by taking their jobs.

Finally, Joseph presented his father to the Pharaoh. Whatever possessed Jacob to bless the Egyptian king instead of bowing low before him? Had the old man been meditating on the Lord's words to Abraham, 'I will bless you, and make your name great, so that you will be a blessing' (12:2)? It was obvious that the Lord had made Joseph a blessing to Egypt and the surrounding nations, all unbeknown to Jacob, and the wonder of the Lord's mastery of events had overwhelmed him to such an extent that Jacob forgot all about protocol. His extreme old age was impressive, but with eastern courtesy, marked still, especially perhaps among the Chinese, he played down any claim to distinction, in the light of the longer life of his fathers. His 130 years had been 'few and evil', but he knew he had the edge over this foreign king. The whole scene rings true.

Joseph settled the family and provided for them as he had promised. The land they occupied, called here *the land of Rameses*,[16] was given them as *a possession* (11). A royal grant of land was indeed a great honour, indicative of the high esteem in which Joseph was held.

The time came when even Egypt, with its perennial water-supply from the Nile, came to the end of its supplies of grain, and the population had spent all its money over the years of famine. Even in their extremity Joseph maintained the principle of selling and not giving the needed grain, and he accepted the value in kind: horses, flocks herds and asses. It is interesting that horses were listed, but no mention is made of camels, which cannot have been a common possession at this time, even for international travel.[17] Eventually there was nothing for it but to accept the land and population of Egypt and Canaan in payment for the essential food, so dangerously exalting the power of the Pharaoh. He was always in theory 'god', a ruler from the realm of the gods. 'By the dogma of the state, the entire land, its properties, and its peoples were his by divine right.'[18] As a result of the famine years theory became fact, and the people of Egypt were reduced to slavery. Joseph's family would be an exception, because they were supplied direct by the vizier himself.

The exception mentioned in our text (47:22) made the priests of Egypt a special case because they were provided for from the royal purse, and so stood in a special relationship with the Pharaoh as advisers. Joseph's wife's family was in this way provided for, and spared the indignity of servitude. The ordinary people, however, grateful to survive at all, accepted the terms with gratitude, and

[16]Since this was the name of pharaohs who reigned in the 14th and 13th centuries, this is an 'updated' name for Goshen. Towns were built, one of them by this name, in the delta (Ex. 1:11; 12:37), presumably during the reign of a Rameses.

[17]Though there is evidence for knowledge and use of this animal in the early second millennium BC and even earlier, 'Only limited use is presupposed by either the biblical or external evidence until the twelfth century BC', K. A. Kitchen, *AOOT*, pp. 79–80.

[18]J. A. Wilson, art. 'Pharaoh', *IDB*, III, p. 773.

worked the fields that had been their own. By way of rent they handed over to the Pharaoh a twenty per cent tax on their crops, which, high as it was, still compares favourably with the taxation in most modern states. Despite his great power Joseph was entirely loyal to the Pharaoh, taking none of the credit for himself, though ultimately everyone was dependent on Joseph's wisdom and organizational ability, and behind that on the provision of his God. Incidentally, there is an indirect admission that sowing and harvesting went on annually in Egypt, as one would expect in view of the irrigation methods made possible by the Nile. These methods continued in use even during the famine years, but with decreasing yields and extra mouths to feed shortages were inevitable.

Genesis 47:27–31

The last years of Jacob

Thus Israel dwelt in the land of Egypt, in the land of Goshen; and they gained possessions in it, and were fruitful and multiplied exceedingly. ²⁸And Jacob lived in the land of Egypt seventeen years; so the days of Jacob, the years of his life, were a hundred and forty-seven years.

²⁹And when the time drew near that Israel must die, he called his son Joseph and said to him, 'If now I have found favour in your sight, put your hand under my thigh, and promise to deal loyally and truly with me. Do not bury me in Egypt, ³⁰but let me lie with my fathers; carry me out of Egypt and bury me in their burying place.' He answered, 'I will do as you have said.' ³¹And he said, 'Swear to me'; and he swore to him. Then Israel bowed himself upon the head of his bed.

For the first time the name *Israel* is used collectively for the family of Jacob, including himself. Despite their uprooting, the famine and life in an alien land, they prospered, and Jacob's seventeen years in Egypt enabled him to witness the extent of the growth in their numbers and possessions. Such remarkable expansion gave him hope as he faced up to the fact that, at 147 years of age, he could not have much longer to live. God had been entirely faithful in making him fruitful (28:14).

Jacob for his part wanted to make the family fully aware that they did not belong to the land of Egypt, lest his successors should forget their commitment to the covenant with the Lord their God, who had promised them the land of Canaan. Nothing could point more forcibly to the land of the promise than a funeral there, in the family tomb, the cave of Machpelah. Joseph's wealth and Egypt's practice of embalming made the expensive journey practicable, and all that new generation would know that their ancestors were buried where they essentially belonged, in the land of Canaan. Joseph's solemn oath, that he would carry through the wishes of his father, meant so much to Jacob that he *bowed himself upon the head of his bed*. Too old to bow himself on the ground in worship to his God, he did the next best thing and leant against the head of his bed as he bowed his head in adoration.[19] In extreme old age life's priorities become crystal clear, and for Jacob nothing mattered so much as the calling of God to him, as Abraham's successor, to inherit the obligation and promises of the covenant and to pass them on to his sons. Here was Joseph, showing understanding of the divine purpose and willingness to go to great lengths to give his father the burial he wanted in the land of Canaan. The Lord was working out his purpose and Jacob could be content.

Genesis 48:1–22

Jacob blesses Joseph's sons

After this Joseph was told, 'Behold, your father is ill'; so he took with him his two sons, Manasseh and Ephraim. [2]And it was told to Jacob, 'Your son Joseph has come to you'; then Israel summoned his strength, and sat up in bed. [3]And Jacob said to Joseph, 'God Almighty appeared to me at Luz in the land of Canaan and blessed me, [4]and said to me, "Behold, I will make you fruitful, and multiply you, and I will make of you a company of peoples, and will give this land to your descendants after you for an everlasting possession." [5]And now your two sons, who were born to you in the land of Egypt before I came to you in Egypt, are mine; Ephraim and Manasseh shall be mine, as Reuben and Simeon are. [6]And the offspring born to you after them shall be yours; they shall be called by the name of their brothers in their inheritance. [7]For when I came from Paddan, Rachel to my sorrow died in the land of Canaan on the way, when there was still some distance to go to Ephrath; and I buried her there on the way to Ephrath (that is, Bethlehem).'

[8]When Israel saw Joseph's sons, he said, 'Who are these?' [9]Joseph said to

---

[19]There is a reference to this incident in Heb. 11:21, where the alternative reading from the LXX is in mind, 'bowing in worship over the head of his staff'. The difference in the Hebrew is confined to the vowel pointing, and either meaning could have been original.

his father, 'They are my sons, whom God has given me here.' And he said,
*'Bring them to me, I pray you, that I may bless them.' * *¹⁰Now the eyes of*
Israel were dim with age, so that he could not see. So Joseph brought them
*near him; and he kissed them and embraced them. * *¹¹And Israel said to*
Joseph, 'I had not thought to see your face; and lo, God has let me see your
*children also.' * *¹²Then Joseph removed them from his knees, and he bowed*
*himself with his face to the earth. * *¹³And Joseph took them both, Ephraim in*
his right hand toward Israel's left hand, and Manasseh in his left hand
*toward Israel's right hand, and brought them near him. * *¹⁴And Israel*
stretched out his right hand and laid it upon the head of Ephraim, who was
the younger, and his left hand upon the head of Manasseh, crossing his
*hands, for Manasseh was the first-born. * *¹⁵And he blessed Joseph, and said,*

'The God before whom my fathers Abraham and Isaac walked,
the God who has led me all my life long to this day,
¹⁶the angel who has redeemed me from all evil, bless the lads;
and in them let my name he perpetuated, and the name of my fathers
Abraham and Isaac;
and let them grow into a multitude in the midst of the earth.'

¹⁷When Joseph saw that his father laid his right hand upon the head of
Ephraim, it displeased him; and he took his father's hand, to remove it from
*Ephraim's head to Manasseh's head. * *¹⁸And Joseph said to his father, 'Not*
so, my father; for this one is the first-born; put your right hand upon his
*head.' * *¹⁹But his father refused, and said, 'I know, my son, I know; he also*
shall become a people, and he also shall be great; nevertheless his younger
brother shall be greater than he, and his descendants shall become a
*multitude of nations.' * *²⁰So he blessed them that day, saying,*

'By you Israel will pronounce blessings, saying,
"God make you as Ephraim and as Manasseh"';
*and thus he put Ephraim before Manasseh. * *²¹Then Israel said to Joseph,*
'Behold, I am about to die, but God will be with you, and will bring you
*again to the land of your fathers. * *²²Moreover I have given to you rather than*
to your brothers one mountain slope which I took from the hand of the
Amorites with my sword and with my bow.'

News of his father's illness was a summons to go to him, and Joseph
knew that he was expected to take his sons with him to hear the last
words of the dying patriarch, and to receive his blessing. 'The
patriarchal blessings of Isaac and Jacob are unique in ancient
literature',[20] which is, after all, what we should expect in view of
the uniqueness of the situation. To no other family had the Lord

[20]M.J. Selman, *EOPN*, p. 111.

given a charge which was to result in the blessing of all the earth. In many respects the patriarchs were people of their time, sharing with their contemporaries (as does every generation) language, culture and skills. But the main reason why the Genesis narratives are still important is that the patriarchs were part of God's plan for the salvation of the world. Through God's dealing with them he continues to speak to us, for he does not change, no matter how great the technological changes that materially separate us from the millennia BC.

Why did Jacob send first for Joseph? From one point of view Joseph's pre-eminence in the land required recognition, and yet this alone would not have influenced Jacob who, in his audience with the Pharaoh, had shown no deference even for royal status. The factor which would have weighed with Jacob was Joseph's part in the divine plan, which had been worked out so wonderfully to save them all from starvation. Surely there was a notable blessing for Joseph and his sons and a particular future for them in the providence of God. This was God's word through Jacob which had to be passed on faithfully before he died. His springboard was that memorable occasion when he dreamed of a ladder from earth to heaven, from the top of which the Lord had first spoken to him. His father Isaac had prayed for God Almighty to bless him, and now Jacob discerns that it was God Almighty, *El Shaddai*, who had appeared to him at *Luz*, the old name for Bethel (28:19), as he ran away from the fury of Esau. The one who had named himself Yahweh, the covenant God of Abraham and Isaac, had shown himself powerful to fulfil his word to the homeless youth, on the run from justice. The substance of the blessing was the promise of many descendants to whom God would give the land, and for Jacob on his deathbed the agenda concerned the naming and the blessing of his sons as tribal heads, each significant as a recognized part of the Abrahamic people, from now on to be known as Israel.

Only in Joseph's case did Jacob accept his grandchildren as if they were his own sons (5). That they were born to an Egyptian mother was not regarded as any disqualification. 'They *are mine*', said Jacob, so adopting them by using an ancient adoption formula.[21] In effect he doubled the inheritance allotted to Joseph, and made the number of his sons who were to constitute 'Israel' thirteen instead of twelve. In honouring them he was honouring the memory of his first love, Rachel, his wife who had died on the homeward journey, some

---

[21]A similar formula is found, for example, in the Laws of Hammurapi, paragraph 170.

distance from Ephrath (35:16–20). Memories flooded back, distracting him so that he could adjust to the present only with difficulty. His question, '*Who are these?*' (8) does not seem strange to anyone who has looked after the very elderly, for whom disorientation is a common problem. At the same time, the question had a certain ritual significance, identifying the ones to receive the blessing, just as Isaac had intended to identify Esau (27:18). Blindness must frequently have afflicted these people, who had no medical help, as it still does the populations of hot, dusty regions of the world.

Joseph's eldest son was Manasseh, but when Jacob mentioned the two he spoke of Ephraim and Manasseh, so putting the younger in first place. The sequel shows that this was no accident. Joseph presented his sons to his father, who embraced them. The ritual of removing the boys *from his knees* (12) is thought to symbolize that Joseph renounced in favour of his father Jacob the right to consider the boys his own offspring (see note on 30:3), and bowed to the earth in worship. When the moment for the blessing had come Joseph took them to his father's bed again, carefully arranging that Manasseh would be close to Jacob's right hand, so that he would receive the blessing intended for the first-born. Jacob, however, deliberately frustrated Joseph's plan by crossing his hands over and putting his right hand on the head of Ephraim. *And he blessed Joseph* (15), that is, his sons, who are now the representatives of their father. Priority goes to the younger son, as had been the divine intention for Isaac's sons, and there is a reminder for Jacob of his own guile in seeing that his mother's plan to achieve it was not frustrated. How faithfully and yet gently the Lord had corrected him over the years.

The blessing he invokes is the blessing of the God whom he describes in three ways. First he is the God of his ancestors, Abraham and Isaac. Jacob-Israel was no innovator, pioneering some new religion; he was the heir to revelation made first to his grandfather, and handed on through his father to himself for the benefit of every future generation. Abraham and his descendants were committed to 'walking before the Lord', which meant living an exemplary life, pleasing to the Lord in whose presence they dwelt. Having been honoured with God's favour, they were obliged to live for him.

This God was also Jacob's personal God, who had *led* him all his *life long to this day*. Despite Jacob's many failings of character and conduct, he was aware that his life had had purpose and meaning, because God had taken him in hand. *The God who has led me* (*the God which hath fed me*, AV) is in Hebrew 'the God who has "shepherded" me'. Jacob had spent his life shepherding, and was not slow to recognize the shepherd care of God in his own experience. But that was not all.

His third invocation was to *the angel who has redeemed me from all evil*. The angel had appeared at three crisis-points in his life, at Bethel (28:13), in Paddan-aram (31:11, 13) and at Peniel (32:24–30). Jacob had recognized this angel as God himself, so that he called the place where he wrestled with the angel 'the face of God' (Peniel). Through the intervention of the angel God had rescued him from both Laban and Esau, and had brought him home in safety, according to his promise. The angel who had so protected him he calls his 'redeemer' (Heb. *gō'ēl*), the one who stepped in to rescue a relative in time of trouble (*cf.* Lv. 25:25–28; Nu. 35:19). It was humiliating to need such help, and Jacob was recalling here the way God had humbled him into submission, when all his instinct had been to work things out for himself.

This then was the God to whom Jacob-Israel prayed as he adopted his two grandsons so that they could play a leading part as inheritors of the promises. Ephraim and Manasseh gave their names to tribes, whereas Joseph renounced that right; moreover they became particularly numerous, to the extent that Ephraim could represent the northern tribes as a whole (*e.g.* Ho. 5:3; 7:1; 10:11). Ephraim and Manasseh also perpetuated Jacob's name by taking the place of Reuben, who had lost his precedence as eldest son and heir. The point is made by the Chronicler, who explains that even Judah, who was singled out for honour, did not receive the birthright, for 'the birthright belonged to Joseph' (1 Ch. 5:1–2). The fact that they are the first to receive the blessing matches their status as 'first-born'.

In this blessing, prefaced as it is by the threefold reference to God's constant care for his people, definition and content is given to the theology of the patriarchs. The new generation could never have known their great-grandfather, Isaac, so the boys needed to be told how God had chosen Abraham and Isaac, and had given meaning to their lives by unmistakable providences. They in their turn were to have their part to play in God's plan of salvation. So numerous would their descendants become that the names Ephraim and Manasseh would in days to come be a kind of prototype blessing, manifested in prosperous and vital family life. At the time of the settlement in Canaan by far the most extensive area had to be allocated to these two Joseph tribes (*cf.* Jos. 17:14–17, and any map of the tribal territories). The blessing worked out in historical expansion, to east and west of the Jordan river.

To Joseph Jacob wished to make one bequest (22). It becomes apparent that at some time Jacob had fought for some land in Canaan which he had won from the Amorite inhabitants. He describes it as a 'shoulder' or *mountain slope* (Heb. *shechem*), and since the word is not used elsewhere in the Old Testament except as the name of the famous old city of Shechem, some scholars have thought that Jacob is referring to this city which his sons had conquered and might have considered they owned (34:25–31). '*I* am about to die', he says, but the descendants of Joseph will be taken back to resume ownership of the one place Jacob could call his own. But Genesis 34 does not suggest that Shechem belonged to Jacob or to his sons after the massacre; though they plundered it they did not occupy it, and it was an incident of which Jacob heartily disapproved. Jacob's bequest, then, is the outcome of another and unrecorded incident in which he took a mountain slope, or a saddle of land between two hills. Any number of sites in the central hills could have been so described. The hill he took *with* his *sword and with* his *bow*, but his camping ground in Shechem he bought (33:18–20). How far apart these two areas were we have no means of knowing, but Joshua, who was of the tribe of Ephraim (1 Ch. 7:27) boldly led all the tribes to Shechem after he had fought for Bethel and Ai (Jos. 8:30–35), though he would appear to have taken a great risk in so doing. He may well have had this claim in mind, as God's law was recited from Mount Ebal and Mount Gerizim, on either side of the city of Shechem. Perhaps the ground Jacob had won was on one of these two mountains.

In giving this land he had conquered to Joseph's sons, Jacob was making provision for the future and declaring his faith in the certainty of God's promises, as the writer to the Hebrews realized when he singled out this incident to illustrate the faith of Jacob (Heb. 11:21). His conviction stood firm that the land would be given to his descendants because God had promised it to them. For this reason his old age was marked, not by regrets, but by hope and assurance. The Christian, who has the whole of Scripture to show how the purposes of God have been worked out over the centuries to find their culmination in the Lord Jesus Christ, has all the more reason for steadfast hope (1 Cor. 15:58).

Genesis 49:1–27

Destiny of the twelve tribes

Then Jacob called his sons, and said, 'Gather yourselves together, that I may tell you what shall befall you in days to come.
²Assemble and hear, O sons of Jacob.
and hearken to Israel your father.

³Reuben. you are my first-born,
my might, and the first fruits of my strength,
pre-eminent in pride and pre-eminent in power.
⁴Unstable as water, you shall not have pre-eminence
because you went up to your father's bed;
then you defiled it — you went up to my couch!

⁵Simeon and Levi are brothers;
weapons of violence are their swords.
⁶O my soul. come not into their council;
O my spirit, be not joined to their company;
for in their anger they slay men,
and in their wantonness they hamstring oxen.
⁷Cursed be their anger. for it is fierce;
and their wrath. for it is cruel!
I will divide them in Jacob
and scatter them in Israel.

⁸Judah. your brothers shall praise you;
your hand shall be on the neck of your enemies
your father's sons shall bow down before you
⁹Judah is a lion's whelp;
from the prey, my son, you have gone up.
He stooped down, he couched as a lion,
and as a lioness; who dares rouse him up?
¹⁰The sceptre shall not depart from Judah,
nor the ruler's staff from between his feet,
until he comes to whom it belongs;
and to him shall be the obedience of the peoples
¹¹Binding his foal to the vine
and his ass's colt to the choice vine,
he washes his garments in wine
and his vesture in the blood of grapes;

12his eyes shall be red with wine,
 and his teeth white with milk.

13Zebulun shall dwell at the shore of the sea,
 he shall become a haven for ships,
 and his border shall be at Sidon.

14Issachar is a strong ass,
 crouching between the sheepfolds;
15he saw that a resting place was good
 and that the land was pleasant;
so he bowed his shoulder to bear,
 and became a slave at forced labour

16Dan shall judge his people
 as one of the tribes of Israel.
17Dan shall be a serpent in the way,
 a viper by the path,
that bites the horse's heels
 so that his rider falls backward
18I wait for thy salvation, O Lord.

19Raiders shall raid Gad.
 but he shall raid at their heels

20Asher's food shall be rich,
 and he shall yield royal dainties

21Naphtali is a hind let loose,
 that bears comely fawns.

22Joseph is a fruitful bough,
 a fruitful bough by a spring;
 his branches run over the wall.
23The archers fiercely attacked him,
 shot at him, and harassed him sorely
24yet his bow remained unmoved,
 his arms were made agile
by the hands of the Mighty One of Jacob
 (by the name of the Shepherd, the Rock of Israel)
25by the God of your father who will help you,

by God Almighty who will bless you
  with blessings of heaven above,
blessings of the deep that couches beneath,
  blessings of the breasts and of the womb.
[26]*The blessings of your father*
  are mighty beyond the blessings of the eternal mountains,
  the bounties of the everlasting hills;
may they be on the head of Joseph,
  and on the brow of him who was separate from his brothers.

[27]*Benjamin is a ravenous wolf,*
  in the morning devouring the prey,
  and at even dividing the spoil.'

A distinction has to be made between the blessing pronounced by
Jacob on the two sons of Joseph and the predictions of this chapter
which outline the future of the twelve tribes as a whole. Blessings
may be incorporated, and indeed might be presupposed, on the
ground that each tribe participates in the initial blessings
pronounced by the Lord on Abraham, but individually some of the
brothers have allied themselves with the enemies of the Lord by
behaving treacherously. Couched in figurative language, these
poetic predictions are none too easy to interpret, and some of the
obscurities may be due to the great age of the text.[22] Uncom-
plimentary references, such as some of the poems contain, are
unlikely to have been incorporated at a later stage, and internal
features of the passage as a whole suggest that the words of Jacob
were memorized from generation to generation, whether or not they
were from the beginning committed to writing. Given Joseph's rank
and skill, there is every reason to suppose that he would have
recorded his father's predictive last words. *Assemble and hear, O sons of
Jacob* is both a formal introduction and a heading by which the
document could later be identified, a 'title'.

Reuben as the eldest son should have inherited a special proportion
of the family estate; this was usual in the ancient Near East, and
resulted from the belief that the first-born inherited the best of his
father's physical strength. He should therefore be well equipped for
leadership in his generation, and Jacob plays on this by saying he

---

[22] H. E. Ryle, for example, speaks of this chapter as 'derived, probably, from a very early
source', *CB*, p. 426. It is generally regarded as an archaic poem.

was *pre-eminent in pride* (in the sense of pride of place) *and pre-eminent in power*. The first three lines are quickly cancelled out by the concluding three, in which all his early promise is lost. *Unstable as water*; the thought is of the power of water out of control, as when dykes burst and reservoirs are breached. Passionate and headstrong, Reuben had committed an offence against his father's concubine, Bilhah (35:22), and by so gravely transgressing had forfeited his privileged place in the family. Moved with indignation, Jacob pointed to the offending Reuben as he exclaimed, 'He *went up to my couch!*' (AV, RV, whereas RSV adopts the less-condemning *you* of LXX). It is a story of a parent's disappointed hopes in his beloved first child, who had grossly wronged his father. When the time came for the allocation of the land of Canaan, Reuben's inheritance was on the east side of the Jordan, somewhat on the fringe of the nation's life. There was an occasion before that when Reubenites questioned the right of Moses to rule, but the disaster that overtook them was such as to deter any further revolt (Nu. 16), and, apart from mention in the Song of Deborah (Jdg. 5:15), the tribe plays little further part in the history of Israel.

Simeon and Levi are dealt with together because their future destiny is bound up with their collusion in the massacre at Shechem (chapter 34). This treacherous attack, which took advantage of an agreement entered into in good faith, now receives its condemnation: *cursed be their anger*. No blessing is promised to either tribe, and the later selection of Levi as the priestly tribe was connected with loyalty to the Lord in another incident (Ex. 32:25–29). Even so, the Levites were scattered among the other tribes instead of enjoying territory of their own. Simeon early lost its separate identity by inclusion with the more powerful Judah.

Though the general meaning of these verses is clear, the details have long posed problems. *Weapons of violence are their swords* is not straightforward, because the word translated 'sword' has not been found elsewhere, which entails guessing the sense. A recent study has suggested the reading, 'Simeon and Levi are brothers, their *kirru*-vessels implements of injustice'.[23] The *kirru* was a flask which had significance in the libations of Mesopotamian marriage rites, and, if this reading is correct (and it makes good sense), Jacob was

[23] Dwight Wayne Young, 'A Ghost Word in the Testament of Jacob (Gen. 49:5)?', *JBL* 100 (1981), pp. 335–342. This involves a re-division of the Hebrew consonants, which were not originally separated into words.

indicting the brothers 'not so much for the slaughter itself as for the desecrated rites and breached vows'. The *kirru* is attested in international use in the second millennium, but later generations evidently failed to recognize the term.

Verse 6 contains a play on words that is not apparent in translation. In the Hebrew *come not* can also be taken to mean 'desire', and *be not joined* suggests also the verb 'rejoice':

'Let my soul not enter/desire their council;

Let my spirit not be united with/rejoice in their company.'[24]

Heart and will are to turn away from the kind of violation of faith of which Simeon and Levi had been guilty, when they carried out their scheme to take advantage of the Shechemites. Man and ox (vivid singulars in the Hebrew) were the victims of their anger; humans were slaughtered and oxen maimed in this unprovoked massacre.[25] Jacob loathes their cruel cunning and indicates that in the long term it will impoverish them and their descendants.

Thus far the dying patriarch has had the sad duty of rebuking his eldest sons, and of predicting for them a future very different from his own hopes for them. The destiny of *Judah*, whose name suggested 'praise', introduced at last an element of hope. The fourth in line will achieve dominance over his brothers and overcome his enemies. Indeed, he is *a lion's cub*, fearing no-one, destined to be supreme, just as lions are more than a match for every other creature and dominate the animal creation. No wonder that the poem, having likened Judah to a lion, exalts Judah to royal prerogatives; *The sceptre shall not depart from Judah, nor the ruler's staff from between his feet*. Statues of enthroned monarchs thus depict their emblems of office, literally between their feet. Up to this point there is no difficulty in understanding the meaning of the poem. Though the tribe of Joseph was in many ways pre-eminent, the kingship was to be entrusted to the tribe of Judah, and the figure of the lion, frequent in poetic imagery and applied also to Gad and Dan (Dt. 33:20, 22), was nevertheless characteristic of Judah in later times (Rev. 5:5). Here the metaphor depicts Judah as a young lion who has learnt to hunt. From this time on he will be feared by all, and he will be 'lord over his brothers' (*cf.* 27: 29).

[24] Gary Rendsburg, 'Double Polysemy in Genesis 49:6 and Job 3:6', *CBQ* 44 (1982), pp. 48–51.

[25] Though the brothers claimed to be vindicating their sister's honour, they were over-reacting, because a marriage agreement had been entered into, and the Mosaic law was to endorse this as the right way forward in the circumstances (Ex. 22:16–17; Dt. 22:28–29).

Until he comes to whom it belongs (10) marks the climax not only of the stanzas addressed to Judah, but also of the whole poem, yet the exact meaning of the words is far from clear, as a comparison of the different English translations will show. The difficulty centres on the Hebrew word *shiloh*, which is not translated in AV, RV, but remains in the text as a personal name, 'until Shiloh comes'. This is unsatisfactory because, though Shiloh was well known as the first sanctuary of Israel after the tribes settled in Canaan, the name is never used elsewhere of a person. 'Till he come to Shiloh' (RV mg.) implies that Judah would hold power till a gathering at Shiloh, possibly that of Joshua 18, but with hindsight we know that Judah's king David, the first of Judah's line to reign, lived at least 200 years after the conquest of Canaan. RSV follows the Syriac version, made early in the Christian era; it accords with Ezekiel's use of our text when, just before the fall of Jerusalem, he called for the removal of the crown from Judah's reigning king, 'until he comes whose right it is; and to him I will give it' (Ezk. 21:26–27). This is as near as it is possible to come to Jacob's meaning.

The prophecy looks forward to a ruler who will descend from Judah, and yet will be so great that he will receive *the obedience of the peoples*. While David established Judah as the ruling tribe, and set up an extensive empire, he could hardly be said to have secured the obedience of other nations; there was serious unrest even within his own family. This coming ruler, moreover, will bring unprecedented prosperity, *binding his foal to the vine*. 'The man who can without a thought bind his mount to a vine and wash his garments in wine is living in paradise.'[26] This poem is looking forward to the day when food shortages are no more, harvests are abundant, and wars have ceased because everyone gives allegiance to God's king, and enjoys the sheer bounty of his provision. God's intention for humanity is nothing less than paradise restored.

The last two lines of the oracle for Judah are not free from difficulty. The word translated *red* is a rare Hebrew word, the meaning of which is therefore obscure. It seems most likely that a comparison is being made here between the colour of eyes and the dark lustre of wine:

    'Darker (?) are his eyes than wine,
    whiter his teeth than milk.'[27]

---

[26] G. von Rad, *Old Testament Theology*, II (English Edition, Oliver and Boyd, 1965), p. 13.
[27] Wilfred G. E. Watson, *Classical Hebrew Poetry* (JSOT Supplement 26, 1984), p. 28. He refers to C. H. Gordon, 'The Wine-Dark Sea', *JNES* 37 (1978), pp. 51–52. Both LXX and

It is fitting that a reference to the ideal ruler should depict him as strikingly attractive, 'altogether desirable' (Song 5:16).

Zebulun, the youngest of the sons born to Leah, is named before his brother, *Issachar*, as in Deuteronomy 33:18–19 and Judges 5:14–15. Zebulun was meant to be associated with the sea, and its commerce, based at Sidon. In the allocation of land (Jos. 19:10–16) the coast was not included, but the tribe may have been enriched all the same by proximity to the markets represented in the port of Sidon, though Asher's territory was nearer as events turned out historically, and Israel rarely possessed the hinterland of Sidon. Issachar, strong but lazy, 'lying down between two saddlebags' (NIV), would find a pleasant land, but rather than conquer it would slave for others. His area of Canaan bordered that of Zebulun and overlooked the Sea of Galilee and the Jordan valley. Interestingly, Issachar is not mentioned in Judges 1:30–36, where other northern tribes are said to have failed to occupy all their territory; was Issachar living out the meaning of his name?

The name *Dan*, Hebrew for 'judge', suggests the calling of this tribe to stand for justice to the needy within its borders, a requirement which applied to all the tribes. But Jacob foresaw treachery in Dan; lordly horsemen riding on the hill tracks would be unseated by the bite of a viper at the horse's heels and the fall of the steed. The prayer of verse 18, '*I wait for thy salvation, O Lord,*' should probably be separated from the words to Dan, with which they have no particular connection. There was little enough to cheer Jacob as he pronounced upon the destiny of his sons, and every reason to reaffirm his confidence in the Lord's deliverance.

Gad's future is suggested by the twofold meaning of his name, 'attack' and 'band of raiders', which makes of the couplet an extended pun. Like Dan, the tribe of Gad will 'raid at their *heels*', just as Jacob took his brother by the heel (the name Gad has the same consonants in Hebrew as the word 'heel'). This tribe elected to settle east of Jordan, where it was exposed to the incursions of marauding bands.

The name *Asher*, 'happy', suggests prosperity, hence the promise

---

Vulgate understood these lines as making comparisons, and NIV has 'His eyes will be darker than wine, his teeth whiter than milk'.

of rich food and 'delicacies fit for a king' (NIV). The fruitful hills overlooking the Mediterranean, to the east of the bay of Acre and Tyre, were allocated to Asher.

Naphtali, 'wrestlings', may suggest struggles for freedom, *a hind let loose*. The second line, *that bears comely fawns*, is more problematic, in that the obvious meaning 'who gives beautiful words' (RSV mg.) has no particular relevance to this tribe, which was notable mainly for providing the liberator Barak (Jdg. 4:6). NIV, like RSV text, prefers the alternative meaning, 'that bears beautiful fawns'. This tribe, allocated to the northern mountains, would over the generations remain true to its calling to liberty.

Despite the special blessing granted to Ephraim and Manasseh, *Joseph* is not omitted from this deathbed pronouncement of future destiny; indeed more is said about him than about Judah, for he had first place now instead of Reuben, and was 'the prince among his brothers' (26, NIV). It is not hard to see what prompted these reflections of Jacob as he considered his son Joseph, who had dreamed that his sheaf of corn received the homage of the sheaves belonging to his brothers. Now he was more like a flourishing, *fruitful bough*, hanging its fruit over the 'wall' or fence intended to support it, and drawing its nourishment from a nearby spring. There is in the word 'fruitful' a play on the name Ephraim (41:52), and a reference, perhaps, to the promise to both of Joseph's sons (48:4-9).

In his youth Joseph had been written off as dead, *the archers fiercely attacked him* (23), *yet his bow remained unmoved* or 'remained steady' (NIV). Hopelessly outnumbered by his older brothers, Joseph had had no chance of defending himself, but, unbeknown to him, the hands of the *Mighty One of Jacob*, the champion of his cause, whom his father had proved when he was equally helpless, had been controlling his own. All the names by which Jacob had come to know his God, and each of which laid stress on some specific attribute, were gathered together in this pronouncement of blessing upon Joseph. *The God of your father* (25) reminded him that he had inherited the blessing of Abraham, Isaac and Jacob; this blessing rested, therefore, on the promises of God, not on human fallibility. Jacob had been impressed by the guidance of God (48:15), hence God was *Shepherd*, and the constancy of God, even through only three generations as yet, suggested that he was *the Rock of Israel*. The

211

word *rock* here is more often translated 'stone'; we meet it, for example, in the name *Ebenezer*, 'stone of help', coined by Samuel to name the memorial he set up to the God who enabled Israel to defeat their Philistine enemies (1 Sa. 7:12). It is rock put to use for building, or precious stone to treasure, and for Jacob both meanings were to the point as he spoke of the upbuilding of the house of Joseph. The imagery of the stone continues into the New Testament, where Jesus depicted his servants as those who build on the rock (Mt. 7:24), and envisages that they will themselves become dependable (Mt. 16:18). Even volatile Peter would grow like the one he served and take on the rock-like character suggested by his Christian name.

Finally Jacob/Israel blesses Joseph by *God Almighty, El Shaddai*, the name which sums up the over-arching providence which had been shaping Jacob's character and guiding his steps throughout his life. That same unmistakable providential care had been evident already in the experience of Joseph, 'for of all the brothers he had gone lowest into human despair and weakness, and was the outstanding illustration of El Shaddai's transforming power'. This name 'El Shaddai undergirded that which later was shown to be at the very centre of the nature of God'.[28] This is the God who will work in wonderful ways for Joseph, and who has worked even more wonderfully in Jesus Christ to bring eternal salvation to all who admit to their need of him.

The *blessings of heaven above* were primarily the rain and dew that ensured a harvest, and the *blessings of the deep that couches beneath* meant that there would be perennial springs, but the opening words to Joseph, *Joseph is a fruitful bough* (22), show that there was also a metaphorical use of the idea in addition to the important, but prosaic, supply of water. Large thriving families and successful farming symbolized blessing which included more besides, in particular, as Jacob goes on to depict, the awareness of having a meaningful part in God's purpose for human history. This is expressed with beautiful subtlety in the first three lines of verse 26. The middle line is the key to the other two because the words *eternal mountains*, or 'mountains of old', can also mean progenitors of old'.[ ] The latter meaning suggests line one, and the former shapes line three.[29] All the wonderful overruling of God seen in the life of Joseph up to this point is part of a total plan for blessing which will

---

[28] J .A. Motyer, *The Revelation of the Divine Name* (Tyndale Press, 1959), pp. 29–30).

[29] *Cf.* Gary Rendsburg, 'Janus Parallelism in Gen. 49:26', *JBL* 99 (1980), pp. 291–293.

now be experienced by his successors. Ephraim and Manasseh inherited the most fertile areas of the land of Canaan and flourished accordingly, but by the time of Amos and Hosea self-indulgence had brought about the ruin of the tribes of Joseph (Am. 6:6), and Ephraim, despite the Lord's gentle upbringing and kind provision, had bitterly deserted the Lord for idols (Ho. 11:1–3). Hosea makes clear how reluctantly the Lord withdrew his hand of blessing (Ho. 11:8–9). The promise stood until its recipients rejected out of hand their father's God who had given them the privilege of the covenant, and even then the exile was not the end, but rather a period of discipline (Ezk. 34:11–16).

Finally Jacob came to his beloved youngest son, whom he had tried to protect from the perils of Egypt, but none of his favouritism is reflected in this little poetic oracle. Emphasis is on the fierce fighting qualities of *Benjamin*, the last-born, who by his aggression would prove the equal of his older brothers. This was the tribe that gave birth to the first king of Israel, but kingship was not envisaged here, and Saul was far from being aggressive at the time of his proclamation (1 Sa. 10:22). Nevertheless Benjamin led the tribes to battle under Deborah and Barak (Jdg. 5:14), and Psalm 68:27 proclaims 'There is Benjamin, the least of them, in the lead', as the solemn procession celebrates a victory in the Temple at Jerusalem.

All these are the twelve tribes of Israel. Though some, like Reuben, forfeited their privilege, none altogether forfeited his inheritance. Most were hardly to be pronounced 'blessed' as they anticipated their future, here outlined by their father; but even if they were disappointed individually, as Israel they entered into the promise to their fathers and knew the guidance of the Mighty One of Jacob. In him, and in his king (10), there was blessing for the future that would know neither restrictions nor boundaries: this is the blessing Christians inherit in the Lord Jesus.

Genesis 49:28 – 50:3

The death and embalming of Jacob

All these are the twelve tribes of Israel; and this is what their father said to them as he blessed them, blessing each with the blessing suitable to him. ^{29}*Then he charged them, and said to them, 'I am to be gathered to my people;*

213

bury me with my fathers in the cave that is in the field of Ephron the Hittite, ³⁰in the cave that is in the field at Machpelah, to the east of Mamre, in the land of Canaan, which Abraham bought with the field from Ephron the Hittite to possess as a burying place. ³¹There they buried Abraham and Sarah his wife; there they buried Isaac and Rebekah his wife; and there I buried Leah—³²the field and the cave that is in it were purchased from the Hittites.' ³³When Jacob finished charging his sons, he drew up his feet into the bed, and breathed his last, and was gathered to his people.

^{50:1} Then Joseph fell on his father's face, and wept over him, and kissed him. ²And Joseph commanded his servants the physicians to embalm his father. So the physicians embalmed Israel; ³forty days were required for it, for so many are required for embalming. And the Egyptians wept for him seventy days.

'*I am to be gathered to my people,*' said Jacob as he contemplated death in a foreign land. True, he wanted to be buried with his fathers, but irrespective of his burial-place, he envisaged a life beyond the grave in continuity with life on earth. This is not the same as knowledge of eternal life, which Jesus came to bring, though the patriarchs' knowledge of the eternal God implied a share in his life, because 'he is not God of the dead, but of the living' (Lk. 20:38). Jacob's charge that he should be buried '*with my fathers in the cave that is in the field of Ephron the Hittite*' (the other details ensure that they will correctly identify the site) was intended to authenticate Israel's claim to the land of Canaan when the time came. Despite the prominence of Joseph in the government of Egypt, the family would never consider its inheritance to be in Egypt. The legitimacy of their claim to Canaan lay with the divine gift of the land to Abraham, the first forefather of Israel. Land tenure in the ancient Near East was dependent on the ability to make proper reference back to the original forefather who held the title authenticating the registration, and from then on transmitting the deeds.[30] The return of the funeral cortège from Egypt for Jacob's burial there renewed the family's claim to the cave, and also to the land. It was a pledge that they would one day return to occupy what had in fact been bestowed on Abraham and Sarah, Isaac and Rebekah. Leah too was buried there (but not Rachel), and Jacob would take his place in the family mausoleum, as one of the three great names for ever associated with God's promise of the land: Abraham, Isaac and Jacob. With such a heritage to pass on to his sons, and with faith in the God of his

[30] D.J. Wiseman, 'Abraham Reassessed', *EOPN*, p. 150.

fathers, Jacob could face death unafraid. His life had had meaning over and above his own personal interests, which in turn had taken on deeper significance. He was not only unafraid but also satisfied.

Though all the sons of Jacob were present at the deathbed, it was Joseph who was in a position to implement the request of his father, and it was he who took the lead in mourning him, as well as in making the arrangements for the embalming, mentioned only in this chapter of the Bible. Though embalming was foreign to Joseph's family, it served the purpose of preserving the body of Jacob (and later that of Joseph) for secondary burial in Canaan. It was an extremely expensive procedure, but Joseph was well placed to ensure that only the very best physicians operated on the body of his father, using all the most fragrant perfumes to replace the organs they removed. The *forty days* were the period needed to ensure the preservation of the body (Herodotus says it was never more than *seventy days*, the period mentioned here for Egyptian public mourning of Jacob).[31] Public mourning for a Pharaoh did not last longer than seventy-two days, so Jacob/Israel was greatly honoured.

Thus funeral rites vary a great deal; we observe differences of practice in Scripture and in different parts of the world today. They matter to the mourners and play an important part in the healing of grief, but there is no one 'biblical' method of disposing of the dead laid down for Christians world-wide. The emphasis is on the change to which the Christian church looks forward, when the dead will be raised imperishable, 'for the perishable must clothe itself with the imperishable, and the mortal with immortality' (1 Cor. 15:53, NIV). This visible transformation will depend, not on the state of the body at burial, but on the believer's union with Christ in God who alone has immortality, and who alone can bestow eternal life (Jn. 17:2–3; 1 Tim. 6:12–16). This is a prospect with the power to assuage grief.

Genesis 50:4–14

The burial in Canaan

And when the days of weeping for him were past, Joseph spoke to the household of Pharaoh, saying, 'If now I have found favour in your eyes, speak, I pray you, in the ears of Pharaoh, saying, ⁵My father made me swear, saying, "I am about to die: in my tomb which I hewed out for myself in the land of Canaan, there shall you bury me." Now therefore let me go

[31] *The Histories* (Penguin Classics edn.) II, 87; p. 133.

up, I pray you, and bury my father; then I will return.' ⁶And Pharaoh answered, 'Go up, and bury your father, as he made you swear.' ⁷So Joseph went up bury his father; and with him went up to all the servants of Pharaoh, the elders of his household, and all the elders of the land of Egypt, ⁸as well as all the household of Joseph, his brothers, and his father's household; only their children, their flocks, and their herds were left in the land of Goshen. ⁹And there went up with him both chariots and horsemen; it was a very great company. ¹⁰When they came to the threshing floor of Atad, which is beyond the Jordan, they lamented there with a very great and sorrowful lamentation; and he made a mourning for his father seven days. ¹¹When the inhabitants of the land, the Canaanites, saw the mourning on the threshing floor of Atad, they said, 'This is a grievous mourning to the Egyptians.' Therefore the place was named Abel-mizraim; it is beyond the Jordan. ¹²Thus his sons did for him as he had commanded them; ¹³for his sons carried him to the land of Canaan, and buried him in the cave of the field at Machpelah, to the east of Mamre, which Abraham bought with the field from Ephron the Hittite, to possess as a burying place. ¹⁴After he had buried his father, Joseph returned to Egypt with his brothers and all who had gone up with him to bury his father.

As a servant of the Pharaoh Joseph had to ask his permission to leave Egypt, and as a mourner he was unclean, so that he could not personally approach the king; hence his indirect request. Joseph was aware that the journey to his homeland would give him an opportunity to 'defect', hence his assurance, *then I will return* (5). Accompanied as he was to be by a cavalcade of Egyptian statesmen and dignitaries, Joseph would in practice have only the slimmest chance of remaining in Canaan, and in any case the families left behind in Egypt would ensure the return of all the brothers. *Chariots and horsemen*, not an everyday sight in Canaan, completed the *very great company*, and made the funeral cortège unusual enough for it to be long remembered.

The lengthy procession halted at *the threshing floor of Atad* (10). Apart from the fact that it was in Canaanite territory and was in the Jordan region, the site is not known, nor is it referred to anywhere else in Scripture.[32] Why is the Jordan mentioned at all in connection with a journey between Egypt and Hebron, in view of the fact that the main route went via the Nile delta and then to east and north round the coast? Perhaps, as was the case at the time of

[32] The Hebrew phrase, usually translated 'beyond the Jordan', has been shown to mean 'in the region of the Jordan' by B. Gemser, *VT* II (1952), pp. 349–355.

the Exodus (Ex. 13:17), that way was endangered by fighting or brigandage. The route across the Sinai peninsula through Kadesh-Barnea, and then northward on the east side of the Dead Sea, was considerably longer and could still have been dangerous, as the provision of chariots and horsemen suggests.

So impressive was the sight of Joseph's company mourning for seven days that the place was renamed *Abel-mizraim*, or 'Egyptian mourning'. But this was not strictly the same as the burial-place, for Jacob was buried in the cave of Machpelah in the tomb he *hewed out* (5). Since the cave was a natural formation the word 'hewed' has been considered an unlikely meaning, but, if tombs which have been excavated are anything to go by, each section of the family had its own extension of a cave, and places were hewn out of the rock for each of its members, so that word is not incongruous. The time had not yet come for the return to Canaan and the whole procession made its way back to Egypt, but the visit had demonstrated that past events were not forgotten, and it was only a matter of time before the descendants of this man Israel would come back to claim their possessions.

Genesis 50:15–21

Guilt continues to haunt the brothers

When Joseph's brothers saw that their father was dead, they said, 'It may be that Joseph will hate us and pay us back for all the evil which we did to him.' ¹⁶So they sent a message to Joseph, saying, 'Your father gave this command before he died, ¹⁷"Say to Joseph, Forgive, I pray you, the transgression of your brothers and their sin, because they did evil to you." And now, we pray you, forgive the transgression of the servants of the God of your father.' Joseph wept when they spoke to him. ¹⁸His brothers also came and fell down before him, and said, 'Behold, we are your servants.' ¹⁹But Joseph said to them, 'Fear not, for am I in the place of God? ²⁰As for you, you meant evil against me; but God meant it for good, to bring it about that many people should be kept alive, as they are today. ²¹So do not fear; I will provide for you and your little ones.' Thus he reassured them and comforted them.

The death of their father inevitably brought about changes in family relationships, and fears arose that all the old animosities would rear their heads again now that their one-time enemy was in the place of supreme power. Without the restraining presence of the old patriarch, what was to prevent Joseph from avenging their treatment of him? That he should actually have forgiven them did not enter their heads, so they concocted words attributed to their father, requesting Joseph to forgive the transgression they had committed. It was their total misunderstanding of his motives that caused Joseph to weep. They were ready to do anything in order to placate him, '*we are your servants*'. But Joseph would have none of it.

In his exalted office Joseph could have become an overbearing tyrant, getting his own back in full measure. This is what his brothers expected him to do, and presumably what they themselves would have done in the same circumstances. Joseph's '*Fear not*' was intended to reassure them that nothing of the sort was in his mind. He freely forgave them, so setting an example of forgiveness unsurpassed in the Old Testament.

By what process of thought did Joseph overcome his natural resentment of the cruel treatment he received at the hand of his brothers? '*You meant evil against me*,' he said. Joseph did not minimize the wrong they had done him, nor pretend that it could be overlooked. On the contrary he stated it plainly, for they needed to be faced with their crime. Joseph's approach had nothing in common with the permissiveness that indulges the wrongdoer and minimizes the need for a change of heart and life. The truth that had gripped him gave him the conviction that *God meant it for good* (20). Despite all the injustice he had suffered, and the years of imprisonment, Joseph could see God's hand at work in the outcome of events. He himself had been vindicated by his promotion to the highest office in the land. His reputation was such that under his regime fair distribution of the emergency food-supplies was never in doubt. Everyone trusted him. But more than that, God had used the evil *to bring it about that many people should be kept alive*. Thousands lived who otherwise would have starved to death, and not least Joseph's would-be assassins, the chosen family.

Over the years Joseph had been moulded by his observation of God's dealings with him, enabling him to endure hardship, resist temptation and keep hopeful even when other people let him down. So overwhelming was Joseph's sense of God's loving-kindness in taking the hatred and incorporating it into his wide purpose of blessing, that Joseph was humbled. In no way could he usurp the place of God by attempting to punish his brothers. Quite the opposite, he wanted to provide for them and their little ones the best that Egypt could supply.

The question arises whether it is possible to attain to Joseph's generosity of heart without his theology, for it is clear that he found the motivation and the power to forgive through God's dealings with him. How else could the strength of human vindictiveness be tamed and transformed? Too often people nurse grievances which they keep secret, but the poison festers and eventually causes a crisis; such grievances have been repressed but not forgiven. Only a deep sense of gratitude for the wonder of our own experience of forgiveness in Christ, and for the provision he has made for others to be forgiven, can break down the barriers we put up between ourselves and others, both those we have wronged and those who have wronged us.

Meanwhile, those who had done the wrong were haunted by their guilt. They could find no ground of appeal against Joseph's justifiable punishment except the request (most probably fabricated) of their dying father, and when Joseph declared that he forgave them they were suspicious of his motives in saying so. Such are the problems that beset efforts to bring about reconciliation between those who have become estranged. Very often the barriers put up by those who have been most to blame are the hardest to remove. 'In Christ God was reconciling the world to himself, not counting their trespasses against them' (2 Cor. 5:19), but the majority of the world's population is unimpressed and unconvinced. So, it seems, were Joseph's eleven brothers, though they depended on him for their supplies of food and were never let down. Joseph *reassured them* by his deeds as well as his words, and *comforted them* (21), or more literally 'spoke to their heart', a turn of phrase which in biblical usage occurs in difficult situations. 'In most cases there is a context of guilt, in which the sense is to seek forgiveness or summon to repentance.'[33] There is no indication that the brothers repented, but had they done so true reconciliation could have taken place, with all the resultant overflow of joyous good will. Instead it seems that they merely rubbed along together as best they could.

---

[33]It occurs ten times: here and in Gn. 34:3; Jdg. 19:3; Ru. 2:13; 1 Sa. 1:13; 2 Sa. 19:7; 2 Ch. 30:22; 32:6; Is. 40:2; Ho. 2:14. *Cf.* Georg Fischer in *Biblica* 65 (1984), pp. 244–250, and *OTA* 7 (1984), p. 271.

Genesis 50:22-26

The last words of Joseph

So Joseph dwelt in Egypt, he and his father's house; and Joseph lived a hundred and ten years. [23]*And Joseph saw Ephraim's children of the third generation; the children also of Machir the son of Manasseh were born upon Joseph's knees.* [24]*And Joseph said to his brothers, 'I am about to die; but God will visit you, and bring you up out of this land to the land which he swore to Abraham, to Isaac, and to Jacob.'* [25]*Then Joseph took an oath of the sons of Israel, saying, 'God will visit you, and you shall carry up my bones from here.'* [26]*So Joseph died, being a hundred and ten years old; and they embalmed him, and he was put in a coffin in Egypt.*

In time the famine was forgotten and the refugees became accustomed to their life in a foreign land. Their children and grandchildren had never known any other country, and could easily have become absorbed into the population, had it not been that the Egyptians themselves were averse to fraternization, and Joseph, taking advantage of this, contrived to keep the family's identity intact (46:34). Joseph himself was blessed in his old age as he had been throughout his life. Two outward signs of this blessing are specified. First, he lived to be 110 years old, an ideal age according to Egyptian lore and therefore a further testimony to the Egyptian people of the commitment of Joseph to the true God. The second sign was made possible by the first: he lived to see his great-great-grandchildren, who would be passing on their memory of Joseph to their children's children nearly a century later.

The continuity was important if the covenant promise and commitment were to be treasured and passed on as the most important family possession. Joseph's dying words were brief and to the point: *'God will visit you, and bring you up out of this land to the land which he swore to Abraham, to Isaac, and to Jacob.'* Incidentally, this reference back to Abraham, Isaac and Jacob at the end of Joseph's life gives us cause for recalling the powerful motif which binds the patriarchal history into a whole; it is the covenant promise, which thrusts forward into the future for its fulfilment. But Joseph had in mind also an outward and visible sign to act as a reminder to each generation that Egypt was not their permanent home.

'God will visit you', he confidently repeated to his brothers as he made them swear, *'you shall carry up my bones from here.'* Joseph was

not committing them to an expensive funeral visit to Canaan, but he was asking that his remains should be kept as a constant memorial of the future removal to Canaan which was as certain as the promises of God. This memorial was made possible by the embalming of his body, so that, though he was put into an Egyptian coffin like the anthropoid ones we see in our museums, he did not need to be buried, but could be kept indefinitely 'lying in state' in Egypt.

Measured by human time-scales the period in Egypt was long, testing both faith and patience. But the last words of the book, *he was put in a coffin in Egypt*, marked not the end of the story but merely the end of the very first episode. In due course a whole succession of circumstances which are recorded in the early chapters of Exodus, contributed to bring about the deliverance under Moses, who 'took the bones of Joseph with him' (Ex. 13: 19). Years later, when Joshua had led Israel into the promised land, the bones of Joseph were buried in Shechem, in the territory of his son Manasseh, but close to the border with Ephraim (Jos. 24: 32). Joseph's faith had not been misplaced, and God did not forget to be gracious nor fail to keep his word.

Retrospect

We have been endeavouring to show that the patriarchal narratives, despite their great antiquity, continue to speak today. Above all they highlight important features of the way God deals with men and women, and it may be helpful in closing to summarize them.

In the first place these chapters clearly show that God takes the initiative in drawing us to himself. It was not Abraham who decided to try to find God, but God who intervened in Abraham's life. There is no suggestion here that mankind gradually evolved through various stages of religious consciousness until he eventually worshipped one God; still less that this particular family, or Abraham in particular, had a flair for religion. From the start the impetus towards salvation comes, not from man, but from God. *The Lord* spoke to Abraham when he sent him from Ur to Canaan and made far-reaching promises which mark the beginning of the history of salvation (12:1–3). At every stage this divine initiative has been maintained: at last God sent his Son, who explicitly stated the same continuing divine initiative, 'You did not choose me, but I chose you' (Jn. 15:16). God both prepared the total plan of salvation and gave us our individual place within it: though it may seem to us that we found God, the truth is that he found us.

Secondly, God's purpose is blessing. In the first place Abraham is the recipient of God's blessing, but not merely for his own sake. The blessing of God is of such abundance that it overflows to others. Abraham will be a blessing, not only locally, but universally. The world-wide scope of God's love is very evident in Genesis.

Thirdly, Genesis shows that, when God is at work fulfilling his great plan for history, he begins with one individual family and continues on a very small scale, not with mighty nations and their accumulated wisdom. Ancient Egypt, with all its famous learning, became dependent for its life on the man of God's choice, the imprisoned and much-wronged Joseph. God begins, moreover, with people who by no means always do his will, who are fearful like Abraham (12:12) and twisty like Jacob. This means that there is hope for all; no-one qualifies by natural gifts. It means also that the church and its effectiveness is not to be judged by its degree of influence or by its numerical strength. It may be tested as Abraham was, but if it is true to its Lord it will be in his hand an instrument of blessing out of all proportion to its size.

The patriarchs and some members of their families found themselves in situations which enabled them to get to know specific attributes of the God they worshipped. Indeed these situations often seemed designed to reveal the character of God, and gave rise to names which highlighted his special qualities. This is outstandingly true of Abraham on Mount Moriah, where he discovered that, when God asks for a costly sacrifice, he provides it himself. This God was to do supremely on the cross. Hagar found that God both sees human need and lets himself be seen. In situations of human helplessness, like the plight of childless Abraham and Sarah, or of Jacob sending off all his sons to Egypt, God reveals himself as the Almighty God, who can not only alter circumstances but also transform people. Thus we are encouraged to see in our adverse circumstances the opportunity to know God better as the one who wants to reveal himself to us in our weakness and need. There are models here in Genesis for our desperate situations today.

We do not know when the book of Genesis received its final form, but it was centuries before the Christian era. The writer cannot have known how the promises of the Abrahamic covenant were going to be fulfilled in Christ, nor how the New Testament writers would hark back to Abraham to point out in Genesis the primary importance of faith. 'Abraham believed God, and it was reckoned to him as righteousness' (Rom. 4:3; cf. Gn. 15:6). Nowhere in the patriarchal narratives is there any suggestion in precept or example that human striving after goodness would of itself make anyone pleasing to God or acceptable to him. Hundreds of years were to pass before the giving of the law through Moses. Its purpose was to specify the fitting response of those who had already been made his people by covenant, and not to make law-keeping a way to God. Salvation has always been a gift of God's grace received by faith.

Nevertheless Abraham and his immediate descendants were

intuitively aware of the character of the God they served; even though they did not possess the law, they knew it was incumbent upon them to live in such a way as to please him. Trust implied obedience and obedience demanded separation from Canaanite practices in order that the whole of life could be lived for God. This total commitment was not very different from the demand Jesus was to make when he said, 'Follow me' (Mk. 1:17), with all its simplicity and at the same time its all-inclusiveness. The God of the Old Testament is also the God of the New; his way of salvation has not changed, and he offers salvation and blessing to all who will receive his gifts in penitence and humility. If this seems simplistic as compared with self-attained goodness by law-keeping, that is because we fail to understand the extent of our past debt to God and our present discredit in his sight.

This failure to face up to our plight is part of our problem. The giving of the law was one means God used to produce conviction of sin; in the event it tended towards confirming self-righteousness. The coming of Jesus cut across the misunderstandings that had arisen over the law, and reopened more fully than ever before the way to God by faith. What the patriarchs had dimly seen the Lord Jesus Christ displayed; he was the righteousness of which Abraham had been aware when he affirmed, 'Shall not the Judge of all the earth do right?' Such is God's mercy that God's righteousness (no less) is bestowed on all who cast themselves on his love, ask for his forgiveness and trust him with their lives. The life of Jacob illustrates how such a commitment can eventually change a person, dealing with the twists of a warped nature as God takes control, while the life of Joseph shows how God's overruling is well able to encompass human wilfulness, correct the wrongdoers, and at the same time provide for their needs.

The patriarchal narratives are, in short, an epitome of the gospel.